Pinter and Stoppard

Pinter and Stoppard

A Director's View

Carey Perloff

methuen | drama

LONDON • NEW YORK • OXFORD • NEW DELHI • SYDNEY

METHUEN DRAMA
Bloomsbury Publishing Plc
50 Bedford Square, London, WC1B 3DP, UK
1385 Broadway, New York, NY 10018, USA
29 Earlsfort Terrace, Dublin 2, Ireland

BLOOMSBURY, METHUEN DRAMA and the Methuen Drama logo are trademarks of
Bloomsbury Publishing Plc

First published in Great Britain 2022

Cover design: Ben Anslow
Cover image © Tom Stoppard, Sydney, June 28th, 1994 (© Fairfax Media
Archives / Getty Images); Harold Pinter (© Hulton-Deutsch Collection / Corbis / Getty
Images); Carey Perloff at the ACT Gala opening of the new Strand Theater,
San Francisco, April 2015 (Photography © Kevin Berne)

A catalogue record for this book is available from the British Library.

A catalog record for this book is available from the Library of Congress.

ISBN: HB: 978-1-3502-4338-5
       PB: 978-1-3502-4339-2
       ePDF: 978-1-3502-4340-8
       eBook: 978-1-3502-4341-5

Typeset by RefineCatch Limited, Bungay, Suffolk
Printed and bound in Great Britain

To find out more about our authors and books visit www.bloomsbury.com
and sign up for our newsletters.

This book is for my mother Marjorie Perloff, critic extraordinaire, who welcomed me into the world of literature, and for my mother-in-law Patricia Giles who welcomed me to all things English, with love and gratitude.

CONTENTS

ILLUSTRATIONS

ACKNOWLEDGMENTS

This book owes its existence to Harold Pinter and Tom Stoppard, whose work has given me inspiration over three decades and whose collaboration was endlessly eye-opening. I would particularly like to thank Tom Stoppard for permission to quote freely from his notes and correspondence pertaining to my productions of his plays.

I owe an immeasurable debt to those who participated in my productions of Pinter and Stoppard's work, including actors Marco Barricelli, Rene Augesen, Steven Anthony Jones, Gregory Wallace, Anthony Fusco, Jack Willis, Manoel Felciano, Jason Butler Harner, Alison Jean White, Brenda Meaney, Dan Clegg, Andrew Polk, Adam O'Byrne, Pamela Reed, Graham Beckel, Jean Stapleton, Peter Riegert, David Strathairn, Firdous Bamji, Rosemarie Harris, Roberta Maxwell, Bill Moor, Scott Wentworth, Art Malik, and Judith Ivey, as well as designers Darron L. West, Alexander V. Nichols, Daniel Ostling, Andrew Boyce, Loy Arcenas, Robert Wierzel, James Ingalls, Douglas Schmidt, Candice Donnelly, Nina Ball, and so many more.

My work on Pinter's and Stoppard's plays was created in collaboration with creative teams at CSC, including Ellen Novack, Patty Taylor, and Lenora Champagne; at A.C.T. I was blessed with dramaturgs Paul Walsh and Michael Paller, Executive Director Heather Kitchen and Publications Manager Elizabeth Brodersen, all of whom helped frame the work by writing extensive dramaturgical packages, elegant program notes, and endless grant applications. In engaging actors-in-training in every aspect of the work, I am grateful to the wisdom and encouragement of Conservatory Director Melissa Smith and Young Conservatory Director Craig Slaight.

For detailed first-hand knowledge of the early period of Pinter's and Stoppard's work, I gleaned invaluable nuggets from my friend and colleague Giles Havergal. I have also benefitted over the years from the acute critical eye of Austin Quigley, the teaching of Martin Esslin, and the invaluable biographical works of Michael Billington on Pinter and of Hermione Lee on Stoppard. Having the opportunity to discuss this project with Hermione Lee in the wake of her masterful study was particularly valuable and enjoyable.

It was director Anne Bogart who generously connected me with her publisher, Bloomsbury Methuen, and urged them to take a look at this manuscript. Editor Anna Brewer, together with Sam Nicholls, combed through every word of the manuscript, gave invaluable advice, and helped make this a better book.

Enormous thanks to Kevin Kopjak for helping me to track down many long-lost photographs, and to Kevin Berne and Tom Chargin for so graciously giving me access to their remarkable archive of theater photos, from which I have drawn.

My agent Leah Hamos provided expert guidance on working with a publisher and encouraged me every step of the way, as did my colleague Brian Kulick who wrote three books to my one during the pandemic and constantly opened my eyes to new ways of thinking.

As always, my mother Marjorie Perloff has been my most rigorous and perceptive reader, giving me fertile ideas about structure, readership, context, and interpretation.

I wrote this book during the pandemic lockdown, which I shared day to day with my brilliant British husband Anthony Giles, who kept me laughing and happy throughout as we read aloud from Pinter's and Stoppard's work and reveled in their linguistic genius, and with my daughter Lexie whose intense work ethic from upstairs in her childhood bedroom inspired me to sit at my desk for longer hours than I would have otherwise, knowing we would meet for lunch, dinner and cocktails when the time came. My son Nick aka Wingtip and my sister Nancy Perloff gave me encouragement over the course of many walks.

More than anything, this book is for future theater artists and future audiences, in the hopes that the work of Harold Pinter and Tom Stoppard will continue to resonate, move, awaken, and delight new generations, and to offer as much invigorating solace and sheer pleasure as it has given me.

Introduction

The Case for a Shared View of Pinter's and Stoppard's Work

On the morning of March 16, 2020, as the effects of the Covid-19 pandemic were beginning to be felt across the world, we were ordered to "shelter in place" in San Francisco. An uncanny feeling of dread had already begun to spread throughout the city. Looking out my window, everything appeared "normal"— skies were blue, cyclists were hurtling through Golden Gate Park en route to the ocean, newspapers were being delivered. But the air was infected. Danger seemed to be lurking everywhere, even if we could not see it or put our finger on it. A kind of heightened silence, an inchoate dread, a palpable menace pervaded the collective psyche. I began thinking about Harold Pinter.

When Harold Hobson reviewed the first production of Pinter's *The Birthday Party* in 1956, he said, "Mr. Pinter's (threat) is of a subtler sort. It breathes in the air. It cannot be seen, but it enters the room every time the door is opened. There is something in your past—it doesn't matter what— which will catch up with you . . . There is terror everywhere."[1] On that first night of the virus lockdown, I pulled my *Collected Plays of Harold Pinter* off the shelf (as I have done during many moments of disruption or change in my life) and spent the evening rereading *The Homecoming* aloud with my husband. The queasy terror of the play's first lines (MAX: "What have you done with the scissors?") brilliantly launches this violent and erotic tale of a seemingly ordinary East End Jewish family after the war. Two grown boys live with their dad, whose brother drives upscale clients around London in his fancy car, and on the night the play occurs, the educated son who has gone off to America comes home for a visit with his wife Ruth. The anxiety of the visitors as they walk into that dark and fraught house is excruciating. What we witness in the course of the play is an entire kingdom collapsing. The World of Max, patriarchal, aggressive, weak, toxic, Jewish, and territorial, succumbs to the World of Ruth, seductive, secretive, sexual, mysterious, and answering to no one but herself. And as that collapse gets under way, the slightest move incites terror.

Pinter knew about the effects of war. He grew up during the Blitz in London and encountered both extreme violence and pervasive anti-Semitism. He understood what it felt like to sit inside a perfectly ordinary room and jump with fear at a knock on the door. He also intuited that terror has an erotic component, and that indeed all human relations are on some level sexual. In Pinter's dramaturgy, power and dominance are the goals by which life is lived. You are either predator or prey. Action reveals character. Truth is fungible. Perhaps this is why Pinter's plays do not "date"—they are metaphoric enough to be eternal, and visceral or "local" enough to be immediate and recognizable. Besides, they are hilarious. For all of those reasons and more, his plays felt like perfect companions in a pandemic.

For me, encountering Pinter was the beginning of my life in the theater. As a Stanford undergraduate, I was introduced to his work by British journalist and critic Martin Esslin, whose *The Theatre of the Absurd* helped define a new kind of dramaturgy that began emerging after the Second World War. If in subsequent decades it became clear that Esslin's categories were somewhat artificial and that they strove to link work that had less in common than he suggested, *The Theatre of the Absurd* was an important introduction to a new kind of theatrical writing and a different way of thinking about the relationship of drama to audience. I had studied Beckett before reading Esslin, but it was Esslin who led me straight to Pinter. Over the course of my career as a director and artistic director, I had numerous occasions to collaborate with Pinter personally and to observe his work up close. The mysterious well of menace and sexuality that lay beneath the surface of his plays became a terrain I knew intimately and have never tired of exploring.

Pinter's impact upon my thinking as a theater director may be outsized in part because I met him when I was so young: I had become Artistic Director of the Classic Stage Company (CSC), an indigent downtown company in New York, in my mid-twenties, and when we produced the American premiere of *Mountain Language*, just after I had given birth to my first child, Pinter came to New York to be part of the rehearsal process. I can only imagine what he must have thought when he walked into the building on 13th Street and encountered a young woman who had a ten-day-old baby girl and was about to tackle the American premiere of his new play in the spotlight of New York theater with the playwright himself in attendance. But he never evinced a moment of doubt in front of me or the cast. Reams have been written about Pinter's temper and oppositional character, but this was not my experience of him. On the contrary, his love of the rehearsal process and his forensic exploration of every theatrical moment put him in a democratic position with anyone in the room willing to be as engaged as he was with the task at hand. I am fully prepared to acknowledge that my perception of Pinter stands in contrast to that of other artists, and certainly I had been warned about his temper, which apparently could erupt with particular virulence when American politics came up. But neither in the rehearsal room nor in my many subsequent encounters with Pinter did the atmosphere ever feel embattled or threatening.

One singular incident may serve to illustrate our collaboration. In the chaos of organizing rehearsals, raising money, casting and designing the production, and experiencing motherhood for the first time, I had not yet had time to organize childcare when we began work at CSC in 1989. I therefore brought my daughter to the theater every day and tucked her into a dressing room backstage, where she slept in her carrycot as we worked (fortunately, she has always been a spectacular sleeper). Pinter never mentioned this fact, and I was not even sure he knew there was an infant back there until one day when we hit a snag in rehearsal for *Mountain Language*.

Mountain Language concerns a "mountain people" who have been forbidden by the government from speaking their own language in the capital of their own country; some of their men have been arrested and held in custody, and the women have come to the prison to try to contact them. Among these is an Elderly Woman who, in Scene 2, faces her son (a political prisoner) across a table and tries to convey to him, telepathically, that "the baby is waiting for you . . . They are all waiting for you." Peter Riegert played the Prisoner, forbidden by the State from seeing his own child. The desperate thoughts of mother and son were revealed to the audience in pre-recorded voice overs, as the two sat silently across from each other; any information the Prisoner could glean about his child had to come from his silent mother's eyes. This scene demanded enormously challenging emotional transparency from both actors. Riegert struggled with how to sustain the tension of the situation without "indicating" his grief. During early days of rehearsal, he constantly felt that he was miscast, being much more accustomed to playing characters with status and control, such as Goldberg in *The Birthday Party*. Try as we might, none of us felt that the despair of the scene was visceral enough.

Suddenly one day, Pinter, who had been watching rehearsals carefully and respectfully, stood up, walked backstage, picked up the carrycot containing my sleeping baby, and brought her onto the stage where we were working. Placing her on the table, he said to Riegert: "This is your child. You have been forbidden ever to see her. Through no fault of your own. Ever. You see? It's not at all abstract, it's very simple. You long for her, and you can't see her. That's what's going on here." The room went very quiet, and Riegert stared at the sleeping child in her carrycot. He nodded. He looked back up at Jean Stapleton, who was playing his heartbroken, frightened mother. We could almost hear their hearts beating. They started from the top and played the scene, fully and honestly. When it was finished, Pinter returned my infant to her dressing room. We never discussed what had happened, but from that point on, the scene was always visceral and real. My favorite opening night photograph from that production was Lauren Bacall cooing over baby Lexie, who remained blissfully unaware of the key role she had played in

FIGURE 1 *Baby Lexie Perloff-Giles with Lauren Bacall, opening night of* The
Birthday Party *at CSC. Photo by Ted Keenan, courtesy of CSC Repertory, 1989.*

excavating *Mountain Language*'s emotional charge. But the playwright
always asked after her in the years to come.

Pinter's plays have loomed large in my life each time I found myself
crossing a difficult juncture or tackling a new opportunity. My first production
of *The Birthday Party* was connected with Lexie's birth, *Celebration* and *The
Room* became entwined with the trauma of 9/11, *The Homecoming* was my
battle cry to sustain a Core Company in spite of the 2008 Great Recession,
and *The Birthday Party* (Take 2) marked my farewell to the leadership of a
theater I had led and adored for twenty-five years. Thus, it was perhaps
fitting that the catastrophe of Covid-19 triggered my desire to write this
book and, ironically, engendered the solitude necessary to finish it.

I like to say that it was Harold Pinter who first got me into the theater and
Tom Stoppard who kept me there. Of the many writers with whom I have
collaborated over my directing career, Pinter and Stoppard are the lodestars,
the constants, the two with whom I have shared the deepest aesthetic
sympathy and enjoyed the most fruitful creative experiences. Why this is true
I am not entirely sure, but every director has a muse or two that activates his
or her imagination unlike any others. Our shared Jewish connection and
intellectual interests were at least a part of the camaraderie we felt, as I shall
discuss in Chapter 1. With Pinter, my collaboration began in New York in

1989. My decades-long collaboration with Stoppard was launched in 1993, during my first season as Artistic Director of A.C.T. (American Conservatory Theater), when I tried to secure the rights to *Arcadia*, which were being held by the Lincoln Center due to the concurrent New York production. Deeply frustrated, I wrote to the playwright to plead my case; the result was a long and wonderful epistolary conversation with Stoppard that yielded not only the rights to produce *Arcadia* in San Francisco but the beginnings of a fruitful collaboration and friendship that continues to this day.

Stoppard's work has informed my own directing and playwriting practice for three decades. Over the course of my tenure at A.C.T., I directed ten productions of Stoppard plays (*Arcadia* twice, *Night and Day*, *The Real Thing*, *Travesties*, *Rock 'n' Roll*, *Indian Ink* twice, *The Invention of Love*, and *The Hard Problem*) and collaborated with him personally on nearly all of them. As with the work of Pinter, I have come to find that Stoppard's plays have given structure to the architecture of my own life. *Arcadia* launched my 25-year tenure at A.C.T., *The Invention of Love* coincided with the dawning of a new century and a major fire in my house, *Rock 'n' Roll* gave us ballast in the midst of the financial meltdown of 2008, *Indian Ink* softened the loss of my father, and *The Hard Problem* helped celebrate the burgeoning musical career of my son Nick aka Wingtip, who sat in the back of the Geary Theater in 2017 and created a score for our production side by side with a writer he had known since birth.

I often wonder what was it about these two extremely different writers that has spoken to me so deeply over the course of my creative life. Aesthetically, Pinter and Stoppard are not obviously connected, although the two men were friendly for most of their careers and at one time played cricket together on a fairly regular basis. Early assessments of their work by theater critics often lumped them together: Kenneth Tynan, who "discovered" Stoppard after *Rosencrantz and Guildenstern are Dead* premiered at the Edinburgh Festival, quickly asserted that "in terms of international prestige, the standard of British playwriting was held by Harold Pinter, Peter Shaffer and Stoppard,"[2] an opinion seconded by mainstream critics who seemed comfortable pairing Stoppard's and Pinter's plays as vital and important British "exports." On the surface, however, they sit on opposite sides of many polarities: Pinter was a dedicated Leftist politically (much more so in his later life) while Stoppard has been considered "conservative" for his resistance to making group statements or avowals; Pinter was lumped from the beginning with "Theater of the Absurd" writers that included Beckett and Ionesco, while Stoppard's work appeared in the West End early on and has always attracted a broad and occasionally commercial audience. One is a minimalist, the other is a maximalist. One is visceral, the other cerebral. One is visually pure, the other is visually outrageous. Pinter's plays are filled with silences, Stoppard's with a torrent of words. Pinter's characters are generally confined to a room, Stoppard's travel the globe, often in the course of a single scene.

Thus, it might appear that the differences between these two writers outweigh the similarities, when viewing them across the landscape of post-war English theater. Pinter is a playwright of intense observation, with an uncanny ability to mine the simplest of situations for the hidden current of menace, violence, and power play underneath. His is a drama of mystery, of subtext, of terror. He writes about what he knows: Jewish patriarchs in the east end of London (*The Homecoming*), sexual politics amongst literary Londoners (*Betrayal*), the terror of artistic independence and rebellion (*The Birthday Party*). His plays usually take place in a single space, in an atmosphere so denuded of superfluous detail that the slightest move is a radical act. He is uniquely able to take seemingly ordinary speech and lift it onto the plane of poetry without ever disconnecting it from the guts and heartbeat of his characters. Stoppard, by contrast, is a writer of ideas. Following his own internal dialectic, he sets off to create characters and situations that can best reveal his own debates in dramatically satisfying ways. "I'm a playwright interested in ideas and forced to invent characters to express those ideas," Stoppard told the critic Mel Gussow in 1979.[3]

Pinter and Stoppard themselves were deeply aware of the aesthetic differences in their work. Indeed, in a 1974 interview with Gussow, Stoppard said, "I don't mean this literally, but I have this feeling that I could've written most other people's plays and most other people could've written mine, because I know how it's done and they know how it's done. But with one or two people—I think Harold Pinter is an example—you don't know how it's done. And I couldn't do it."[4] In an earlier interview with Gussow in April 1972, Stoppard elaborated:

> I think Pinter did something equally important and significant. He changed the ground rules. One thing plays had in common: you were supposed to believe what people said up there. If somebody comes on and says, "Tea or coffee?" and the answer is "Tea," you are entitled to assume that somebody is offering a choice of two drinks and the second person has stated a preference. With a Pinter play, you can no longer make that assumption.[5]

Stoppard told a wonderful story to Shusha Guppy in *The Paris Review* about Pinter:

> The first time I met Harold Pinter was when I was a journalist in Bristol and he came down to see a student production of *The Birthday Party*. I realized he was sitting in the seat in front of me. I was tremendously intimidated and spent a good long time working out how to engage him in conversation. Finally, I tapped him on the shoulder and said, "Are you Harold Pinter or do you just look like him?" He said, "What?" So that was the end of that.[6]

Stoppard passionately defended Pinter's work and has made it clear that he never felt he came near to the elder writer in terms of contributions to the theater. He was dismayed when Christopher Hitchens wrote a dismissive column about Pinter on the occasion of Pinter's winning the Nobel Prize; Stoppard wrote Hitchens a four-page letter trying to explain what was unique and irreplaceable about Pinter:

> It was—at the time—counter-intuitive to see that a shortfall of information, rather than a surplus, is what can make the theatre hold up the mirror, and that the effect is dramatic—funny, disturbing, fascinating . . . and not because the writer is withholding information tactically, but because he doesn't know the answers. Not knowing the answers is the modus vivendi . . . It opened up a different street.[7]

I'm not sure this argument convinced Hitchens; nor, perhaps, did it quite address the core of Pinter's genius, which to my mind is the way in which he articulates unconscious appetites in highly specific idiomatic language that is simultaneously mythic and meticulous.

Hermione Lee's masterful 2020 biography of Stoppard makes much of the closeness between the two writers, although I rarely experienced that personally—certainly, they spoke highly of each other, but mostly stayed in their own lanes. However, Stoppard was devastated when Pinter died (on December 24, 2008), writing a beautiful condolence letter to Pinter's wife Antonia Fraser and then, a year later, a wonderful poem entitled "Another Time" about the intimidating process of dropping in on a Pinter rehearsal. The poem ends:

> was it? was it?
> was it what for fucksake
> oh open yes I see yes
> how very pinteresque
> but haroldly he broke for tea
> for he was always kind to me
> I wish I'd brought a cake.

If queried about Stoppard, Pinter may well have conveyed the same sense of both admiration and distance, from his own unique point of view. "I think I am in a trap, always. I sometimes wish desperately that I could write like someone else, *be* someone else. I often feel that about waking up with myself in the morning. You're trapped with yourself all your damn life . . . If I were someone else I would probably create a different air."[8] Pinter marveled at writers who invented new worlds or set their plays in exotic locations, as Stoppard did, but that was never where his own instincts lay. Each of them carved out a language that was utterly distinct and sui generis. Both have had endless imitators, yet no real peers; in each case, a few lines of dialogue from the plays suffice to identify the author.

Why, then, couple these two writers in a single study? I would like to argue that when Pinter and Stoppard are considered together, facets of their work are revealed which have hitherto been less examined and which shed light on both. If the form of their work is different, their biographies and their passion for the actual making of theater become surprisingly complimentary when viewed through a shared lens. My understanding of the "rules of play" that pertain to each was abetted by having worked so extensively on the work of both; I carried my lessons from Pinter into my exploration of Stoppard's work and vice versa. In the same way, Pinter and Stoppard learned from and admired each other's work over the course of many decades. On the occasion of Stoppard's fiftieth birthday in 1987, Pinter wrote something about Stoppard that could equally have been said about himself,

> He is his own man. He's gone his own way from the word go. He follows his nose. It's a pretty sharp one. Nobody pushes him around. He writes what he likes—not what others might like him to write. But in doing so he has succeeded in writing serious plays which are also immensely popular. You can count on the fingers of one hand those who have brought that off. But, indisputably, he's one of them. He doesn't look fifty either.[9]

What I learned from Pinter during rehearsals in New York gave me a set of parameters that I have used when staging his work ever since. The same happened when I first got into the studio with Stoppard. Obviously, the presence of the writer is not a necessary nor, often, a possible condition in a working director's life. And it is not always a boon; there are writers who are so prescriptive that the creative life of the rehearsal room gets stifled by their involvement. Directing is an iterative process in which a script slowly reveals itself on stage through rigorous examination and the freedom to play and fail until solutions are reached which feel true to the spirit of the text. The direct involvement of Pinter and Stoppard during this process of discovery was invaluable to me. How does a director uncover the laws governing the unique and mysterious world of a given play? What is the roadmap that will help guide the journey into that unfamiliar landscape? And how do the specific and idiosyncratic laws of a given play inform how that play gets cast, designed, rehearsed, imagined on stage? These questions are particularly challenging when dealing with a dramaturgy that is not, strictly speaking, "realism." If one cannot rely on certain accepted truths or realistic markers to navigate a play, what path does one follow? Equally importantly, if one is part of the American theater tradition in which psychology, confession, and the tropes of naturalism are almost always the starting positions from which a play is explored, how does one approach the unique worlds of Pinter and Stoppard? This is when it is a particular privilege to be in the rehearsal room with writers who are able to bring the "laws" of their plays into focus in ways that can then be remembered and activated in subsequent productions of that writer's work.

This is not to say that the playwright is always "right" or that there is a single correct way to stage a play. But an active spirit of collaboration on the part of the playwright helps ensure that all the artists involved are pursuing the same quarry. Pinter and Stoppard, from the advent of their very first plays, shared a delight in and forensic pursuit of the perfect *word*, the richest possible use of language. There is a distilled poetry in Pinter's work that is as vivid and meticulous as Shakespeare's blank verse. ("I suppose Shakespeare's dominated my life the way he's dominated many people's lives," Pinter told Gussow in 1988. "We don't recover from Shakespeare."[10]) Embedded in Pinter's language, if you know how to find them, are all the clues an actor needs to understand the "meaning" of the text. "The music and the rhythm will tell you what you mean," he explained. "You can work yourself into the ground, and you won't ever get anywhere unless you get the precise emphasis, and then the sense of the sentence will become clear."[11] The sound of a word or a phrase in Pinter is as crucial as its meaning; this may stem from his earliest schooldays in which he apparently conversed in an almost private language of invented words and puns with his friends, one of whom, Mick Goldstein, later explained,

> It is useless to try to recall the effect these phrases had on me now, since then, I was hearing them for the first time. I could appreciate Harold's use of the type of language that would result from the occasional distortion of using nouns, adjectives and verbs indiscriminately. It was possible to invent a completely private language. I am not saying that I immediately understood what it was that was being said, but there was a lack of concern if the meaning of a phrase eluded one's attempt to interpret it, provided that it had a life of its own.[12]

Similarly, there is a complex and highly crafted elegance to Stoppard's language that lifts ideas to the level of desire. In our collaborations, both writers gave explicit instructions in the rehearsal room about how their language was to be accessed and through what methods the force of their words could best be activated.

Furthermore, from their earliest days as young writers, both Pinter and Stoppard were inherently suspicious of *theory*. They were not aiming for abstract or existential truths but for theatrical events that would rivet an audience's attention. Pinter quipped in his speech "On Being Awarded the German Shakespeare Prize in Hamburg": "Someone asked me what my work was 'about'. I replied with no thought at all and merely to frustrate this line of enquiry, 'The weasel under the cocktail cabinet'. That was a great mistake. Over the years I have seen that remark quoted in a number of learned columns . . . But for me the remark meant precisely nothing." (Actor Peter Riegert, who memorably played Goldberg for me in *The Birthday Party* at CSC, felt the "weasel" description really referred to the experience of seeing a play; he believed the "cocktail cabinet" represented the polite veneer of the theater, where a well-behaved audience came to watch a play, and the "weasels" were the actors who inevitably wreaked havoc on the proceedings.) Literal biographical interpretations annoyed Pinter as much as theoretical ones; Hermione Lee relates a story about a dinner table argument in the early 1970s in which Miriam Stoppard asked Pinter whether he believed a writer drew more upon his life or his imagination to inspire his work. "Pinter, outraged, at once lost his temper and berated her," relates Hermione Lee. "Miriam cried." Apparently, Pinter was defending his point of view that he never planned his characters' lives or knew how they were going to behave in any given moment, but simply followed his instincts. This was not Stoppard's experience of writing, and he allowed his wife to argue it out alone with his fellow playwright. Later Pinter sent Miriam flowers in apology.[13]

Stoppard is similarly resistant to academic or biographical analysis; the first time I ever queried Stoppard about a given moment in one of his plays (*Arcadia*), he replied bashfully that it was about sex. Stoppard's antipathy to personal disclosure mirrors Pinter's; "Biography is the mesh through which real life escapes," Eleanor Swan says tartly to her sister's biographer Eldon Pike in *Indian Ink*. Indeed, when Stoppard writes biographers into his plays (from Pike to Bernard Nightingale in *Arcadia*) they are notoriously unreliable. "Perhaps I'll get him a reporter doll for Christmas," says Ruth in *Night and Day*. "Wind it up and it gets it wrong." This is not to say that the lives, loves, and losses of both writers have not found their way into the fabric of the plays, on the contrary. The more deeply I got to know Pinter and Stoppard as human beings, the more their plays revealed themselves to me; those discoveries are, in part, the subject of this book. In both cases, I have found the psychological depth of their writing breathtaking. But the connections between fiction and life are mysterious and subterranean, and rarely present obvious equivalences. Now that Hermione Lee's biography has come out, perhaps scholars will start analyzing Stoppard's plays with a finer biographical comb.

From their first forays into theater, both Pinter and Stoppard have displayed wicked senses of humor that often mask dark and complex themes. (The critic Kenneth Tynan made a famous assessment that the playwrights of his time fell into two categories: "the hairy men—heated, embattled, socially-committed playwrights, like John Osborne, John Arden, and Arnold Wesker"; and the "smooth men—cool, apolitical stylists, like Harold Pinter, the late Joe Orton, Christopher Hampton, Alan Ayckbourn, Simon Gray and Tom Stoppard."[14]) Comedy can be chilling or it can be reassuring, but much of what makes both Pinter and Stoppard's work funny is *subterfuge*. These are not *confessional* playwrights. For me, this is one of the most salient aspects of their work.

In Stoppard's universe, *thought* is paramount. His characters are what they think. The erotic charge, which is considerable, is connected to the force of their ideas. You cannot separate Thomasina from her intellectual passions, no matter how much her desire for Septimus colors her words. *Arcadia* is a love story, but it is as much a love story about mathematics and fractals as it is about the momentary coming together of a nineteenth century girl and her tutor. Stoppard's reverence for a richly imagined linguistic life means that even his minor characters display a kind of verbal dexterity rarely seen in the actual world, but that is what makes his writing unique and compelling. He pays more attention to the necessary "gear change" (his term) engendered by the word "if" than most writers pay to entire sentences. As with Pinter's work, biography and confession, the tools of the trade in American drama, prove less useful in staging Stoppard's work than behavior, desire, and an almost athletic approach to language.

When you read about Pinter's youth, his gang of friends describe how they learned to "take the piss," using language to deflect, distract, and delight, but rarely to "reveal." The gap between what is said and what is meant in a Pinter play, or what lies buried beneath a Stoppardian joke, is thus terrain worthy of exploration. Stoppard shared Vaclav Havel's theory that humor is based in "incongruous juxtaposition" or an excess of literalism, which leads to delicious lines like Thomasina's "Septimus, what is carnal embrace?" to which he replies, "The process of throwing one's arms around a side of beef." Directing Pinter's and Stoppard's work inevitably involves figuring out how to activate complex language in a way that keeps the surface structure (or the joke) taut but allows the underlying emotional energy to move forward. I have spent many rehearsals trying to help psychologically trained American artists find their way into the mysteries of Pinter's or Stoppard's work without overburdening it with their own "feelings" or their desire for a more naked emotional expression and a more visible arc of experience.

I remember assuring Pinter's agent Judy Daish in 1988 that if she would grant me the rights to *The Birthday Party* at CSC, I would get the comedy right, as I was married to a Brit and would not burden the plays with too much earnest American psychology. That made her laugh, but still it took extensive persuasion by the poet and playwright Tony Harrison (whose *Phaedra Britannica* I had just directed) before she finally agreed. Like Pinter, Stoppard has been known to say that he believes most Americans are missing the "irony key" on their keyboard, and thus he is meticulous about helping actors access the humor in the language of his plays, down to the last syllable. I recall an incident in which the actress playing Ruth in *Night and Day*, which is set in a fictitious African country, was not getting her laugh in an early exchange, a laugh built on Guthrie's assumption that Ruth had not returned to her native London in years: "CARSON: Actually, Ruth was born in London. GUTHRIE: Really? Well, you wouldn't know it now. When were you last there? RUTH: Friday." Stoppard patiently explained to

Rene Augesen that she was dropping the second syllable of "Friday" and was thus eviscerating the desired comedic result.

Because the work of these two writers has always felt so congenial to me, it was only recently, in discussing Pinter and Stoppard with directors, actors, and designers less familiar with their plays, that I realized how oblique they could feel from the outside, at least in North America. Hence the impulse for this book. Each time I collaborated with Pinter and Stoppard, the landscape of the plays became both more familiar and more exhilarating to explore. Eventually, I stopped being anxious about "not knowing" underlying meanings in advance, and trusted that, over time, I would accrue enough tools to find my way through the mysteries of even their most difficult plays. I had also learned rehearsal techniques that I believed might be valuable to share. This is thus a study by a working theater artist, not an academic; it attempts to interpret and reveal the essence of the plays by exploring how they actually function on stage. It has been my experience that although Pinter's and Stoppard's plays are a staple of theaters around the world, the critical discourse around their work, based primarily on a reading of their texts, has not, with a few notable exceptions, proved useful for theater practitioners. Why has this been the case? Perhaps because drama is rarely part of the curriculum of English departments, at least not in America; drama is simply not considered a "serious enough" art form to merit the kind of analysis given to poetry and the novel. Robert Brustein articulated this unfortunate situation so clearly when he described his interview to join a literature seminar at Columbia taught by his mentor Lionel Trilling: "He (Trilling) was not happy about my theatrical interests. Drama for him was what Sir Philip Sidney called a poor stepsister of the arts, not a serious literary pursuit."[15] Conversely, when it comes to pre-professional drama departments, at least American ones, the work of dramatists like Pinter and Stoppard is rarely central to training that is either focused on Stanislavskian psychological techniques or on issues such as representation, identity, authenticity, and social justice. While I believe that both Pinter's and Stoppard's work requires actors of capacious psychological range and while their work expresses significant thinking about injustice, censorship, a free press and individual expression, it has become increasingly clear to me that, with some exceptions, young actors and directors are given few if any tools with which to approach what I consider to be some of the great theatrical writing of our era. I hope this book may help to change that situation. More than anything else, I have wanted to share these thoughts because my collaborations with Pinter and Stoppard have consistently pushed me to become a better, more imaginative, and more rigorous artist.

As I began, in preparation for writing this book, to look back over decades of collaboration and to contemplate what I had learned, I occasionally wondered why I had not felt terrified to be in the rehearsal room with those two writers. It was not as if I had either experience or theatrical training to boast of when I began working on their plays. But neither seemed to care that I was young and inexperienced; both had started their careers in their twenties without having gone to graduate school or having had any connection to the professional theater, so my own unorthodox career trajectory—I have no formal theater training—must have felt familiar to them. They certainly had no bias against youth. "There was something else I found very gracious," Jean Stapleton (who played Meg in the CSC production of *The Birthday Party*) said of Pinter. "He did not encroach on Carey's turf. He did it so graciously. He respected her position as director."[16]

This graciousness toward his collaborators seems to have been part of Pinter's make-up from the beginning. The director Giles Havergal tells a wonderful story about Pinter coming to play Lenny in *The Homecoming* at the Watford Palace Theatre (where Havergal was Artistic Director in the 1960s). The director of the production was a very young and inexperienced man, Stephen Hollis, whose first professional outing this was. According to Havergal, Pinter treated Hollis with generosity and deference throughout the process. However difficult Pinter could sometimes be, he seemed to understand intuitively that a productive rehearsal room was one in which the actors respected the director, and he was going to set the tone.

As a female director, I realize this courtesy cannot be taken for granted. On many occasions in my theatrical career, I have known what it feels like to be rendered invisible by "great men." Nor do I mean to sound pollyannaish about the situation of being a woman director in rehearsal with two of the

FIGURE 2 *Tom Stoppard and Carey Perloff in rehearsal at A.C.T. 2004. Photo courtesy of David Allen.*

most powerful men in British drama. It did make me laugh when I read Hermione Lee's account of Trevor Nunn taking Miriam Stoppard aside, shortly after she and Stoppard had got together, and saying to her, "You will look after him, won't you?"[17] The idea that anyone would say this to the male partner of a female artist, no matter how famous, is impossible to imagine. Regardless, because of our mutual intellectual interests, our mutual sense of humor, our shared aesthetic, and perhaps because of our mutual backgrounds, I was able to work with both writers as colleagues in an atmosphere of mutual respect. On every occasion, the experience was one of joy and discovery, never of intimidation or fear. We felt like congenial artists in pursuit of the same goals.

Given that my process for exploring the plays of Pinter and Stoppard is so connected to my knowledge of the two writers themselves, this book is in part a portrait of the artists as they revealed themselves to me in rehearsal. As such, it is by no means objective or complete; it was built up through pre-production correspondence, rehearsal experiences, notes from run-throughs and performances, and the many meals, drinks, phone calls, and panel discussions we engaged in together. My goal here is not so much to add to the broader biographical material available on Pinter and Stoppard or to comprehensively discuss all the plays, but to shine a light on specific working methods discovered in production, and to argue that the surest way to understand the plays is to figure out how to make them come alive onstage.

Central to the successful staging of a playwright's work is an intuitive understanding of that writer's individual *voice*. This is abetted not only by a comprehensive knowledge of the writer's whole oeuvre but a sense of the formative cultural factors that underlie the work. As I suggested earlier, my interpretation of, and personal connection to, Pinter's and Stoppard's aesthetic, humor, and creative impulse is connected to a biographical fact that is often overlooked, namely that both are Jewish. Thus, the first chapter of this book argues that their connection to Central European Jewish culture and their childhood wartime experiences helped shape their plays in crucial ways. Chapter 2 looks at the broader cultural landscape of post-war England and the environment that shaped Pinter's and Stoppard's arrival on the scene. While British readers may have a deeper knowledge of this period of cultural history than most Americans, I believe it is valuable for all those interested in the work to understand not just how radical Pinter's and Stoppard's plays felt when they first emerged, but how connected they were to a theatrical tradition that we may have forgotten today. Chapter 3 provides an overview of the "rules of play" (from casting to design to choreography to shaping of language) that I employ as a director when approaching Pinter's and Stoppard's work. The second half of the book (Chapters 4–7) focuses on individual plays (starting with Pinter's *The Birthday Party* and Stoppard's *Indian Ink*) as they revealed themselves to me through specific rehearsal experiences. The book does not cover Pinter's and

FIGURE 3 *Harold Pinter, Carey Perloff and cast members at the Perloff-Giles apartment in the East Village, 1989, Photo courtesy of Tom Chargin.*

Stoppard's whole oeuvre; I have focused on those plays I have staged which have most deeply involved the participation of the playwright and for which I feel I have something valuable to add. More time is spent on some of the lesser-known works, such as Pinter's *Celebration* and *The Room* or Stoppard's *Rock 'n' Roll, The Invention of Love*, and *The Hard Problem* than on masterpieces such as *Betrayal* and *Arcadia*. But I hope that the principles elucidated will be useful to an understanding of their writing as a whole.

Over the course of their many decades in the theater, any number of cliches and myths have grown up around Pinter and Stoppard; they are legends who seem to engender hyperbole and anxiety in equal measure. I will feel gratified if this book helps to humanize two playwrights whom I found to be passionate, collaborative, endlessly curious, devoted to their work, and always up for a laugh. During a year of pandemic isolation in which live theater seemed impossibly remote, the writing of this book re-engaged me with the joy and vitality that rehearsals with Pinter and Stoppard brought to my life and to the lives of countless other artists. For that, I am eternally grateful.

1

The Jewish Connection

If finding a playwright's "voice" is a key to realizing their work onstage (see Chapter 2), a crucial aspect of both Pinter's and Stoppard's life histories is that both are Jewish. Not only Jewish, but Central European Jews who came of age in the traumatic period of the Second World War and the Holocaust. This salient fact has begun to be more deeply explored in recent years; for me, the "Jewish thread" has consistently informed my own understanding about, and interpretation of, their work. In the New York theater, where Judaism is pervasive, the fact that these two major figures happened to be Jewish may seem inconsequential. But in the universe of post-war Britain which Pinter and Stoppard entered as young men and young writers, it was significant. I would like to argue that Pinter's and Stoppard's Jewish heritage ultimately had a profound impact upon their plays and is a useful angle to explore in the rehearsal room.

I first met Stoppard in a bar in the lobby of the National Theatre in London in 1994. The "Jewish question" had not really surfaced for him in the way it would after his mother died in 1996, but I sensed even then that we had a particular bond. He asked me about my family, about my children and my English husband, and also about my parents. I explained that they were vigorous Jewish intellectuals with distinguished careers, my mother (a Viennese refugee) as a literary critic, my father as a cardiologist, both professors. Stoppard and I were pleased to discover early on that both of our fathers had been physicians who specialized in diseases of the *heart*. While my family was entirely secularized (as was Stoppard's), a consciousness of being Jewish was central to my upbringing and to the narrative of my family's life. Education, family, language, and knowledge of our past were of paramount importance. The family religion was *culture*. My Viennese grandfather (who could spot a "hidden Jew" a mile off and always knew when someone had changed his name from "Ben'levi" to "Benoliel" to avoid the "taint" of Judaism) knew every single painting in Vienna's Kuntshistorisches Museum and told me that when he closed his eyes, he could move from art work to art work in his mind and experience them all perfectly. I was raised as an avid museum-goer, book-lover, and believer in the life of the mind. At the same time, I became highly accustomed to

"Englishness," having wed a British man, Anthony Giles, whom I had met at Oxford during my Fulbright year in 1980; I have spent more than thirty-five years of marriage reveling in his wit, irony, charm, and linguistic dexterity. (When I first brought Anthony home to meet my parents, I was worried that they would be unhappy he was not Jewish, but since my parents were great Anglophiles—my father always treasured his year at the National Heart Hospital on Wimpole Street—Anthony's Englishness trumped his non-Jewish status and they embraced him immediately.)

Clearly, by the time I met Stoppard he had mastered "Englishness" better than most Englishmen. Yet underneath was something different. It was not just the slight hint of an Eastern European accent, it was a warmth, a sexuality, an eccentricity, a shyness (that "outsider" status), a verbal panache and an intellectual curiosity that felt familiar. And somewhere, there was sorrow, a sorrow that reminded me of my beautiful Viennese grandmother, on whose face there was always the trace of a memory about what she had lost. In addition, Stoppard had an Eastern European sense of the absurd: the first plays I had ever directed were by Slawomir Mrozek (*Tango* and *Lost at Sea*) and Witold Gombrowicz (*The Marriage*), and I was not surprised to discover that one of Stoppard's first theatrical assignments was to create a version of *Tango* for the Royal Shakespeare Company (RSC) in May 1966. Kafka was another link. Perhaps because he was, at heart, more Central European than English, Stoppard's demeanor and outlook seemed even on the surface quite different from the cadre of "second wave" British playwrights of that period (David Hare, Howard Brenton, Snoo Wilson, David Edgar, and so on) with whom I felt little affinity. In some strangely atavistic way, Stoppard and I valued the same things and knew how to talk to each other.

I had a similar sense of recognition the day I first met Harold Pinter. The tone of that encounter was quite different: my meeting with Stoppard was instantly congenial and chatty, whereas my first meeting with Pinter was slightly terrifying. At CSC (the Classic Stage Company) where I was Artistic Director, I had directed a successful production of *The Birthday Party* in 1988 which Pinter had heard about. As the *New York Times* reported it,

> Last Spring Harold Pinter sent Lauren Bacall down to Manhattan's East 13th Street to take a look at CSC Repertory's production of his play "The Birthday Party." Her report so intrigued the playwright that when visiting New York in November he arranged to see the small, 180-seat theater and meet CSC's 29-year-old artistic director, Carey Perloff. Pinter was impressed enough, in fact, that he asked Carey to take on the first American production of his newest play, "Mountain Language," the following season.[1]

So it was that, one afternoon, the door to CSC opened and in strolled a tall striking man with a baritone voice who announced himself as Harold Pinter.

He strode through the lobby with vigor and curiously began looking at what was on the walls, sniffing us out. Just like Goldberg arriving at Meg's. He was gracious but laconic. No small talk. A deep voice and a weighty presence. A lady's man. Assertive. Suave. Clearly a theater animal. He surveyed the space and asked all the right questions. Pinter, less loquacious than Stoppard and more averse to small talk, was not there to chat but to work. Because we were preparing to remount our production of *The Birthday Party* in preparation for the double bill with *Mountain Language*, we were already reveling in the singularly Jewish wit, wordplay, and linguistic experimentation Pinter had put into that play, particularly in the mouth of Goldberg (played for us by Peter Riegert, an actor steeped in Catskills comedy). When Pinter arrived at CSC that afternoon, Riegert rushed forward and exclaimed, "Harold! Welcome!" as if meeting a long-lost member of the tribe.

As we began talking about the play, Pinter's eyes lit up and his wicked sense of humor emerged. It was immediately clear that he was an inherently theatrical animal and loved being in the company of actors. As I said in the "Introduction," much has been made of his temper and irritability, but perhaps because we met him in the context of rehearsal, we encountered him at his most open and receptive. I cannot help but think that the Jewish connection may have played a role in that ease as well. The night Pinter arrived in New York, we went for a drink with the cast. What I remember most is how his eyes fastened on the young actress playing Lulu. Her name

FIGURE 4 *Peter Riegert, Carey Perloff, and Harold Pinter on the streets of the East Village, 1989. Photo courtesy of Tom Chargin.*

was Wendy Makkena. Something puzzled him. "Makenna, Makenna . . ." he mused, looking at her curiously. "Irish?" "No," she replied. "Makkena. Scottish?" "No," she demurred. He knew there was a secret there, and did not stop querying until he discovered that she was really Wendy Rosenberg, a young Jewish woman who had changed her name when she became an actress (just as Pinter himself had changed his name to David Baron). He was delighted at this discovery. Unmasking what lurked beneath seemingly banal reality was a central part of his game. It was a game I recognized.

In the post-war period of British playwriting a few other Anglo-Jewish playwrights had emerged: Arnold Wesker, who grew up in Stepney Green (near Pinter's childhood neighborhood) and wrote plays with specifically Jewish themes and characters (*Chicken Soup With Rice, Shylock*); Ronald Harwood (aka Horwitz, born in South Africa); and Steven Berkoff, an actor, playwright, and director whose visceral theatrical language (*East, Greek, Decadence*) inspired a cult following in the eighties. But these were the exceptions to the rule; of the first wave of British playwriting in the late fifties and sixties that included Alan Bennett, David Storey, Edward Bond, Alan Ayckbourn, Michael Frayn, John Arden, Simon Gray and Caryl Churchill, very few were Jews. Regarding attitudes toward Judaism in British theater, Berkoff himself commented, "They quite like diversity and will tolerate you as long as you act a bit Gentile and don't throw your chicken soup around too much. You're perfectly entitled occasionally even to touch the great prophet of British culture, Shakespeare, as long as you keep your Jewishness well zipped up."[2] But Pinter never kept his Jewishness "zipped up." And later in his life, Stoppard has made an enormous effort to explore his own Jewish roots. While neither would have characterized himself as a Jewish writer, I have come to believe that being Jewish defined the gestalt of Pinter's and Stoppard's plays in specific ways that provide access and insight in the rehearsal room. And I would argue that, unlike the Jewish-American writer Arthur Miller who consistently "deracinated" his characters in order to achieve a desired universality (more about this shortly), Pinter's and Stoppard's work has become universal through the creation of highly specific and idiosyncratic characters tied to their pasts and their personae. For this reason, I think their work is less likely to date.

Of the two writers, Pinter was the more "visibly" Jewish, having been raised in Hackney in London's East End by parents whose lives were very much bound up in their Jewish heritage. About his identity Pinter said, "I've no religious beliefs whatsoever, but I'm still Jewish. I don't know what that means, really, nobody ever does." Yet by his own admission, being Jewish had a lasting impact upon Pinter's writing and world view, despite being ignored by most critics; characteristically, in one of the first full-length studies of Pinter's work, *Harold Pinter* by Arnold Hinchcliffe, the assertion is made, "Harold Pinter is quintessentially the *English* (I am tempted to say 'London') representative of the Absurd Theater."[3]

Pinter's father, Jack Pinter, was an Orthodox Jewish tailor; his parents were Central European Jews (of Pinter's grandparents, three were from Poland and one from Odessa) who emigrated to England with few resources and no knowledge of English. A master cutter, Jack Pinter's knowledge of the ins and outs of the garment trade is deliciously echoed by Goldberg in *The Birthday Party*: "Do you like my dress, Mr. Goldberg?" asks Meg in Act 2. "It's out on its own," replies Goldberg. "Turn yourself round a minute. I used to be in the business." Pinter's intense affection for, and connection to, his father is well documented; one story that particularly moved me comes from the filmmaker John Boorman, in whose memoir I found the story about a role Pinter was asked to play in Boorman's film *The Tailor of Panama*: "I recalled that Harold Pinter's father had been an East End tailor, and so I asked him to play the part," Boorman explains. "On the first day he sent word that he wished to see me in his dressing room. I found him studying the script. He was at his most self-important, addressing me in his pompous upper-class voice. He was so far from the East End." But when shooting began, "Harold arrived for the first scene. The elegant playwright had metamorphosed into a small cockney Jewish tailor. He was brilliant."[4] The highly specific behavior and belief-system of his father never left him.

Pinter's mother, Frances Moskowitz, more secular and skeptical about religion than her husband, was the daughter of an entrepreneurial spirit from Odessa, Harry Moskowitz, who could barely write his name when he arrived in London in 1900 but immediately began to make his way in the clothing business. Harry married Polish-born Rose Franklin (Rose became the name of the central character in Pinter's first play, *The Room*) and had four children, one of whom turned out to be an East End boxer who was surely an inspiration for Joey in *The Homecoming*. While the Pinter side of the family was erudite, musical, and Orthodox, the Moskowitz clan was boisterous, gregarious, and more secular. Although Pinter himself was an only child, his youth was spent in the company of a large extended family. "There were constant get-togethers at the paternal grandparents' in Amhurst Road until Nathan's death in 1939," Michael Billington tells us in his biography of Pinter. "Passover . . . was always a big event. The young Harold participated in the ritual of the symbolic descent of the Angel of Death which was always followed by a long, and significantly dramatic, pause."[5]

In his unpublished autobiographical memoir *The Queen of all the Fairies*, Pinter described his childhood neighborhood thus: "Many Jews lived in the district, noisy but candid; mostly taxi drivers and pressers, machinists and cutters who steamed all day in their workshop ovens. Up the hill lived the richer, the 'better-class' Jews, strutting with their mink coats and American suits and ties . . ."[6] So close was only child Harold to his parents that it was deeply traumatic to be sent away to Cornwall (and later to Reading and then Norfolk) during the war, far from family and friends. "There was no fixed sense of being . . . of *being* . . . at all," Pinter told Billington about that extremely alienating period of his life. Later, he reiterated those feelings in an interview with Mel Gussow: "It was—very traumatic. At the time I was only 9 or 10. I missed my parents. We missed each other very much."[7] I found this extremely moving; Pinter's writing is so unsentimental, and his live presence was so powerful and seemingly fearless, it is difficult for me to visualize him as a child who loved and needed his parents so enormously that he risked everything to return to London at the height of the Blitz rather than remain apart from them. No wonder he had such an intuitive understanding of the young Marcel in Proust's *A La Recherche du Temps Perdu*.

The complex nature of the nuclear family, both its potent ties and its destructive energy, is a theme that runs throughout Pinter's work. "The importance of the family, the tribe, of preserving continuity and hierarchy within the cohesive repeating patterns of family life, does seem to be something foreign to British drama in general but powerfully felt in works arising out of a specifically Jewish social and cultural heritage," the critic John Russell Taylor has commented.[8] As if to acknowledge this truth, when Pinter wrote his epic family drama *The Homecoming*, he explained that the play was "about love and lack of love. There's no question that the family does behave very calculatingly and pretty horribly to each other and to the returning son. But they do it out of the texture of their lives and for other reasons which are not evil but slightly desperate."[9] And again in 1980, to Miriam Gross in the *Observer*, "In *The Homecoming*, for example the violence of the family towards their son . . . comes about because they don't know where to *put their love*"[10] (my italics). "I think there's a great deal of love in that play but they simply don't know what to do with it." Lenny expounds upon this theme when reminding Teddy of his betrayal in leaving the family: "When we all sit round the backyard having a quiet gander at the night sky, there's always an empty chair standing in the circle, which is in fact yours," he tells his brother, with echoes of the Prophet Elijah and Passover. The deep ties Pinter felt to his parents and the complex nature of love, loyalty, and betrayal in a Jewish immigrant family are tropes that provide a crucial roadmap for all his plays, right through the later *Moonlight* and *Celebration*, plays which explore the rupture between parents and children when childhood bonds are forgotten or ignored.

Surrounding the complex but mostly loving atmosphere of Pinter's extended family and community was a toxic anti-Semitism that had characterized British culture for decades and was disturbingly present amongst supposedly enlightened post-war thinkers and intellectuals. As recent incidents with Jeremy Corbyn and the British Labour Party continue to remind us, anti-Semitism has lurked beneath the surface of the English left wing for generations. Not only has the literary world rarely acknowledged this, it has often been complicit. In a recent article about his father in *The Tablet*, Jewish writer Jonathan Wilson (aka "Wilsick") writes scathingly about the Bloomsbury group in general and Virginia Woolf in particular when it came to her corrosive attitudes toward Jews, including her own husband, Leonard Woolf, during the period between the wars:

Virginia's obsession with Leonard's Jewishness generated from the very beginning of their relationship one nasty remark after another: "uninhibited racial slurs", as the critic John Gross describes, "corrosive contempt" as Leonard's biographer Victoria Glendinning has it, both to her relatives, friends and to Leonard himself, frequently about her husband, relentlessly about his mother and siblings, and broadly about more or less every Jew with whom she came into contact. She doesn't like the "Jewish voice" or "Jewish laugh" and she specializes in erroneous downgrades. Sir Philip Sassoon, Eton- and Oxford-educated and one time minister for the air force, is "an under-bred Whitechapel Jew". Middle-class Leonard, son of a distinguished barrister when she met him (a QC) was, she liked to say, "a penniless Jew", and Virginia's nephew Quentin Bell reports that at mealtime she would tell the servants to "give the Jew his food".[11]

This is how it was in "educated" Britain between the wars. Pervasive anti-Semitism continued after the war from both sides of the political spectrum; even when both Pinter and Stoppard "married up" and lived the elegant lives of London literati, this was the atmosphere they inherited. Austrian and German Jewish intellectuals who ended up in England during and after the war were viewed with a mixture of admiration and skepticism, and usually tried to assimilate as quickly as possible into British culture. "In England, impecunious foreigners were admitted if they were prepared to work as domestic servants," describes Amos Elon in his landmark study of German Jews from 1750 to 1945, *The Pity of it All*. "The difficulties exiles encountered in even this most liberal of European countries were evident in the case of one upper-middle-class Jewish doctor who applied for an entry permit as a tutor. Alas, the British visa officer in Paris informed him that work as a tutor did not constitute 'domestic service', and he was rejected."[12]

Pinter's "oppositional" status as a Jew was baked into his mindset early on. So was his relationship to violence and dislocation. Having been evacuated to Cornwall during what came to be called the "Phoney War" in 1940, Pinter quickly returned to London, where he lived through the worst of the Blitz at the epicenter of the bombing and witnessed enormous destruction and loss. Nevertheless, he had not the slightest doubt that he needed and wanted to be with his family, no matter how dangerous it was. There was always a sense in Pinter's childhood of belonging to a tightly knit tribe, with its own rules, expectations, and ways of demonstrating affection. Those rules of inclusion could sometimes be oppressive for an iconoclast like Pinter: indeed, the theme of the Jewish son who is pilloried when he brings home someone "outside" the religion to meet the family would be vividly brought to life in *The Homecoming*. As his childhood friends Henry Woolf and Mick Goldstein attested, Pinter witnessed occasions when someone married outside the faith and was treated as if dead by their families from that point forward. "In post-war Hackney, marriage between a Jewish boy and a *shiksa* was still the exception rather than the rule,"[13] a fact that Pinter discovered when he brought his Irish-Catholic girlfriend, the actress Pauline Flannigan, home to meet his parents. To their relief, he did not marry her (Vivien Merchant was yet to come). But the message was clear: to feel centered in oneself as a human being, it was important to *belong*. In his later plays, Pinter returns again and again to the crisis of parents separated from their children, from *Moonlight*, in which a dying father longs for his sons to come home and see him before he dies, only to be met with distance and derision ("Chinese laundry," one son replies to a phone call from his mother), to *Family Voices* in which a mother tries repeatedly to connect with a son who has become lost to her, while he writes her letters that are either never sent or never arrive, describing his new life. For Pinter, the deep pain of family dislocation that followed the loss of home and community was a wartime memory that never went away. In viewing a character like Davies in *The Caretaker*, a man robbed of his name and identity and desperate to find a way to get to Sidcup to get his papers, one realizes how deeply the fear of "non-belonging" had permeated Pinter's consciousness, a non-belonging he shared with his beloved Kafka. "They prove who I am! I can't move without them papers. They tell you who I am," Davies says to Aston in despair, adding that the man who has got his papers has had them, "oh, must be . . . it was in the war . . . must be . . . about near on fifteen years ago." The war and the loss of identity are intimately bound up; it was as if that period of time, and the concomitant sense of personal vulnerability as a Jew, was always with Pinter ("The past is always present," he was fond of saying).

In a similar vein, Pinter's memories of the actual bombing of London were graphic and specific. "At one point we were all evacuated from our house when there was a raid and we opened the door and that famous garden I told you about was alight all along the laundry wall including the lilac tree. We were evacuated straight away. Though not before I took my cricket bat."[14] The fact that the East End, home to the preponderance of London's Jewish population, sustained the heaviest bombing, was not a coincidence. The East End was the locus of docks, harbors, and railway installations that were natural targets of the Germans, but the large Jewish population that lived there was, as it were, an added bonus for the Nazis. Pinter's rage against the nuclear aspirations of Britain and the US in the 1990s was surely shaped by his childhood terror of being bombed. "I was brought up in the Second World War," Pinter always reminded people. "I was about fifteen when the war ended; I could listen and hear and add two and two, so these images of horror and man's inhumanity to man were very strong in my mind as a young man."[15]

The violence that Pinter witnessed as a child during the Blitz gave way to a different kind of violence post-war, as Oswald Mosley and the anti-Semitic British fascists returned to the streets and to Speaker's Corner to propound their noxious views. As Billington explains, "In the 1920s the *Hackney Gazette* fulminated against the presence in the borough of '30,000 Jewish and other aliens' turning the area into 'a sort of Middle East' and depriving locals of jobs and decent housing."[16] There were more and more Fascist bookstores, Fascist newspapers and Fascist debating societies seen in the area. A group of Jewish ex-servicemen who called themselves the "43 Group" emerged in opposition to the far right, and waged physical battle with fascists on the streets of London. The 1947 killings in Palestine of two British sergeants by the Jewish fighter group Irgun triggered violent anti-Semitic riots across Britain that year. This atmosphere of fear and intimidation against Jews, even in the country that had fought so hard to liberate them from German fascism, is described in detail in Daniel Sonabend's fascinating *We Fight Fascists: The 43 Group and Their Forgotten Battle for Post-War Britain,* and must have made a deep impression on the teenage Pinter growing up in Hackney.[17]

It is thus no surprise that violence is a central theme in Pinter's work; one could argue that Pinter always wrote from a place of *opposition,* that he needed an enemy to energize his activity in the world. In an interview with Laurence Bensky in 1966, Pinter commented,

> Everyone encounters violence in some way or other. It so happens I did encounter it in quite an extreme form after the war, in the East End, when the Fascists were coming back to life in England. I got into fights down there. If you looked remotely like a Jew you might be in trouble. Also I went to a Jewish club, by an old railway arch, there were quite a lot of people often waiting with broken milk bottles in a particular alley we used to walk through.[18]

Of course, the flip side of violence was a kind of sexual charge that Pinter talked a great deal about when remembering his wartime life in London. Many years later, I wrote to him about a speech in *Old Times* in which Anna, trying to persuade Kate not to go out walking in the park that evening, says, "The park is dirty at night, all sorts of horrible people, men hiding behind trees and women with terrible voices, they scream at you as you go past"; I wondered at the tone of the speech, the graphic violence in it, and asked Pinter for his thoughts. He wrote back immediately, "I don't understand why you don't understand the speech 'The park is dirty at night'. It seems simple enough to me. The park embodies a menacing, alien world, violent, sinister, dangerous, as opposed to the comfort, peace and security of their room. The speech actually refers to the atmosphere of Hyde Park in the 50s and 60s quite accurately." But he went on to say, "The park was full of prostitutes then, men behind trees etc. It was a very ugly and—to some, very exciting place. Our conversation definitely revealed something else, which is that Anna is expressing her *own* revulsion and fear in the speech." The fraught atmosphere of his youth became the visceral reality of his characters, for whom the outside world is almost always a place of threat and potential danger.

Being alert to attack was part of Pinter's DNA; opposition gave him adrenaline. When he came to write *The Birthday Party*, Pinter explained that the impetus for the play was an image of a man sitting alone in a room, startled by a knock at the door. "The idea of the knock came from my knowledge of the Gestapo," Pinter told Gussow in 1988. This aggression was not an abstract or metaphoric notion to Pinter, it grew out of his lived experience. As critic Francesca Coppa points out, "The plotline of *The Birthday Party* was being played out as the most utter realism throughout Europe during Pinter's childhood and teens."[19] Thus, when Barry Davis of *The Jewish Quarterly* asked Pinter in 1992, "In the final analysis, you feel a Jew when you feel beleaguered?" Pinter replied that he identified "with Jewish suffering . . . particularly in relation to the Holocaust. I find that the poetry, the art that has come out of the Holocaust, is very strong and leaves a very strong impression."

In 1990, Pinter was asked to adapt Fred Uhlman's novella *Reunion* (which tells the story of the friendship between a Jewish boy and a pre-Nazi Christian in 1932 Germany) for film in 1990; he was immediately clear about why it interested him. "I'm Jewish."[20] In his screenplays and subsequent stage plays, Pinter became increasingly interested in the politics of the aftermath of the Second World War and the lasting effects of both psychological and actual torture on the population. While in his early plays, the violent assault on vulnerable individuals is by authority figures whose source of power is less defined, by the time Pinter writes *One for the Road* in 1984, the torture has become much more graphic. "*The Birthday Party* . . . has a central figure who is squeezed by certain authoritarian figures," he explained.

> There are at least ninety countries that practice torture now quite commonly—as an accepted routine . . . Certainly in terms of actual physical brutality, by which I mean murder and rape, which are the given facts in *One for the Road*. However, the distinction between then and now is that then, in 1957, the concentration camps were still an open wound which it was impossible to ignore, whereas now it's only too easy to ignore the horror of what's going on around us.[21]

If there was violence and dislocation in Pinter's formative years, there was humor and loquaciousness as well. So many of the nuances and rhythm of Pinter's language have their roots in Jewish comedy, as well as in the vaudeville/music hall tradition Pinter had inherited after years of comic banter with his best friends Mick Goldstein and Henry Woolf as a young man. When Bel, Andy's wife in *Moonlight*, says, "The term 'taking the piss,' however, was not known to us," Andy furiously explains, "It means mockery! It means to mock! It means Mockery! Mockery! Mockery!", a skill Pinter had honed carefully in his youth with his "gang of seven." As soon as he began to write, Pinter's characters, from Mr. Kidd in *The Room* to Goldberg in *The Birthday Party* to Max in *The Homecoming*, echoed the kinds of

Jewish patriarchs Pinter encountered growing up. To understand the origins of their unique idiolect, one has only to listen to Pinter describe his own experience. In "A Speech of Thanks," given in March 1995 upon receiving the David Cohen British Literature Prize, Pinter told the following story:

> When I first had a poem published in a magazine called *Poetry London* my parents were quite pleased . . . There was only one member of my family who appeared to be at all well-off, my great-uncle, Uncle Coleman, who was 'in business.' He always wore felt carpet slippers and a skull cap at home and was a very courteous man. My father proposed that I show Uncle Coleman my poem in *Poetry London* when we next went to tea. I agreed, with some misgivings. My poem was called 'New Year in the Midlands', and was to do with a young actor's vagabond life in rep. It was heavily influenced by Dylan Thomas. It contained the following line: 'This is the shine the powder and blood, and here am I,/Straddled, exiled always in one Whitbread Ale town,/Or such.' My father and I sat in the room in silence while Uncle Coleman read this poem. When he reached those lines he stopped, looked over the magazine at us and said, 'Whitbread shares are doing very well at the moment. Take my tip.'[22] [A Goldberg line if ever there was one].

Goldberg's "arias" in *The Birthday Party* represent horrifying and hilarious attempts to construct a persona appropriate to the occasion; his relish for philosophizing and moralizing is clearly and deliberately redolent of the community from which he sprang. "How can I put it to you?" he asks in his birthday toast to Stanley:

> We all wander on our tod through this world. It's a lonely pillow to kip on. Right!. . . But tonight, Lulu, McCann, we've heard a lady extend the sum total of her devotion, in all its pride, plume and peacock, to a member of her own living race. Stanley, my heartfelt congratulations. I wish you, on behalf of us all, a happy birthday. I'm sure you've never been a prouder man than you are today. Mazeltov! And may we only meet at Simchahs!

This perverted ode, welcoming Stanley into the closeness of the human (Jewish) community, is chilling because it feels so "authentic," full of alliteration, exhortation, and bonhomie. It implies a shared history and a shared vocabulary, although of course only the Jewish Goldberg would know that "Simchahs" means joyful occasions, or indeed that "Mazeltov" is an expression of congratulations. No wonder Meg is seduced; listening to Goldberg is like entering a secret world, a private fraternity with its own language and code. Not only the vocabulary itself but his means of expression and locution define Goldberg's way of thinking. "Is the number 846 possible or necessary?" Goldberg demands of the terrorized Stanley, a number which the critic Leslie Kane believes is "not random. Goldberg is employing

"Gematriya," she argues, "the non-verbal Jewish preoccupation with the numerical value of words. The number $846 = 8 + 4 + 6 = 28$, the letter value of the Hebrew word *Chai*," which may be translated: "Life."[23] This is, of course, the subject of Goldberg's supposed speech at the Ethical Hall, Bayswater, "A wonderful opportunity," he tells Lulu. "I'll never forget it. They were all there that night. Charlotte Street was empty. Of course that's a good while ago." When Lulu breathlessly asks what he spoke about, Goldberg replies, "The Necessary and the Possible. It went like a bomb." Which is a terrifying echo of Pinter's wartime debates with his friends.

The weaponizing of language is directly connected to a belief in the potency of language, in its power to both reveal and to destroy. In her article "Marginal Writers: Or, Jews who Aren't," Debra Shostak describes the verbal impulse in the work of American novelist Paul Auster: "Insofar as Jews have been the People of the Book, with a long rabbinic tradition of word-obsessed exegesis, Auster's preoccupation with how language constructs order as a stay against such absence (*i.e. the absence of God in a post-Holocaust world*) marks his Jewishness."[24] The same could be said about Pinter. The Jewish, Viennese-born actress Susan Engel (who starred in the first production of *The Room* at Bristol University) attempted to articulate what she saw as the particularly Jewish quality that defined Pinter's sense of language: "There's a joy in language, and there's a joy in imitating for Jews. They're very good at quoting from the Bible, the Talmud, and quotations have an important place in Jewish culture ... there aren't many Jewish characters in Harold's plays, but the attitude remains, the sense that it is part of everyday life to use strange words, the words of others."[25] She gives a wonderful example of this linguistic "strangeness" in *The Room*, which begins when the landlord Mr. Kidd says about his mother, "I think my mum was a Jewess. Yes, I wouldn't be surprised to learn that she was a Jewess. She didn't have many babies"; this leads to a discussion about Kidd's sister, who "always used to tell me how much she appreciated all the—little things—that I used to do for her. Then she copped it. I was her senior. Yes, I was her senior. She had a lovely boudoir. A beautiful boudoir." Of all the words one expects to come at the end of that speech, it is unlikely one would anticipate "boudoir." But the strangeness of its sound adds to the sexual mysteries surrounding the sister (what were those "little things" Kidd did for her?) and draws one into frightening speculation about life in that "boudoir." Kidd's exotic vocabulary is the opposite of Rose's, which is blunt and direct. It is this linguistic disconnect that unsettles Rose so completely: in the impoverished boarding house in which Rose rents a single unadorned room, how could there ever have been something as exotic as a "boudoir"? She has no idea what to make of it.

An obsession with the use and misuse of language, and the delight in the sound and structure of words, is central to Pinter's work. A desperate desire for *clarity* is coupled with the impossibility of ever achieving a true connection between thought and speech: "I don't think she's got it clear," Max frets in *The Homecoming*. While the Jewish-American linguistic tradition belonging to novelists like Philip Roth and Bernard Malamud was quite different from Pinter's own creative impulses and while he never characterized himself as an "Anglo-Jewish writer," there is no doubt that his passionate love of language and his ability to mine emotion with the precise and often surprising word is closely connected to the language he heard and studied during his Jewish upbringing. To *speak* in Pinter is rarely to confess or to reveal; it is to bear witness, to remember, to hide, to protect, to play games, to interrogate, to debunk, to learn, to query, to attack, to destabilize. Perhaps this is why so many exchanges in Pinter's dialogue are non sequiturs—speech acts do not follow each other in a predictable way. It is certainly why Pinter's texts are so hard for actors to memorize. Pinter's acute focus on the shape and possibilities of the English language was connected to his opposition to cliché, cant, and political obfuscation.

Years later, in the wake of fascism and the horrors of war, the poet Spooner will lament to his host Hirst in *No Man's Land*: "All we have left is the English language. Can it be salvaged? That is the question." The implication is that the right words can save us from barbarity. In the context of this discussion about Jewish identity, it is also interesting to remember that Pinter's school, the Hackney Downs Grammar School which had been founded in 1870, was, as Billington explains, "in exact imitation of a Prussian prototype ... In the 1940s, by virtue of Hackney demographics, it had an over 50 percent Jewish intake and a high regard for learning. In its time it has produced two life peers, two university vice-chancellors and two famous actor-playwrights in Pinter and Steven Berkoff."[26]

At Hackney Downs, Pinter formed a circle of close male friends with whom he remained in vigorous touch throughout his life. Within this group, conversation was a sport second only to cricket. Language and the written word were revered, argued over, shaped, and celebrated. Words *mattered*. Pinter tells a wonderful story of going to visit his friend Henry Woolf one evening; upon finding Henry was out, he was invited by Henry's parents to wait, and he asked for a piece of paper so that he could write a poem while anticipating his return. "Occasionally I'd be aware of them and look up," he says of Henry's parents. "They were really pleased because they came from a Continental tradition in which writing was really good. Henry's father knew the Bible. He was a great Talmudic scholar too. The point of the story is that they delighted in the fact that their son's friend was actually engaged in the act of writing." Language could be a weapon, a punchline or a poem; the young Pinter excelled at it all. Years later, Pinter nods to his childhood affection for Jewish comedy in an exchange in Act One of *The Birthday Party*, when the hulking Irishman McCann effusively tries to thank his killer boss Goldberg for all his support over the years, an exchange that plays exactly like a vaudeville routine:

Goldberg   I would never deny that I had a position.

McCann   And what a position!

Goldberg   It's not a thing I would deny.

McCann   Yes, it's true, you've done a lot for me. I appreciate it.

Goldberg   Say no more.

McCann   You've always been a true Christian.

And then the punch line (requiring exquisite timing):

Goldberg   In a way.

Teasing out the particularities of Pinter's language is fascinating, and very useful for the actors involved. In *A Casebook of Harold Pinter's The Homecoming*, Paul Rogers, who originated the role of Max in Peter Hall's production of *The Homecoming*, was interviewed by John Lahr, who asked him, "Do you think that the family is Jewish?" Rogers replied,

> Harold has not made this evident, except in terms of the language . . . If we believe that Jewry is a condition of religion and not race, then they're English. But to an English actor, it leaps out of the text—the facility of speech, the quality of speech and the area: North London, Hackney. Far more important than this family being Jewish is their instinct for family, family unity. In Anglo-Saxon terms, this isn't part of the blood and being. This to an English audience would telegraph a Jewish heritage. Our London Jews have more than a melodic line in the voice, there is a speech shape, it isn't a dialect, the speech is, at it were, foreign, in the way that English is foreign to a Welsh tongue. Not in terms of syntax or shape of the sentence but merely in the sound. . . . The repetitions, the emphasis upon certain aspects. The ironies, that curious, very unEnglish working of the mind.[27]

I found this analysis of the Jewish idiolect of Pinter's language apt, particularly coming from a non-Jewish actor. The music of the language was everything to Pinter, and clearly it was a music he remembered from his youth.

If Hackney was a place of friendship, jocularity, and intellectual growth for the young Pinter, it was also, as I have described, a place where disguise and quick-wittedness were often necessary for survival. This subterfuge or protectiveness leads characters in Pinter's plays to be cagey about their identities. The changing of names in order to "pass" or to protect is a trait any diaspora Jew recognizes immediately. As Ian Smith relates,

> Another feature of the Hackney Jewish community that echoes in the plays is the frequency with which names are changed. In the 1980s an old

school contemporary saw Pinter on television and wrote him giving brief details of what had happened to a number of classmates. Several had changed their names—names that in the first place had only been Anglicizations. A long-standing verbal trick, used by anti-Semites and others, is to create mock-Jewish names like "Krapstein," and in letters and conversation, Pinter's friends would make this device their own.[28]

Of course, Pinter's own "name change," once he'd become a working actor, was well-known: he performed under the name "David Baron." Baron was his grandmother's maiden name; far from trying to disguise his Jewish identity via his stage name, Pinter often remarked that his stage name was perhaps more Jewish than his given name. He only left the name "Baron" behind when the two sides of his own being collided in a theater poster at Cheltenham's Theatre Royal in September 1960 that announced, "David Baron and Patrick Magee in *The Birthday Party* by Harold Pinter," at which point he decided it was time for the invented "David Baron" to finally yield to the genuine "Harold Pinter."

It is often the case that "naming" someone is an act of aggression or exposure in Pinter, a dangerous assault on individual freedom or a frightening incursion into private territory. In *The Birthday Party*, Goldberg is seen to possess a number of names as the play progresses: "Up the street, into my gate, inside the door, home. 'Simey,' my old mum used to shout, 'quick before it gets cold.' And there on the table what would I see? The nicest piece of gefilte fish you could wish to find on a plate." To which McCann replies, "I thought your name was Nat." "She called me Simey," insists Goldberg. But later, it appears that his childhood name was "Benny": "My father said to me, 'Benny, Benny he said, come here.' He was dying." Goldberg's lack of fixed identity is bewildering and threatening to the Irishman unversed in Jewish name-games; McCann does not know what to make of these multiple names or how to behave around his protean and unknowable boss. Finally in Act 3, when McCann desperately tries to get Goldberg to "finish the bloody thing" and go, and Goldberg refuses to answer to the name of "Nat," McCann tries to get his attention by calling out in desperation, "Simey!" A murderous moment follows. Goldberg, who has been sitting slumped at the table, slowly opens his eyes and stares at McCann.

Goldberg   What—did—you—call—me?

McCann   Who?

Goldberg (*murderously*)   Don't call me that! (*He seizes* **McCann** *by the throat.*) NEVER CALL ME THAT!

The danger of having one's true identity exposed, particularly as a Jew, cannot be overestimated. In the vicious interrogation scene in Act 2 of *The Birthday Party*, during which any crime Stanley could possibly have committed is thrown in his face, we hear the following exchange:

Goldberg Webber! Why did you change your name?

Stanley I forgot the other one.

Goldberg What's your name now?

Stanley Joe Soap.

Goldberg You stink of sin.

McCann I can smell it.

Pinter once said to us in rehearsal that "if you accuse someone of enough things, he will be guilty of one of them." By acknowledging that he has changed his name and/or is currently operating under a false identity, Stanley is forced into an admission of guilt in spite of the fact that he has most likely committed no crime. In this way, Pinter actually *dramatizes* the action of naming, recognizing it as a complex tool of control and assertion. An equally dangerous "frisson" happens in *The Homecoming* when Ruth exposes Lenny by calling him "Leonard," which engenders an ominous pause. "Don't call me that, please," Lenny begs. "Why not?" challenges Ruth. "That's the name my mother gave me," he replies. As such, it is forbidden territory, it is a personal side of his identity over which she has no right to take control. By co-opting the name his mother gave him and using it against him, Ruth has located exactly where Lenny is vulnerable, and he knows it.

In the climactic last scene of *The Room*, a mysterious blind man named Riley enters Rose's room. "Come home Sal," he begs her. When this private name is spoken, there is a moment of silence. Rose is completely taken aback. Finally, she gathers her strength and asks, "What did you call me?" Riley repeats, "Come home, Sal." Rose resists the name: "Don't call me that." "Come, now," Riley begs. "Don't call me that," Rose insists. Why is she so threatened by being called a different name? Who is Sal? What does the use of the name tell us about a possible prior relationship between Riley and Rose? It is interesting to note that the name "Sal" can be seen as a diminutive of "Sarah," which is a clue to Rose's possible Jewishness; Jewish women in Nazi Germany were forced to put the name "Sarah" in their passports for rapid identification. Regardless, for Pinter, a change in name can open a window into a character's most vulnerable and "unmasked" soul.

However, a change in name can also be the start of a new future, as it was for Tomas Straussler when he became Tom Stoppard and for Harold Pinter when he became, temporarily, David Baron. This is true for theatrical characters as well. In *No Man's Land*, Hirst upends the dynamic between himself and Spooner by returning to the room and suddenly calling Spooner by a different name: "Charles. How nice of you to drop in," he exclaims. "Have they been looking after you all right?" And then, turning to Briggs, he says, "Denson, let's have some coffee." By choosing to employ new names all round, Hirst is able to shift the landscape of the room, conjuring a scene of two elegant old Oxonians catching up about the war. Following the rules of improvisation, when one character takes charge of the situation by changing the name of his antagonist, the other character must say "yes" in order to stay in the game. This causes a new power dynamic to emerge, based on a new set of coordinates.

Just as we put on "faces" to suit every occasion, the characters in Pinter put on alternative names to protect their innermost beings from exposure and assault. The issue in *The Room* is not whether Rose is perhaps Jewish (although as noted, she does share a name with Pinter's grandmother, and, coincidentally, with my own), it is that she has clearly re-made herself in order to escape something about her past that would be dangerous to reveal now that she is living with Bert. That "something" is housed in the dark, dank basement which Rose seems to know all too well. To feel safe from whatever is lurking down there, she must bury the past, climb the stairs, hold on tight to Room 7, and resolutely call herself "Rose." But, as Pinter reminds us, the past will always come back to bite us, and the weapon of choice is often a childhood name. Alternatively, in the endless search for control in Pinter's universe, a fantasy name can open up new potential identities. As Max and Lenny negotiate a future for Teddy's wife Ruth (a nice Jewish name) in *The Homecoming*, they consider whether it might render her prostitution practice swankier if she had a more elegant appellation: "You've got to be reserved about it, Dad. We could call her something nice . . . like Cynthia . . . or Gillian." "Gillian," Joey echoes, savoring the decidedly non-Jewish, upscale English name in his mouth, just as Hirst savored "Annabelle." Ultimately, however, Ruth is always Ruth. That is where her power lies, and Max knows it. "But you . . . Ruth . . . you're not only lovely and beautiful, but you're kin. You're kith. You belong here."

Pinter did not have to label a character Jewish or to expound upon Nazism to create an atmosphere of assault that felt authentic to him. When, during rehearsals for *The Birthday Party*, we asked Pinter whether Stanley was meant to be Jewish, he replied carefully, "It's possible." Certainly, the name "Stanley Webber" implies that he might be. Regardless, the terror of being caught and the subterfuge Stanley must employ to stay alive in a hostile world were redolent of a Jewish experience during and after the war that Pinter knew to be true. From the first days of rehearsal, I found that Pinter's personal antennae were always out, always on the alert for an attack. Although, as I have said, he was consistently gracious, kind, and forthcoming to all the artists in the room, there was one occasion in which his temper erupted at the outside world. It happened the day *The New York Times* sent a writer and photographer down to CSC to cover our production. Pinter's oppositional ire had already been roused by the *Times'* insistence that the story be about the production rather than focusing on Pinter's current political beliefs; this proscription enraged him. "Arts and *Leisure?*" he fulminated, decrying the name of the culture section of *The New York Times*. "Since when do the arts have anything to do with *leisure?*" He

FIGURE 5 *David Strathairn, Peter Riegert, Carey Perloff, Richard Riehle, Harold Pinter, Miguel Perez, Jean Stapleton, Bill Moor, and Wendy Makkena at CSC Repertory during rehearsals for* The Birthday Party *and* Mountain Language, *1989. Photo by Martha Swope, courtesy of the New York Public Library.*

wanted to talk politics as well as theater, and did not see how one could profitably be separated from the other. The celebrated *Times* theater photographer Martha Swope arrived and, setting up her photo shoot, asked Pinter to hold a script of the play as if he were referring to it in rehearsal. Pinter immediately tossed the script away and snarled, "I wrote the bloody play. I don't have to refer to it!" He agreed to one (stiffly) posed photo with the cast (see Figure 5), and then sent Swope on her way. It was clear that in Pinter's mind, *The New York Times* represented the enemy, the state, coercion, judgment, all those aspects of repression and censorship that he intuitively and valiantly railed against. As Petey exhorts Stanley, he was not going to let them "tell him what to do."

As soon as the "enemy" had left our rehearsal room, Pinter's good humor instantly returned. The altercation had energized him, and he was ready to get back to work. We were his tribe, and he was there as our ally and protector against the forces of idiocy arrayed against us. He looked around the room and spotted a young man named Tom Chargin who was quietly watching the proceedings, camera in hand; he had been hired to document our rehearsal process, but had graciously given way that afternoon to the legendary Martha Swope. "Okay, Tom, she's gone! You can have a go now!" Pinter chortled. We got down to work, and over the course of the next week,

Chargin took some of the most remarkable, candid rehearsal shots I have ever seen. Pinter clearly liked having him around—he was an unpretentious working-class guy with a cheerful manner and a deep intuitive understanding of "Harold" and his work. During breaks, we would find Pinter in intense conversation with this young photographer, as if he had met a new character in one of his plays. It was clear Pinter thought Chargin was on "our side."

Years later, I read an interview Pinter had given to the *Daily Mail* in 1964, in which he described being insulted in a pub for being Jewish and responding very violently. When asked why he had hit his assailant so hard for his anti-Semitic remarks, Pinter had explained: "I laid into him, forgetting who he was and what the whole thing was about entirely ... I wasn't insulted personally but I was insulted on behalf of someone or something." In other words, when Pinter received what he felt to be attacks on himself, he instinctively responded on behalf of a larger community whom he felt compelled to defend, just as he had in Hackney when confronted with anti-Semitic attacks, or in our case at CSC, when confronted with a reporter whom he believed was standing in the way of artists speaking their minds.

This is not to say that Pinter was interested in victimhood or in creating Jewish characters who were simply oppressed. On the contrary. When Arnold Wesker accused Pinter of having written a negative example of Jewish experience in his character of Goldberg in *The Birthday Party*, and argued that the play would have been stronger if given a completely Jewish setting, Pinter said that the play was not intended as a specific criticism of Jewish society, but "if you're going to say anything about my attitude toward society, then for God's sake don't leave out Jewish society."[29] He did not want to write an insular Jewish play, but by the same token he was not afraid of exposing negative aspects of Jewish behavior by creating a violent and dangerous character who is clearly a Jew. What is fascinating about Goldberg is the multiplicity of "selves" that emerges within the single character, as he offers up different versions of his past to different people at different moments in the play: to Meg, he is the avuncular party host, to Petey an elegant and well-paying client, to McCann, a demanding and powerful boss, to Stanley, a vicious torturer. Pinter's premise in *The Birthday Party* is that this time it is the Jew who behaves like the Gestapo, wreaking havoc on an innocent man not for what he has done but simply for who he is: an artist, a rebel, an anarchist, and, by analogy, a Jew. As with the European Jews who suffered in the Holocaust, it was the way their Jewishness was viewed in the eyes of their oppressors that mattered, just as it is Goldberg's perception of Stanley that seals his fate.

Pinter began his career as a writer not of "themes" or of "ideas" but of dramatic situations between deeply felt characters; as such, he benefitted from an uncanny ability to remember visual detail, vocal nuance, surrounding sound, physical behavior, light and smell, all the imagery that gives his theatrical worlds such texture. Part of his genius was his ability, like Proust's, to mine his subconscious for the treasure of *specificity*. Which is why it is unsurprising that his Jewish upbringing finds its way into his work in such vivid ways, linguistically, emotionally, psychologically, and physically. I would contrast this, as I noted at the beginning of this chapter, with the seemingly deracinated work of Pinter's Jewish-American counterpart, playwright Arthur Miller. Although Miller had a background not dissimilar to Pinter's, with a Jewish father in the women's clothing business and a life (post-crash) of financial struggle and family tension, Miller's most famous plays all strive for a level of ethnic anonymity which "transcends" their Jewish roots. In an interview in *Jewish Life* in 1948, Miller put the following spin on this fact: "I was afraid that even an innocent allusion to the individual wrong-doing of an individual Jew would be inflamed by the atmosphere, ignited by the hatred I was suddenly aware of, and my love would be twisted into a weapon of persecution against the Jews." Certainly, Miller had felt the sting of anti-Semitism, and his caution may be understandable. But to my mind, the fact that Miller took the landscape of his childhood in Brooklyn and tried to blanch it of Jewish rhythms, contexts and references in order to render it "universal" (i.e. not Jewish) is a serious limitation. Mary McCarthy, reviewing *The Death of a Salesman* for *The Partisan Review* in 1949, agrees: "Willy Loman could not be Jewish because he had to be 'American' . . . he is a capitalized Human Being without being anyone . . . Willy is only a type." When *The Death of a Salesman* was put on in a Yiddish production starring Joseph Buloff in 1951, George Ross felt that in Yiddish, one could see the roots of Miller's drama for the first time:

> The vivid impression is that translating from his mixed American-Jewish experience, Miller tried to ignore or censor out the Jewish part, and as a result, succeeded only in making the Loman family anonymous. What we saw on Broadway was a kind of American Everyman, an attempt at generalization which in fact ended in limitation . . . Arthur Miller, one feels, has almost deliberately deprived himself of some of the resources of his experience. Buloff has caught Miller, as it were, in the act of changing his name.[30]

This strategy on the part of Arthur Miller to render his plays more palatable to the broader Broadway audience by "changing his name" is a fascinating contrast to that of Pinter, who understood the power of name changing all too well and used it to dramatic advantage in his plays. As we have just seen, the subtle terror of unmasking or re-framing identity became a potent tool for Pinter, whereas for Miller, the desire to impart a message about such universal themes as the evils of capitalism or the horrors of war meant choosing to bury specific identity markers. Miller's own sense of shame is always evident; in his autobiography *Timebends*, he relates a story about trying to apply for a library card but being ashamed to speak aloud his father's Jewish-sounding name "Isidore" to the librarian. Thus, although the title character in *The Death of a Salesman* was modeled, by Miller's own admission, on his Jewish salesman uncle Manny Newman, in the play he becomes "everyman" Willy Loman, head of a "universal" family filled with names like "Linda," "Happy," and "Biff."

Therefore, to my mind, what makes Pinter's work more vibrant than Miller's is the muscular specificity of past memory becoming present life. Pinter's characters are speaking for no one but themselves. If they are reprehensible and thus reflect badly on their own ethnicity or identity, so be it. At least they are true. Pinter has spoken movingly about the pain he senses in a character when he or she is being manipulated by the author to fulfill an external function; it seems clear that the respect he felt for his characters was ultimately too great to rob them of their roots. A writer with a profound connection to his own unconscious, Pinter allowed images of war, rituals of his family, the language and violence of youth, and the sense of his own Jewish identity to percolate in surprising ways throughout his work without explanation or apology but with extraordinary potency. He does not have to tell us, as Miller puts into the mouth of Linda Loman, that "attention must be paid"; we pay attention to Pinter's characters because their secrets arrest us, their actions terrify us, their sexuality arouses us, and their motives elude us. Throughout, they are utterly, three-dimensionally, themselves. In the midst of subtlety and subterfuge, a little specificity helps.

Let me turn, then, to the question of Jewish identity in the life and work of Tom Stoppard. Here, the legacy is more elusive and subtle, but the dislocation caused by being Jewish in the war was perhaps even more profound than it was for Pinter. Born in Zlin, Czechoslovakia on July 3, 1937 (seven years younger than Pinter) and named Tomas Straussler, Stoppard (then called "Tomik") was the son of Eugen and Marta Straussler; Eugen was a young Jewish surgeon employed by the company hospital of the Bata shoe factory headquarters. Evidently as early as 1932, the enlightened founder of Bata Shoes had developed a plan for how to help his Jewish employees escape if Hitler's rise culminated in a takeover of Czechoslovakia; when the time came, those employees were evacuated to various locations that were part of the company's network of shoe factories around the world, including Kenya, the Philippines, and Singapore, where Stoppard's family (the parents and two boys, Tomik and Petr) ended up. After two years in Singapore, as the war in the Pacific escalated and the Japanese began closing in, Marta and the boys got on a boat headed for Australia for safety while Eugen stayed behind and volunteered in the war effort, only to be killed when Japanese planes torpedoed and sank the ship he was on. By then, Marta and the boys, having been diverted from Australia to India, had settled in Darjeeling (where Stoppard was then called "Tommy"); it took two years for the Straussler family to discover what had happened to Eugen. When Stoppard was finally told by a family friend of his father's death, he said, "For my part, I took it well, or not well, depending upon how you look at it. I felt almost nothing. I felt the significance of the occasion but not the loss. How had my father died? At sea? No one seemed to know. As far as I was told, he had simply disappeared."[31]

I have always wondered whether this feeling of emptiness and "not knowing" was in the back of Stoppard's mind when, in his first major play *Rosencrantz and Guildenstern are Dead*, his character Guildenstern watches the Player trying to "enact death" and emphatically corrects him: "No, no, no ... you've got it all wrong ... you can't act death. The *fact* of it is nothing to do with seeing it happen—it's not gasps of blood and falling about—that isn't what makes it death. It's just a man failing to reappear, that's all—now you see him, now you don't, that's the only thing that's real: here one minute and gone the next and never coming back". The mysterious disappearance of his father, and by extension of his whole personal history, would prove to be a crucial theme for Stoppard throughout his playwriting career. So was the notion of *luck*. After all, it was in some ways an act of luck that the Straussler family landed in England after Eugen's death, just as in *Rosencrantz and Guildenstern are Dead*, it's luck that determines whether the coin lands on "heads" or "tails," and a lucky accident in *Travesties* that maroons a group of famous artists safely in Zurich during the war. For Stoppard, strange and surprising moments of luck reverse the course of action just when you think you see where things are heading, in life as in art.

After age five, there was nothing left of his father in Stoppard's life. With his mother Marta and his brother Peter, the Strausslers remained in India for the duration of the war; Marta worked for the Darjeeling outlet of the Bata shoe corporation. It must have been a desperate time for her, although Stoppard's own memories of Indian are happy ones. In 1945 Marta met and married Major Kenneth Stoppard, returning with him to England after the war with her sons, who took her new husband's surname. That seems to have been a given, but Hermione Lee reports that in the journal he kept for his son Ed in 1975, Stoppard wrote that he regretted losing his original surname, and wished that he had learned more about his family history: "Mummy has a curious reluctance to talk about the past. I intend to persuade her to do so."[32]

Once in England (Retford, Derbyshire, to be precise), Stoppard's elder brother Peter was called "Stoppard One" at school and Tom was "Stoppard Two." It is hard to even conceive of what the dislocation must have been like for the Straussler family, although Stoppard seems to have immediately relished being British, and grew up with an avid love of the English language, the English parliamentary system, and the English way of being. His sheer resilience in the face of so much dislocation is astonishing. "Until I went to the bad, and the first sign of that was when I turned out to be arty," he says in *Talk Magazine*, "I was coming on well as an honorary Englishman." Adopting an entirely new language and persona was probably much easier than trying to hang on to despairing remnants of the past; as Amos Elon writes of German refugees who kept their language, "The fact that the exiled writers remained chained to the language of their tormentors added to their pain and trauma." Being English was Stoppard's salvation. But it was never a perfect fit, as much as he longed for it to be his new identity. He articulates this longing through the character of Jan (originally called, like Stoppard, Tomas), a Czech graduate student in the 2006 play *Rock 'n' Roll* who chooses to return to Prague after the war. "Your problems are yours, you fix them, okay?" Jan tells Max, the English Marxist: "I love England. . . . If I was English, I wouldn't care if communism in Czechoslovakia reformed itself into a pile of pig shit. To be English would be my luck. I would be moderately enthusiastic and moderately philistine, and a good sport. I would be kind to foreigners in a moderately superior way and also to animals except for the ones I kill, and I would live a decent life, like most English people."

Unlike Jan, Stoppard did have the "good luck" to become English, yet as much as he wants to belong in England, he has never stopped being something of an outsider. "I fairly often find," he told *Guardian* interviewer Maya Jaggi, "I'm with people who forget that I don't quite belong in the world we're in. I find I put a foot wrong—it could be pronunciation, an arcane bit of English history, and suddenly I'm there naked, as someone with a pass, a press ticket."[33] Of course, identity is a very fluid concept, and Stoppard's own sense of self has undergone a radical transformation as he has become older and begun to explore his roots more rigorously. But the fascination with an unstable self seems to have been a valuable trigger in Stoppard's work; in the same *Guardian* interview he notes that his own sense of dislocation is reflected in his characters, who "are constantly being addressed by the wrong name, with jokes and false trails to do with the confusion of having two names." Like the great composer Elgar (who wrote "Pomp and Circumstance" and many oratorios beloved by Church of England choral societies but who was, in fact, a Catholic outsider with no formal musical education), Stoppard's assumed "Englishness" always has a wonderful undercurrent of "outsider" doubt. As his friend the playwright James Saunders once remarked, "He's basically a displaced person. Therefore, he doesn't want to stick his neck out. He feels grateful to Britain because he seems himself as a guest here, and that makes it hard for him to criticize Britain."[34]

Stoppard's fluid and seemingly contradictory identity is clearly reflected in his first successful play, which revolves around two hapless men, Rosencrantz and Guildenstern, who are uncertain about who they are and at a loss as to how to behave, who to believe or how to fit in to the court in which they unwittingly find themselves. "I recognized you at once," The Player tells Rosencrantz and Guildenstern. "And who are we?" asks Rosencrantz hopefully. "—as fellow artists," finishes the Player. To which Rosencrantz replies, "I thought we were gentlemen." The "double act" of Rosencrantz and Guildenstern finds parallels in many of Stoppard's subsequent plays, which often revolve around double/fractured identities or twinning (e.g. Rosencrantz and Guildenstern, the old AEH and the young Housman in *The Invention of Love*, or the twin Russian agents and double Hapgoods in *Hapgood*). In part this divided self is an ancient theatrical trope that nearly always provides rich comic fodder. But the longing to determine "who he is" has carried on throughout Stoppard's life; it is interestingly revealed in an interview Stoppard did just after the success of *Rosencrantz and Guildenstern* when asked how he was enjoying his new-found fame: "Oh, I like it. The advantages are psychological, social and material. The first because I don't have to worry who I am—*I am the man who has written these plays.*"[35]

Identity is thus nerve-rackingly mutable in the Stoppardian universe, just as *naming* proved to be in Pinter's. While for Pinter the "bait and switch" of introducing a new name or new persona often signals danger, Stoppard delights in mining the comic potential of characters whose identities keep shifting. In *Indian Ink* (1996), one of the most hilarious and moving passages revolves around the attempt by an aged Englishwoman (Eleanor Swan) to understand the identity of a young Indian man (Anish) whom she is hosting for tea. The conversation devolves into a series of misunderstandings, as the nature of identity in general and Anish's identity in particular become increasingly hard to pin down:

> **Swan**   You are a painter like your father.
>
> **Anish**   Oh . . . yes. Yes, I am a painter like my father. Though not at all like my father, of course.
>
> **Swan**   Your father was an Indian painter, you mean?
>
> **Anish**   An Indian painter? Well, I'm as Indian as he was. But yes. I suppose I am not a particularly *Indian* painter . . . not an Indian painter *particularly*, or rather . . .
>
> **Swan**   Not particularly an Indian painter.
>
> **Anish**   Yes. But then, nor was he. Apart from being Indian.
>
> **Swan**   As you are.
>
> **Anish**   Yes.
>
> **Swan**   Though you are not at all like him.
>
> **Anish**   No. Yes. My father was quite a different kind of artist, a portrait painter.

This was a remarkable scene to explore in rehearsal: Eleanor and Anish want desperately to understand each other, but Anish's identity is so elusive Eleanor cannot grasp it, or at least, cannot place him in a continuum that might include her sister and his father. Perhaps this scene could only be written by someone whose own identity was as unsettled as Stoppard's. But the inability to pin down someone's identity is not always comic. In one of his earliest plays, *Cahoot's Macbeth*, the Soviet-style inspector makes the playwright Cahoot so miserable he "howls like a dog, barks. Falls silent on his hands and knees." When the Inspector demands the name of this "dog," Macbeth answers, "Cahoot." The Inspector asks, "The social parasite and slanderer of the state?" to which Cahoot retorts, "The writer." A devastating reply. What is identity? Particularly for an artist? And who gets to determine it? Is it where you were born? What you believe? What language you speak? What history you carry with you, knowingly or unknowingly? Stoppard never stops asking that question. "I'm not having him foul the system let alone the pavement just because he's got an identity crisis," retorts the indignant Inspector about the abject specimen Cahoot.

It is hard to be clear about one's identity when one has so little knowledge of one's past, and this pertained to Stoppard well into adulthood. The lacuna seems primarily driven by his mother's own reticence to discuss the family history; when he finally met his distant cousin Sarka one afternoon at the National Theatre, his mother came along and was visibly distressed by the conversation about their Jewish past, even though she had been in fairly regular correspondence with Sarka for years. In an interview with Hermione Lee, Stoppard described the painful moment in which he asked Sarka "how Jewish were we?" only to be told that he was completely Jewish and had lost nearly his entire family to the gas chambers. How had he not known? Why was the past so opaque? When his parents had left Zlin in 1938, what did they think was going to happen to their parents, for example, and to their other relatives who were less "lucky" and were not saved by being part of the Bata Shoe empire? When Stoppard met Vera Somen, daughter of Marta's best childhood friend Nelly Gellert from Zlin, she was (according to Hermione Lee) "amazed that ... Stoppard had no idea about his mother's Jewishness, since it was something she had known all her life. She (Vera) had often looked at the headlines about Stoppard which called him a 'Czech-born English playwright' and asked herself, 'Why don't they say Czech-born *Jewish* playwright?'"[36] It was Vera, with her son Alexandr and his cousin Sarka, who took Stoppard to the Pinkas Synagogue, next to the famous Old Jewish Cemetery in Prague. Hand-painted on the walls in the 1990s were the names of 80,000 Czechs murdered by the Nazis during the war—among them were the Becks (under Zlin) and the Strausslers (under Brno) with the dates and details of their deaths in the camps. These deaths were news to both Stoppard and his brother Peter.

In his most recent (and most Jewish) play *Leopoldstadt*, Stoppard puts this sense of disconnection into the mouth and hands of the matriarch Emilia, a woman who spends the first act of the play holding a family photo album. As she looks at the small black and white snapshots, she remarks sadly, "You don't realize how fast they're disappearing from being remembered ... Here's a couple waving goodbye from the train, but who are they? No idea! That's why they're waving goodbye. It's like a second death, to lose your name in a family album." By the time he wrote the heartbreaking ending of *Leopoldstadt*, Stoppard was in the midst of a long journey of self-discovery, part of which involved a meeting in 1999 in Prague with the widow and two daughters of his father's boss at the Bata hospital.

ɔry in an essay written for *Talk Magazine* entitled "On
e Jewish." It seems that one of the daughters, Zaria, showed
ɾ hand which she had received from having walked through
a child; she told Stoppard that it was his father (everyone's
ɔr at the hospital) who had stitched her wound. Stoppard
ιs he touched her scar, he realized it was the only thing of his
father's   had encountered since leaving Zlin as a child. This was a
wrenching Proustian moment for a person who had barely evinced sorrow
upon learning of his father's death the first time round. "In that moment, I
am surprised by grief, a small catching up of all the grief I owe," he wrote
about the incident.[37]

This prevailing sense of loss (and survivor guilt) underlies much of his
work; Stoppard seems both preoccupied by and reconciled to the despair
that comes with a culture being lost over time, as his past (and the language
and world view attached to it) was to him. Imagine it. In May 1933, four
years before Stoppard was born, fifty thousand books by Jews and other
"traitors" were burned in Berlin, in a fanatic attempt to eradicate Jewish
culture. As Amos Elon describes it, "the Nazi propaganda chief, Joseph
Goebbels, led the proceedings proclaiming the 'end of the age of Jewish
intellectualism'. . . . That night, the flames consumed works by Thomas
Mann, Lion Feuchtwanger, Bertolt Brecht, Erich Maria Remarque, Albert
Einstein, Vicky Baum, Robert Musil, Ernst Toller, Heinrich Heine, Emil
Ludwig, Stefan Zweig and many others." Stoppard, full of a Central
European love of culture, is obsessed with lost artifacts and with the
fragments of ancient writing that have survived. There is a crucial scene in
Arcadia in which a young pupil, Thomasina, despairs about the disappearance
of so much Greek literature: "Oh, Septimus!—can you bear it?" she exclaims.
"All the lost plays of the Athenians! Two hundred at least by Aeschylus,
Sophocles, Euripides—thousands of poems—Aristotle's own library brought
to Egypt by the noodle's ancestors! How can we sleep for grief?" To which
her tutor Septimus replies, "By counting our stock. . . . We shed as we pick
up, like travellers who must carry everything in their arms, and what we let
fall will be picked up by those left behind. The procession is very long and
life is very short. We die on the march. But since there is nothing outside the
march, there is nothing lost to it." I remember the day we staged that scene
when I rehearsed *Arcadia* in 1994. It is a scene filled with despair in spite of
its comic overtones, and as we worked, it was hard not to hear, in Thomasina's
outburst, an echo of those burned Jewish books, written by an artist who
understood in a profound way that knowledge and writing will keep being
lost or destroyed and then rediscovered, generation after generation, by a
people obsessed with learning and always on the march. Another beautiful
articulation of this idea can be found in *The Invention of Love*: "Have you
ever seen a cornfield after the reaping?", asks Housman. "Laid flat to
stubble, and here and there, unaccountably, miraculously spared, a few
stalks still upright. Why those? There's no reason. Ovid's Medea, The

Thyestes of Varius . . . the lost Aeschylus trilogy of the Trojan war gathered to oblivion in sheaves." The mourning for a lost culture and the gratitude for fragments left behind has characterized Stoppard's work from the beginning.

Stoppard has an almost Talmudic belief in the power of language to impart knowledge, as did Pinter. Jews, after all, are the people of the *word*. We are obsessed with education because we are wanderers: education is the only thing we can carry with us in diaspora. In *Dear Zealot,* Israeli writer Amos Oz quotes a teacher of his who told him, "If you seek shelter from the wind and rain, erect yourself a tent. . . . If you seek a place to dwell in for the rest of your life, build a house of stone. If you wish to take care of your sons . . . build a walled city. But if you want to construct a building for future generations, write a book."[38] Twentieth century European Jews, particularly German Jews, worshipped culture at their peril, believing that their devotion to Goethe and Schiller would render them safely "German" in a world of anti-Semitism. Alas, there was no protection. But in nearly every Stoppard play, it is the *quest for knowledge* and for free expression that animates the work. *Arcadia* is perhaps the most salient example of this: the play centers around a precocious teenage girl in nineteenth-century England who has a premonition about chaos theory, and the quest of an independent scholar in the twentieth century to use the trope of a nineteenth century hermit as a "peg for the nervous breakdown of the Romantic imagination . . . I'm doing landscape and literature 1750 to 1834," while her rival is researching a lesser known poet connected to Byron. The dogged pursuit of knowledge butts up against the hilarious egotism and blindness of academe, and in the end, a young girl burns up in her quest for understanding. As with Pinter, Stoppard's work is consistently steeped in the nineteenth century Central European belief in *culture* as the saving grace of humanity. Even his 2016 play about neuroscience, *The Hard Problem,* actually revolves around a heroine whose belief in *consciousness* is set against scientific colleagues who mock and humiliate her humanistic convictions.

Although Stoppard did not live in the shadow of war violence and the Holocaust as Pinter did, his work inevitably deals with moral questions about what it means to live a "good life" and how one can deploy language as a bulwark against fascism, cliché, and repression. True passion in a Stoppard play always lies in *thought* and *speech*. As Young Housman tries to parse a Catullus Ode with his older self in *The Invention of Love,* he asks, "The point of interest is—what is virtue?, what is the good and the beautiful really and truly?" Alan Jones, Dean of Grace Cathedral in San Francisco during my tenure at A.C.T., believed that the key to understanding Stoppard was his "brilliant rabbinical method of endless interpretation," which is most passionately realized in *The Invention of Love,* in which young Housman says, "Scholarship doesn't need to wriggle out of it with a joke. It's where we're nearest to our own humanness. Useless knowledge for its own sake. Useful knowledge is good too, but it's for the faint-hearted, an

real thing, which is only to shine some light, it doesn't
vhat, it's the light itself against the darkness, it's what's left
when you take away God." For all his silliness, words and
e always been sacred to Stoppard. In the 1980s, when he
ed with campaigns to support dissident Soviet and Eastern
ters, Stoppard began to experience first-hand the dangerous
ways .   ;h political regimes distort language to mean its opposite; such
a misuse of language leads to peaceful protestors being called "agitators" at
the same time that political dissidents are forced to become garbage
collectors and menial laborers. One of the first jokes Stoppard heard when
he went back to Prague in 1977 was "Definition of a pessimist? A well-
informed optimist."[39] The deployment of language both as a legacy and as a
mordant means of resistance has been central to Stoppard's aesthetic and
life's work.

As we shall find over and over again in Stoppard's plays, the relationship
of knowledge to love is rich, surprising, and occasionally painful. Observing
Stoppard's writing process over three decades, I have seen him fall in love
with new subjects and fields of inquiry with as much passion as with genuine
love affairs. At the end of the day, to "know" is always in some way carnal,
as Henry points out to Debbie in *The Real Thing*: "It's to do with knowing
and being known. I remember how it stopped seeming odd that in biblical
Greek knowing was used for making love ... Carnal knowledge." The
hunger for knowledge is connected with a hunger to know oneself, and it is
useful when staging Stoppard to remember what is at stake in that perilous
but thrilling endeavor. Even though Stoppard often says that he has no idea
what it means to "be" Jewish since he does not practice the religion and does
not feel part of any coherent group, there is something in his delight in
pedagogy, dialectic, argument, and finding the perfect word that connects
him clearly to a long line of Jewish thought and intellectual behavior. His
sense of loss when culture is destroyed by philistinism or violence is not only
palpable but personal. "We literally worship culture," says Herman in
Leopoldstadt. "When we make money, that's what the money is for, to put
it at the beating heart of Viennese culture. This is the Promised Land, and
not because it's some place on a map where my ancestors came from. We're
Austrians now. Austrian Jews."

Leopoldstadt, which was enjoying a successful run in London in the
winter of 2020 when the pandemic abruptly closed the theaters, is set in a
world reminiscent of my own family history, as articulated in my mother's
memoir *The Vienna Paradox*. Having grown up in a highly cultured and
educated household of assimilated Jews, my mother escaped from Vienna in
March 1938, immediately after the Anschluss; her trajectory was very
different from Stoppard's in that she and her extended family managed to
get out just ahead of the Nazis, and thus did not end up killed in the camps
as so many of Stoppard's relatives were. Although my mother's family was
left with almost no resources, they held on fiercely to their own history.

But clearly the prevarications must have weighed on Stoppard; he says that after meeting Sarka, he had been in a state of "almost willful purblindness," a strange admission for a writer so obsessed with other people's pasts. He was not alone in this myopia; the two other survivors of his Jewish-Czech family (Sarka Gauglitz and Alexandr Rosa) were also the children of silent parents who had never spoken about their history. Was it survivor's guilt? Was it a desire to "fit in," particularly in a country like England that had continued to display its share of anti-Semitism? Was it self-loathing on his mother's part, a latent anti-Semitism even amongst those who were obviously Jewish? Probably all three things pertained. To understand it better, Stoppard finally began to dig more deeply.

The search for a more integrated "self" may be something that happens naturally as one ages, yet it is somewhat surprising that it took Stoppard so long to interrogate his "Jewish connection," particularly because his second marriage was to a Jewish woman, Miriam Stern. Miriam's parents were working-class Orthodox Jews; in fact, her mother Jenny was a convert, and clearly the family valued their Jewish heritage enough to be upset that Miriam chose, as her first husband, a Quaker, by the name of Peter Moore-Robinson. Once Stoppard and Miriam were married and living at Iver Grove in 1981, Miriam's parents came to live with them on the grounds. As Hermione Lee describes it, "Sid and Jenny Stern moved down from Newcastle to live near them in what had been the gardener's cottage. . . . They kept up the devout Jewish practices which had been the context of her childhood, with a mezuzah on the cottage door, celebrating shabbas on Friday nights, in the grounds of their daughter's very secular household."[44] Perhaps what happened in the gardener's cottage stayed in the gardener's cottage, but did the grandparents never want their grandchildren to know that their heritage was Jewish? And what reaction if any did Stoppard's Jewish mother have to his second wife and her parents? Did the subject of the Straussler emigration never come up between them? If not, what a strange and fascinating gap.

Making order out of chaos is a worthy Stoppardian ambition; once he began the search for his origins, he did it with a strong sense that the past (about which he has written so much) is not only worthy of exploration but demands a certain leap of imagination. "Fiction is unrebuttable in the way that history isn't," he said recently when asked about his past. Turning the murky facts of his personal history into drama was a way of both wrestling with and acknowledging the unverifiability of the past. Thus, in the 1999 inaugural issue of Tina Brown's *Talk Magazine* to which I have referred above, Stoppard wrote an essay entitled "On Turning Out to Be Jewish" which was the beginning of his public exploration of this fact, an exploration that has continued in a theatrical way through *Rock 'n' Roll*, *The Coast of Utopia*, and *Leopoldstadt*. In the essay, he quotes his mother, who when asked to write about her past, said: "The move to England had been so sudden, unplanned and drastic that I—perhaps subconsciously—decided the only thing to make it possible to live and truly settle down (I mean the three of us) was to draw a blind over my past life, start so to speak from scratch." It was an astonishing and brave attempt, to bury memory and the past, particularly when one of your children turns out to be someone who lives in his imagination and has a great obsession with other people's pasts, if not his own. In the essay, Stoppard adds, "She describes her parents and my father's parents but does not say when or where or how they died. The word Jew or Jewish does not occur." Yet as I have said, both Stoppard's maternal and paternal grandparents died at the hands of the Nazis. The shame that he must have felt, as a hugely successful Englishman, about not being attuned to the tragedy of his family seems palpable by the time we arrive in 2019 with *Leopoldstadt*, his self-described "Jewish play."

Leopoldstadt follows an extended Viennese family from 1899 to 1955; Stoppard deliberately avoided setting the play in his native Czechoslovakia (too much self-exposure, or just a desire to partake of the elegant cultural world of Vienna before the war?), and as I have noted, many of the details about the Viennese family in the play are redolent of my mother's own history. Even the play's title has echoes: in her memoir, she quotes a heartbreaking letter her mother wrote about their escape, when the Nazi soldiers mocked her family as they desperately tried to cross the border in March 1938: "Aha, from Vienna? Surely from the Leopoldstadt," they had sneered. My mother explains that to my elegant, assimilated grandparents, this was a terrible insult: "the Leopoldstadt was the enclave of the unassimilated Eastern Jews— men and women in strange garb who spoke Yiddish and went to the Synagogue, men and women who were entirely 'foreign' to us."[45]

In Stoppard's play, the individual members of the extended Merz clan, having moved far from the Leopoldstadt themselves, wrestle with what it means to be Jewish, try to convince themselves that assimilation and a reverence for German-language culture will save them from discrimination, choose whether or not to convert and to emigrate, and struggle to raise their children and grandchildren in an increasingly Nazified Austria, as options narrow and violence threatens to erupt. Many of the situations mirror those described by my mother, including a story she tells of a distant Austrian cousin who had converted and joined the Nazi party as a close confidant of Goring and his wife, only to be "outed" by the SS after the Anschluss as having three Jewish grandparents, at which point his mother tried to claim an affair with an Aryan as proof that he was not actually Jewish. (All inventions failed, and he ended up dying at Auschwitz.) In *Leopoldstadt*, there is a similar desperation on the part of some members of the family to "pass," to feign an Aryan affair, to do whatever it would take to escape the net of the Nazis. Questions of Zionism loom large, as well as an almost perverse denial of the fact that their precious and sophisticated Vienna could have fallen into the hands of barbarians.

The last scene is the most devastating: a young Viennese-born Englishman (Stoppard's proxy if you will) named Leonard Chamberlain (aka Leopold Rosenbaum) finds himself in Vienna in the early 1950s for a work-related event (not entirely plausible, but nonetheless) and meets, quite by chance, his Aunt Rosa and cousin Nathan. ("History knocks at a thousand gates at every moment, and the gatekeeper is chance," Stoppard says in *The Coast of Utopia*.) Rosa has escaped to New York before the Anschluss and works as a psychiatrist, Nathan is a mathematician who never left Vienna. Right away, both are stunned by Leo's lack of understanding of his own history, beginning with his offhand remark to Nathan, "I'm sorry you had a rotten war" (a wonderful echo of Hirst's question to Spooner in *No Man's Land*: "You did say you had a good war, didn't you?" "A rather good one, yes," Spooner replies).

In response to their outrage, Leonard asks, "What have I done wrong?" And of course, the answer is, he has failed to be the least bit curious about the tragedy of his Jewish past and in particular, about the actual fate of his own family. Leo has lived a peaceful life of ignorance in England, a life made possible by the lucky fact that his mother's second husband was English, like Kenneth Stoppard, and could save him. Leo makes a speech about loving England which feels familiar to anyone acquainted with Stoppard's oeuvre, but this time it feels willfully myopic, almost laughable. "My mother didn't want me to go to school with a German name," Leo says to justify his lack of knowledge. "I was Leonard Chamberlain from when I was eight. She never talked about home and family. She didn't want me to have Jewish relatives in case Hitler won. She wanted me to be an English boy. I didn't mind, I was pleased." When Rosa attacks his lack of self-awareness, saying, "That's not an excuse, Leo! You knew you were Jewish," Leo replies, "When? Yes, obviously I knew. But you don't understand. In England it wasn't something you have to *know*, or something people had to know about other people." This is clearly not true for many people; as I have described above, anti-Semitism is as alive and well in England today as it was in the 1950s. But Stoppard is writing about his own personal perception of the situation; an understanding of Jewish history, of the legacy of the Jewish people in diaspora, did not seem to have shaped Stoppard's life in any literal or substantial way, at least up until the point when it suddenly began to matter. When Leo says, rather cavalierly, "I was quite pleased to have Jewish blood. To my mind it's a little bit of a distinction . . . an exotic fact from my life gone by," he is echoing a point of view Stoppard himself had taken. In an interview with James Fallon in *W* in 1993, Stoppard said about his past, "Abroad was a very exotic idea in England after the war. People didn't go on holidays and were in awe of someone who had lived in all those places. I liked that." Earlier, in an interview with Shusha Guppy, Stoppard went as far as to say that being Czech (or by extension, Jewish) was completely irrelevant to him:

> The whole Czech thing about me has gotten wildly out of hand. I wasn't two years old when I left the country and was back one week in 1977. I went to an English school and was brought up in English. So I don't feel Czech. I like what Havel writes. . . . I met other writers there I liked and

admired, and felt their situation keenly. But I could have gotten onto the wrong plane and landed in Poland or Paraguay and felt the same about the writers' situations there.[46]

The intense and often violent anti-Semitism experienced by Pinter during the war, a violence that left its mark quite clearly on Pinter's plays, may not have been part of Stoppard's immediate experience when he arrived in England (although he had certainly experienced the intense bombing of Singapore by the Japanese); after years of disruption, it must have felt like a relief to be somewhere permanent, although he speaks of his early years in Indian with great affection and very little memory of trauma. Having a Czech Jewish past seems to have been an exoticism to be worn lightly for at least the first half of Stoppard's life, as it was for his character, Leo; indeed, Stoppard used to joke about being a "bounced Czech," and found great comic potential in the confused identities and fragmented selves of his characters. But finally, the chickens came home to roost. It takes courage to write about a profound lack of self-awareness. Stoppard must have known that in giving these lines to Leo in *Leopoldstadt*, he was in some way exposing his own myopia. Leo was "someone who was close to my conscience," Stoppard told Hermione Lee, "a triumph of assimilation of Jew into Englishman." Stoppard had said on dozens of occasions that he felt he had lived a charmed life; now he began to cringe at the expression as he forced himself to ask, at what cost? In 2012, he read Dasa Drndic's novel *Trieste* about a Jewish-Italian woman whose son (which she had by a German officer) later commanded the Trieste concentration camp. At one point in the novel, this woman lashes out at those who subsequently discovered their family histories but said nothing. The list of those bystanders included Madeleine Albright (who claimed amazement later in her life about discovering she had been Jewish), Herbert Von Karajan, and Tom Stoppard. Drndic tells Stoppard's own story: "He learns that his grandfathers and grandmothers, uncles and aunts, all of them disappeared as if they had never lived, which, as far as he is concerned, they had not, and he goes back to his lovely English language and his one and only royal homeland."
As Lee recounts it,

Reading this, Stoppard accepted the charge. . . . He felt that Drndic was justifiably blaming him for excluding from his 'charmed life' all those others who had 'disappeared'. . . . He felt regret and guilt. . . . He went back over his family history, and his Jewishness. It seemed to him that he had been in denial about his own past. He increasingly felt that he should have been ruing his good fortune in escaping from those events, rather than congratulating himself. As a playwright, he needed to inhabit those lives he never lived, in his imagination.[47]

Yet even then, he was ambivalent; what did it mean to be Jewish, when he had no faith, no dogma, no connection to Israel, and no sense of the Jewish identity that comes from family? It is so telling to me that even when he finally wrote *Leopoldstadt*, he did not make an obvious connection to his own family and did not set the play in Czechoslovakia but in the glittering world of Hapsburg Vienna which he had so admired from his days of translating Schnitzler and reading Joseph Roth, Stefan Zweig, and Wittgenstein. For Stoppard, it has always seemed more intuitive to place his own emotional conflicts inside the envelope of a different culture and time, and *Leopoldstadt* is no exception. Yet ironically, it is in the closing scene, which is taken absolutely from Stoppard's own life, that the play cracks open. Perhaps self-examination is too painful and can only come in very small doses.

Regardless, the past catches up with you in the end. By the late seventies, Stoppard was saying, "I am Czech, through and through." As my mother articulates in her memoir, "Jewish identity can never be expunged, for the simple reason, as refugees from Hitler were forced to learn the hard way, one is always a Jew in the eyes of the Other."[48] Choices had to be made, some of which Stoppard shows us in *Leopoldstadt*, about who would get to escape and how. Those that survive will carry that guilt with them forever. In the moment after Leo makes his trivial assertion about Jewish exoticism, Rosa walks out, enraged. She cannot bear to keep talking to this fatuous, privileged English boy. She leaves it to Nathan to explain to Leo that history, one's own history, *matters*. It matters more than anything. "No one is born eight years old," Nathan tells Leo. "Leonard Chamberlain's life is Leo Rosenbaum's life continued. His family is your family. But you live as if without history, as if you throw no shadow behind you." This, from the playwright for whom the weight of history and the passion for knowledge, if not self-knowledge, has always been a primary driver.

But words can only penetrate so far. It is when Nathan points out Leo's scar, in an extraordinary moment of stagecraft perfectly echoing Stoppard's own experience touching the scar his father had stitched, that Leo is reminded of his last night in Vienna, when he sliced his thumb with a broken piece of china in his terror at being confronted by a Nazi soldier in his own home. Only then does Leo begin to weep, and Stoppard's unique personal story comes to the fore. As the ghosts of the family swirl around the room, Rosa sits Leo down and draws his family tree on blank piece of paper. She proceeds to tell him the destiny of each family member. The play ends with the word "Auschwitz," spoken over and over again. Jewish intellectuals may have dreamed of utopia, but many ended up in gas chambers. When Hermione Lee asked Stoppard whether writing *Leopoldstadt* had somehow "appeased the emotions which went into it," Stoppard immediately said no. No aesthetic catharsis can make up for an entire generation lost.

Stoppard sent me *Leopoldstadt* in manuscript (with a copy for my mother as well, to see whether the Viennese context felt convincing to her) and I read it in England at my mother-in-law's in Dorridge just after my beloved father-in-law Brian Giles had died. I thought about that reckoning, and also about how retrospectively surprising it was that Anthony's parents had never once questioned his desire to marry a Jewish woman and had, on the contrary, always been entirely warm and welcoming to me. I remembered the hilarious moment at our Registry Office wedding in Warwick in 1984 when I decided, in honor of Jewish tradition, to break a glass, an event that completely mystified the prim Mrs. Finlayson who was presiding over the ceremony. I thought about Stoppard and his strange journey toward Jewishness via an obsession with England that bordered on the fanatic. Reading the last scene of *Leopoldstadt* (which Stoppard at one time considered calling *A Family Album*), I was reminded of the ghosts that inhabit Pinter's *No Man's Land*, a heartbreaking play in which two old men who may or may not have a long history of literary and personal association find themselves in an elegant library in a North London home, exchanging views about the war and the past. Like the matriarch in *Leopoldstadt*, Hirst, the owner of the house, repeatedly returns to the only source of personal connection he seems to sustain in the world: his photograph album. He tells Spooner:

> I might even show you my photograph album. You might even see a face in it which might remind you of your own, of what you once were. You might see the faces of others, in shadow, or cheeks of others, turning, or jaws, or backs of necks, or eyes, dark under hats, which might remind you of others, whom you once knew, whom you thought long dead, but from whom you will still receive a sidelong glance, if you can face the good ghost.

Hirst mesmerizes Spooner with an image of the dead caught in chains or imprisoned in glass jars, longing to be set free by the memory of a living person. Finally, he urges Spooner: "And so I say to you, tender the dead, as you would yourself be tendered, now, in what you would describe as your life."

This is, in essence, what Rosa asks of Leo in *Leopoldstadt*. To tender the dead. To free them from erasure and forgetfulness, to let them live again in memory. Rosa invites Leo to acknowledge his place in history, his connection to a group of people who have seemingly played little role in his life and yet are part of its very fabric. For Jews who came of age after the war, "tendering the dead" was a painful if necessary reminder of the six million killed at the hands of the Nazis, and the resulting dislocation and loss of history that ensued. It was also a way of being part of the narrative of history. We have no idea what Hirst's background is in *No Man's Land* and no reason to assume he suffered the same fate as the young Viennese ex-pat in Stoppard's play who lost his family to the Holocaust. But Pinter places his two protagonists, Spooner and Hirst, in a "no man's land" of post-war emptiness not unlike Leo's. (Antonia Fraser once remarked that the house in which Pinter was living with Vivien Merchant when he wrote *No Man's Land*, "was the grandest house I've ever been in. I went there once and it was absolutely, totally silent. I don't think I'd have understood *No Man's Land* if I hadn't seen it. Every room was immaculate with this terrible silence."[49]) And yet as Pinter constantly reminds us and Stoppard reveals in *Leopoldstadt*, the past never really disappears, its traces remain ever-present in the bodies of the living. "We're talking of my youth, which can never leave me," says Hirst. "No. It existed. It was solid, the people in it were solid, while . . . transformed by light, while being sensitive . . . to all the changing light." And just as Stoppard celebrates Britishness in order to transcend the darkness of the past, Hirst conjures a vision of life defined by a bucolic and almost laughable "Englishness," an Englishness as artificial a construction in many ways as Stoppard's. "What happened to them? What happened to our cottages? What happened to our lawns?" Spooner asks Hirst. "Be frank. Tell me. You've revealed something. You've made an unequivocal reference to your past. Don't go back on it. We share something. A memory of the bucolic life. We're both English."

But are they? Is a "memory of the bucolic life" something Spooner and Hirst actually share, any more than Leo in *Leopoldstadt* can convince us of the reality of his supremely English demeanor and affect? In Pinter's play, when Hirst makes the statement "we're both English," there is a pause, not an affirmation. Hirst considers the proposition. He then briefly describes his village church. He is laconic, barely forthcoming. Spooner presses him: "Tell me more. Tell me more about the quaint little perversions of your life and times. Tell me more, with all the authority and brilliance you can muster, about the socio-politico-economic structure of the environment in which you attained to the age of reason." And with those words, a bridge is crossed and we are suddenly back in Hackney Downs with Pinter and his gang of seven, expounding philosophy and taking the piss as Jewish boys, not in a bucolic village but in an East End immigrant neighborhood.

What does it actually mean to be "English"? In the case of *No Man's Land*, from the pen of the writer who never went to Oxbridge comes hilarious parodic dialogue about the life of university men in love with women possessing absurdly Cowardesque names like Arabella Hinscott and Stella Witstanley, names that seem as invented as that of Hirst's amanuensis Foster: "I'm Mr. Foster. Old English stock." Rereading *No Man's Land* in light of Hermione Lee's biography of Stoppard, it struck me as surprising that (like fantasy-prone Hirst), the Jewish Czech playwright Tom Stoppard chose to live for two decades on English country estates that were almost parodies of a bucolic British past, replete with ponds and pansies and hand-drawn book plates indicating "Fernleigh." He had "colluded" with being English in every possible way; that included getting married (the first time) in a Christian church. But the more the old men of *No Man's Land* assert their "Englishness," the more remote that fact appears; and I wonder if to some extent, Stoppard felt the same about living as a country squire. He certainly seemed relieved when, after separating from Miriam, he gave up country life for an anonymous flat in Chelsea where he could finally live exactly as he pleased, inhabiting the world of his writing in whatever way he chose. With Spooner, Stoppard might have been thinking, "All we have left is the English language. Can it be salvaged? That is my question."

The saving of lost things is a central motif for Stoppard; he would go on to write a three-part epic about Russian Utopianists (*The Coast of Utopia*) whose third part is called, fittingly, "Salvage." The disconnect between memory and the present, and the question of what can be salvaged from the ruin of the past, is as aching in *Leopoldstadt* as in *No Man's Land*. This is probably why the characters in both plays expend so much effort avoiding thoughts of the past, while staring obsessively at faded snapshots in a photo album. "For a playwright, the relationship between the author and what is being transmitted is like a blurred photograph," Stoppard told Hermione Lee. The past, even when unknown or misunderstood, is the most fertile of material, particularly for two outsiders who were able to write both about what they saw when they looked through the window onto the landscape of English culture, and about what it felt like to know that there was another nearly lost world behind them, waiting to be re-imagined in the theater.

My sense of the role of Jewishness in Pinter's and Stoppard's work evolved slowly. Over time, I have grown to understand the roots of their imaginations, their unique senses of humor, the nature of their subterfuges, the specificity of their loss and their passion for the *word*. Much of what I discovered about how to unlock Pinter's and Stoppard's plays in rehearsal was connected to my understanding of their "outsider" status, which was impacted by their being Jewish and by having an ever-shifting relationship to the complex and heartbreaking tradition of Central European culture, and to the after-effects of the war. I came to view Pinter's innate reflex against violence and obsession with family, and Stoppard's fascination with fragmented selves and lost knowledge, as terrain to be carefully mined. Initially this was just an instinct on my part, but it was an instinct powerfully felt, and it offered a way into the world of their plays that I have followed subsequently. Just as one can never direct Beckett's *Happy Days* the same way once one knows about the physical privations of Beckett's wartime experience, so Pinter's encounters with anti-Semitism or Stoppard's childhood in exile in Darjeeling become useful keys to unlock their dramaturgy. The more I understood about Pinter's and Stoppard's psychic inheritance, the richer the plays became.

2

The Launch:

Pinter and Stoppard in Context

As radical as Pinter's and Stoppard's contributions were to Anglophone drama in the twentieth century, their plays grew out of a relationship to English theatrical tradition which was subversive in some ways but also surprisingly respectful. In order to understand what shaped their early work, it is useful to briefly examine the "theater scene" into which these two writers emerged. By the late fifties, as Dominic Shellard has so clearly articulated in his study *British Theatre Since the War* (Yale 1999), the landscape was finally being reconfigured, as the legacy of the "well-behaved" West End plays of the pre-war years began to be dismantled. This is not to say that there was not a vigorous tradition of writing on the British stage between the wars and just after: Noel Coward was still a regular presence in the West End, as were Terrence Rattigan, N.C. Hunter, Graham Greene, and J.B. Priestly, whose explorations of moral crises and sexual repression could be potent when well played. But there was a sense, by the late forties and early fifties, of stagnation and stasis in British drama.

For a start, one had to account for the ongoing effects of censorship: this was still a period in which the Lord Chamberlain played a crucial role in determining which plays could be licensed for production. In a recent conversation with the British director Giles Havergal, who ran the Glasgow Citizens Theatre from 1967 to 2002, I learned that when he applied for a license to produce *Who's Afraid of Virginia Woolf*, the standard rider demanded the following substitutions: "Cheese" for "Jesus" and "bastard" for "bugger"; there was no substitution for "prick". Thus, it was an ongoing challenge for English post-war playwrights to introduce subject matter or language which might fall foul of the Lord Chamberlain; why risk writing a "subversive" play if one could never be sure that a license to produce it would be granted?

Furthermore, the financing for theater in Britain after the war was mostly through commercial management, most notably H.M. Tennant, Ltd., led by the extravagantly named Hugh "Binkie" Beaumont. The general method of the Tennant management was to envelop a literate play in gorgeous scenery and costumes, deploy several well-known stars, and make sure that the atmosphere stayed resolutely upper middle class. Plays that wrestled with contemporary issues, foregrounded politics, upended the form or, in particular, focused on the working classes, were almost invisible in the London theater scene of that period; as critic David Thompson reminds us, "By the 1950s the well-made play, craftsmanlike and tidily constructed but uninventive technically and too derivative in its inspiration, formed the staple diet of theatre audiences and seemed to have lost touch with reality."[1] For a serious critic like Kenneth Tynan, this was a source of enormous frustration:

> The leading dramatists of this period, like Priestly, Rattigan, Coward, Greene, Hunter and Ustinov, were writing well-constructed plays on familiar themes whose main fault, but it was a serious one, was that those themes did not correspond with the mood of frustration prevalent in the 1950s. Individuals sensed that they were caught up in some action where the causes were too large and remote to be useful either in life or the theatre.[2]

For every Rattigan or Priestly offering, there was a seemingly endless supply of farces, sentimental romances and Agatha Christie thrillers. All one has to do is look at which plays Pinter himself performed in rep during the fifties to get a sense of the theatrical diet. It should be noted, however, that while the distance from his acting work to his early writing may seem astonishing, traces of Pinter's exposure to the "rep" of the fifties can be found throughout his plays, including his preference for strong curtain lines, rising suspense, carefully calibrated punch lines, and a tight three-act structure.

This is not to say that classics were absent from the canon during Pinter's and Stoppard's formative years: the beginnings of the Royal Shakespeare Company (originally called the Shakespeare Memorial Theatre) were emerging, and the Old Vic had become a home for Laurence Olivier and Ralph Richardson to star in everything from *Oedipus* to *Richard III*. Pinter himself, as will be discussed subsequently, had begun his acting career playing Shakespeare in the Irish touring company of Anew McMaster, a larger-than-life actor manager for whom Pinter had enormous affection and admiration; he also had one season with the famed Donald Wolfit, whose *Oedipus at Colonnus* captivated the young Pinter. And Stoppard's theatrical awakening was shaped immeasurably by watching Peter O'Toole perform numerous roles at the Bristol Old Vic.

The arrival in London in August 1956 of the Brecht's Berliner Ensemble, with its landmark production of *Mother Courage* starring Brecht's wife Helene Weigel, as well as the visits of Jean Louis Barrault's company from

Paris in *Hamlet* and *The Misanthrope*, began to reveal to the British public a new European dramaturgy that was visceral and physical, that used direct address and song to surprise and disrupt audience expectations, and relied upon spare but beautifully crafted set pieces to stand in for the whole. The notion that drama could speak to its own time with vigor and provocation, rather than exist to reassure a middle-class audience of its worthiness, had been largely absent in England in recent decades (with the notable exception of the work of director Joan Littlewood, whose own production of *Mother Courage* at Theatre East in 1955 was an important milestone). Upon returning from a visit to Paris in 1952, the *Sunday Times* critic Harold Hobson wrote, "I came back to a country whose newspapers are mainly filled with tidings of war, insurrection, industrial unrest, political controversy and parliamentary misbehaviour, and to a theatre from which it seems to me, in the first shock of re-acquaintance, that all echoes of these things are shut off as by sound-proof walls."[3] How fascinating that this could be said of the country that had nurtured Shakespeare, a dramatist whose work deliberately appealed to every social strata of society. But that was a long time ago.

The steady diet of West End comedies in the post-war period left no one prepared for the shock of John Osborne's *Look Back in Anger*, which premiered in 1956 at George Devine's newly formed English Stage Company. Osborne's explosive play is centered around a testosterone-filled drifter named Jimmy Porter who subjects his marriage to the resentment of class conflict and the dreary emptiness of 1950s Britain. Nothing ever satisfies the enraged Porter, whose heart and talent (or so we are meant to believe) are bigger than the constricted bourgeois universe in which he has found himself. It is interesting to note that David Baron (aka Harold Pinter) played Porter's roommate Cliff in a 1958 production of *Look Back in Anger* at the Intimate Theatre, Palmers Green, and received excellent notices for his performance.

Look Back in Anger, like many conventional domestic dramas, is structured in three acts, the dialogue is naturalistic, and the plot is pure melodrama. From a contemporary vantage point, the play can appear both misogynistic and predictable. But in 1956, Jimmy Porter's *cri de coeur* felt new and radical. The character's emotional and sexual violence sat right on the edge of "acceptable" behavior; his cruelty was novel, edgy and immediate, and the metaphor of a suffocating culture in which all ideals were wantonly destroyed felt resonant to an audience dealing with rationing, poverty, the disaster of Suez, the end of the empire, and the despairing sight of Soviet tanks crushing a popular revolt in Hungary. It was an angry play for an angry, disaffected time.

It is hard to imagine, pre-"Coronation Street" (or, in the US, pre-"All in the Family") that working-class characters (and regional dialects) almost never figured except in minor or comic roles in British drama in the forties and fifties, but such was the case. Stylistically, Pinter's Max in *The Homecoming* might be a far cry from Jimmy Porter, but they both represent a class whose theatrical moment had finally come. While Pinter's characters "moved up" in class as the plays evolved from *The Birthday Party* to *Betrayal*, it is indisputable that his early work opened up received notions of who and what was "acceptable" on the English stage. As his friend Henry Woolf commented about his inaugural production of Pinter's explosive one act *The Room*, "On the first night the audience woke up from its polite cultural stupor and burst into unexpected life, laughing, listening, taking part in the story unfolding onstage. They had just been introduced to Pinterland, where no explanations are offered, no quarter given, and you have the best time in a theatre you've ever had in your life."[4]

Richard Hoggart's landmark 1957 study *The Uses of Literacy* strove to articulate the particularities of a whole sector of British culture that had been invisible on stage for decades. When I revisited Hoggart's book recently, one thing struck me as particularly apropos when considering how to approach Pinter's work. In rehearsal, Pinter constantly urged actors to approach each moment as a fresh start rather than as the accumulation of a series of moments of a clearly calibrated "arc" (which is how American Stanislavski-trained actors generally proceed). Hoggart describes the "climate of life" in working class England in the 1950s in exactly the same way: "One moves generally from item to item. Wage-packets come in weekly and go out weekly. . . . Life goes on from day to day and from week to week. . . . In general the striking feature is the unplanned nature of life, the moment-to-moment meeting of troubles or taking of pleasure; schemes are mostly short-term."[5] I found this to be a brilliant clue for how to approach Pinter's dramaturgy.

Even more genuinely radical and transformative to the English stage in the 1950s was the initial (and initially disastrous) English run of Beckett's *Waiting for Godot*, which appeared in an English-language production directed by Peter Hall in 1955. Unlike *Look Back in Anger*, which was formally fairly conventional, *Waiting for Godot* introduced English audiences to a completely new kind of theatrical language and dramaturgy; it was untethered from realism, it was comic and existential, its language had the shape of poetry, it had no linear plot, and it refused to explain itself. The daily critics were nearly unanimous in their vitriol for this "incomprehensible" piece of work, but as would happen with Pinter's work soon enough, The *Sunday Times* critic Harold Hobson came to the rescue. In a review entitled "Tomorrow," Hobson said that he felt he had seen the future, writing about Didi and Gogo with admiration and passion: "their conversation often has the simplicity, in this case the delusive simplicity, of music hall cross-talk, now and again pierced with a shaft that seems for a second or so to touch the edge of truth's garment. It is bewildering. It is exasperating. It is insidiously exciting."

The arrival of American musicals such as *Oklahoma!* and *Carousel* in the late 1940s and early 1950s also had a galvanizing effect on the landscape of British drama: here were "low life" American characters singing their hearts out and longing for a better world. Thus it was that by the late 1950s, the ground was fertile for change on the theatrical front; the combination of

European influences, the energizing arrival of American musicals, and the desire to revitalize classical plays through new interpretations and new ways of speaking opened the door to a raft of new writers (later called the "First Wave") ready to expand the purview of what had been considered "acceptable" plays before the war. Among this cohort were two supremely talented self-taught theater artists with very different world views but a huge appetite to become a central part of British drama.

That their arrival on the scene was concurrent with the rise of subsidized theater in Britain is significant. Stoppard's first successful play, *Rosencrantz and Guildenstern are Dead* (1966), received its London premiere at the brand-new National Theatre, after a try out in a student production at the Edinburgh Festival Fringe. (It is notable that Pinter's career began with a student production as well, Henry Woolf's staging of *The Room* at Bristol University in 1957.) This meant that the extended rehearsal time and considerable resources of the National Theatre were made available to this delicious new comedy, a play that managed to fuse Beckettian lack of certainty with Shakespearean extravaganza. Having survived the humiliation of launching *The Birthday Party* in a commercial venue, Pinter's third major work *The Homecoming* premiered at the other important subsidized theatre, the Royal Shakespeare Company (RSC), a year before Stoppard was at the National. For the first time, there was an alternative to both the commercial theater of the West End and the impoverished repertory companies that had proliferated in small towns in England before the arrival of television. Slowly, the notion that theater was a cultural treasure and should be supported by government grants was becoming more widespread, along with the crucial notion that numbers of tickets sold was not the only metric by which one should measure the worth of a new play.

The impact of these new subsidized houses on the careers of Pinter and Stoppard cannot be overestimated, concurrent with the notion that the value of a piece of drama was measured, at least in part, by whether it had sufficient literary and theatrical value to speak to a new audience hungry for meatier fare. After the West End debacle of his first play, it was crucial for Pinter's growth and development as an artist to have a producing venue that was invested in his work for the long term. The same can be said for Stoppard: he has been able to consistently write long complex plays requiring dozens of actors (and, in the case of *The Coast of Utopia*, a nine-hour running time) and to know that these plays would get produced in large part because of his relationship with the National Theatre. Reviewing Hermione Lee's biography of Stoppard for *Commentary*, drama critic Terry Teachout wonders whether the canon of Stoppard's work will ultimately survive in a woefully unsubsidized American theater: "Regional revivals of Stoppard's plays . . . are less common, in part because so many of them are 'big machines' written for England's government-subsidized theater and calling for large, costly casts."[6] Producing this kind of work is extremely challenging in contemporary America.

It was valuable that both Pinter and Stoppard ended up writing for organizations that had a commitment to both classical plays and premieres of contemporary writing; RSC Artistic Director Peter Hall's belief that "the textual discipline of the classics could and should be applied to modern drama"[7] meant that new work was treated with the seriousness of a classic, and classics were explored with as much energy and discovery as a new play. It poses a wonderful challenge for a contemporary writer to be programmed alongside Shakespeare or Sophocles; equally, it must have been a great pleasure for audiences to encounter Stoppard's first play (in which two minor characters in *Hamlet* try to figure out what they are doing in that bewildering world) at a theater known for incisive Shakespeare productions, just as it was for the audience at the Royal Shakespeare Company to be able to compare Pinter's *The Homecoming* with a play like *King Lear*, which Pinter's play often echoes. The classical/contemporary juxtaposition always inspired my own mandate as an Artistic Director, but in the United States, such aspirations are difficult to realize. Federal arts funding is so minimal that artists have to either hope for commercial success or write work that is modest enough to find a home in the under-funded non-profit arena. This has had a marked impact upon the breadth and scope of new American plays, hamstrung by a Broadway culture that does little to encourage contemporary writers to create anything with the ambition of the classical canon that came before them. Our desire to "grow" the career of playwrights and other artists constantly runs headlong into the commercial imperatives that demand a quick return on investment. Such was not, crucially, the case for Pinter and Stoppard.

When Stoppard left school at seventeen, he initially became a journalist in Bristol; the fact that he ultimately chose drama as his *metier* had a lot to do with the rising currency of drama as a "status art" in the English cultural scene of the time. "I really think I'm a playwright by historical accident," Stoppard told Mel Gussow in 1972. "In the late 1950s anybody of my age who thought he could break free of the city room started writing plays. It used to be books; I think it's going to be books again. There was an enormous interest in the theatre. The least fashionable playwright was as fashionable as the most fashionable novelist."[8] Although this assertion was somewhat tongue in cheek, there is truth to his description of historical happenstance. John Russell Taylor, in the "Introduction" to *Anger and After*, describes the remarkable shift in priorities: "writers who fifty, fifteen or even five years before would probably have adopted the novel as their chosen form . . . now, all of a sudden, were moved to try their hand at drama and, even more surprisingly, found companies to stage their works and audiences to appreciate them."[9] The environment was ripe for Stoppard and Pinter to emerge.

For Pinter, the path to playwriting was somewhat less surprising than for Stoppard: at eighteen, he was an indigent actor in repertory theater (in Ireland, for the most part) who desperately needed money, and writing plays was where he thought he could make it. The fact that he was already embedded in the theater is crucial to Pinter's development as a writer, although it must be said that Pinter had been writing poetry and short prose pieces since adolescence. He describes his first foray into playwriting thus: "I went into a room one day and saw a couple of people in it. This stuck with me for some time afterwards, and I felt that the only way I could give it expression and get it off my mind was dramatically. I started off with a picture of two people, and let them carry on from there. It wasn't a deliberate switch from one kind of writing to another. It was quite a natural movement." When his old school friend Henry Woolf invited him to write a play for the Bristol Drama Department, he initially said it would take him six months. Four days later, Pinter had written *The Room*.

Neither Pinter nor Stoppard were academic writers; they were both happiest inside the blood and guts of making theater, and became playwrights in part as a way to participate in that communal effort. Pinter was a commanding actor and a masterful director, which meant that as he was writing, he was staging the plays in his mind, creating vivid roles for actors and inventing indelible stage pictures to be sculpted in rehearsal. "The question of using language every night, really having to use it and go with it," Pinter explained of his acting life, "was very very strong and I'm sure it somehow quickened my mind."[10] Stoppard, while neither an actor nor (with some exceptions) a director, has also relished and truly profited from the tangible, collaborative process of bringing his plays to life onstage. He gleefully describes his early writing process as scribbling drafts longhand on yellow pads and then reading them into cassette tapes, with himself performing all the parts. Because, for both artists, each play has always been viewed as a blueprint for production, the practical considerations around *staging* are not secondary but, in fact, central to their thinking. "A writer should think of himself, apart from anything else, as a professional craftsman," Stoppard told Mel Gussow in 1974, "You call in a plumber—or a writer."[11]

Never have I seen a playwright enjoy the actual details of technical rehearsals more than Stoppard has in all the years we have worked together: our long note sessions at midnight in the basement bar of the Geary Theater after finishing technical rehearsals were always assiduously attended by the chain-smoking playwright, who listened carefully as the lighting designer wrestled with a difficult cue or a prop master figured out how to finesse a piece of stage business. "It's the equivalent of the potter and the clay," Stoppard once said (again, to critic Mel Gussow). "I just love getting my hands in it. Clearly there are many writers who can mail the play in. . . . It stays the way they write it, I am told. I think they miss all the fun. I change things to accommodate something in the scenery, or in the lighting. Happily. I love being part of the equation. I don't want it to be what happens to my text. I like the text to be part of the clay which is being molded."[12] Because there is much less of a tradition of "workshopping" new plays in England than in America, Stoppard is used to hearing his plays for the first time only when they are actually in rehearsal, whereas with new American plays, there are usually several readings and "development opportunities" beforehand. Perhaps this is why Stoppard continues to work on his complex scripts long after they have gone into production: his plays reveal themselves to him in the process of being staged.

It is precisely because Pinter and Stoppard have always been highly *practical* artists that one discovers the meaning of their work best by staging it, by discovering the specific theatrical imperatives that allow the plays to flourish in production. As Stoppard remarked before the first production of *Indian Ink*, "*Indian Ink* is still, as it were, a potential play ... the text becomes a record of the event, but at the moment *Indian Ink* is not a record of an event except an imaginary event. It's more like the book of instructions for the event."[13] Having directed two productions of *Indian Ink* separated by twenty years, I can affirm that we were still decoding the "instructions for the event" well into the second rehearsal process, when the design and the writing finally came together in a magical and satisfying way. So involved is Stoppard in the day-to-day rehearsals of his work that the text often changes considerably from production to production, as I will discuss in Chapter 5. It does not seem to bother Stoppard that there are multiple versions of his plays floating about—he views them like bespoke suits, tailored to fit the occasion. In this way, he is unlike Pinter, for whom the text was definitive and almost always unchanging (an exception was the marvelous addition he made for our CSC production of *The Birthday Party*, as described in Chapter 4). For both writers, each play emerged almost sui generis, a new experiment in human experience. "I use everything I've got hanging around," Stoppard told Elizabeth Brodersen before *Indian Ink* was staged in San Francisco, "so that whenever I finish a play I have absolutely nothing left at all. I just use it up and move on."[14] Fortunately, his relentless curiosity has always managed to find the next source of inspiration.

As we examine the surprising connections between Pinter and Stoppard and their evolution as artists in the context of post-war Britain, it is notable the degree to which they were both autodidacts. They were not alone in having left school at seventeen; few of their peers at that explosive moment in English playwriting, from Edward Bond to Alan Ayckbourn, had actually attended university (it would be different with the "Second Wave" of post-war playwrights such as David Hare and Pam Gems). But the depths of self-learning that Pinter and Stoppard have evidenced over their careers is remarkable. Pinter had the luck to attend Hackney Downs Grammar School at a time when his teacher Joe Brearley instilled in the students a passion for philosophy, poetry, and drama; Pinter describes long walks from Hackney Downs along the River Lea, reciting the verse of John Webster loudly into the wind. "That language made me dizzy," he later recalled. "Joe Brearley fired my imagination. I can never forget him"[15] One of Pinter's best friends at the time, Mick Goldstein, explains the impact of their Hackney education thus: "In my view, Hackney was a decisive factor, in the kind of rarified breakdown and rebuilding of a language that was foreign to Henry's and Moishe's parents and not that natural to mine either. Hackney Downs school was a decisive factor in the nature and quality of its teaching staff and the natural acceptance by the non-Jews of its large and undoubtedly talented Jewish content."[16]

Pinter's formal education ended at eighteen. "In those days, 1948, the only universities you wanted to go to were Oxford and Cambridge. Those were the attractive ones, but you needed Latin. My Latin was non-existent."[17] But in spite of his lack of a university education, Pinter was a voracious intellectual from his teenage years onwards; "one who scrutinizes and mediates his experience through a body of knowledge and critical apparatus acquired and developed through learning and debate," as his friend Ian Smith described him in *Pinter in the Theatre*. In particular, it is worth noting how deeply he absorbed the Modernists at a very young age: "And then I was very excited by the discoveries one makes. I discovered and read Joyce very early on, and Eliot and Dostoevsky, Hemingway and Sartre, etcetera etcetera. I had a pretty vigorous time with them all, I used to discuss them at great length with my friends."[18] By the time Pinter was a working actor in Irish rep companies, he had already devoured Beckett, Kafka, and the major modernists, and become, all on his own, an expert in avant garde film (especially Bunuel), while acting in Shakespeare plays and teaching himself what he needed to know in order to pursue the kind of writing he was hoping to do.

Stoppard too left school at seventeen; he had not enjoyed it and was eager to make his way in the world. Later he regretted this: "I have a sort of fascination for academics," he said in an interview for the A.C.T. program of *Indian Ink* in 1998. "I never went to university, and I think that was very bad for me. I think it's left me with an attitude towards university people." It is difficult to believe that the author of a play like *The Invention of Love* never attended Oxford or Cambridge himself, since he is such a devotee of scholarship and eager to master everything from Sappho and Housman to neuroscience and political philosophy. But such is the case. Over the years, Stoppard's self-education has led to writing about chaos theory, fractals, neuroscience, altruism, artificial intelligence, and a host of other complex subjects. The bookshelves in Stoppard's house in Dorset are meticulously organized room by room, and to all appearances, the books have actually been *read*. It is through endless intellectual curiosity and random discoveries that Stoppard's plays are born. Each new adventure requires extensive and voracious research; this research often leads to surprising discoveries that help shape the plays. For example, because he had such fond memories of growing up in India, Stoppard was always eager to find a way to make India the central location of one of his plays. He began developing the story of an English poetess and an Indian painter in 1930 without knowing where it would lead; during this process, he happened to find himself in a bookshop on Charing Cross Road one day while waiting for an appointment nearby, and picked up a volume about Indian art. It was thus that he discovered the concept of *rasa,* which became a central metaphor of *Indian Ink.* "It's quite alarming how casually one trawls the ocean for things that end up important in one's work," he commented in the A.C.T. program. "I just blindly stumble forward, relying on destiny to bring me what I need. I'm completely shameless that way. I just grab what I need while I'm working on it."

Because the content of Stoppard's work covers a vast terrain, the rehearsal process can be like taking a graduate seminar: one spends months in advance reading up on whatever the subjects may be, in order to compete with a playwright who travels the world with a magical little trunk that opens up to become a library shelf, always crammed with new and interesting books which just might spark an idea for the next play. But their personal intellectual appetite never prevented either Stoppard or Pinter from being extremely suspicious of academic theory, and both very often lampoon academics: from Bernard in *Arcadia* to Teddy in *The Homecoming,* from Eldon Pike in *Indian Ink* to Edward in *A Slight Ache,* academics are characterized as blowhards with an ego, or disassociated individuals with little understanding of real life. On the rare occasions when either Pinter or Stoppard was asked to address an academic convention or symposium, both professed anxiety and a lack of ease. And when Stoppard knew that an academic named Ira Nadel was attempting to write his biography (well before Hermione Lee began to write the "authorized" life), he told me that he hoped it would be as inaccurate as possible.

Absent a reliance on academic analysis, we must begin in the rehearsal room, with the creative act itself. Repeated exposure to the plays in performance leads to a kind of road map for understanding the work. Staging the plays of Pinter and Stoppard is a bit like learning to play a demanding and meticulous sport; it helps to practice it, over and over again. Slowly, the sound of a voice emerges that is distinct, vivid, and insistent. It is our job to follow the writer's voice wherever it takes us, discovering new and surprising landscapes along the way. Let us now turn to that process and to the discoveries it yields.

3

Finding the Voice in Rehearsal

If one has the good fortune to work with a playwright in the rehearsal room, the key is to listen not only to *what* the writer says but *how* it is said. The goal is not to look for answers but for clues. In searching to discover what the "voice" of the play is, a director begins by asking questions like: What does the music of the play's language "sound" like? What's the tempo? The volume? The inflection? How does its comedy function? Its sexuality? Its danger? Where is it silent? Where does it reveal vulnerability? When the writer is in the room, he or she usually reveals the essential tone of the work within five minutes, even without knowing it. Through this process and through my own encounter with the two writers over four decades, certain overall precepts became clear. In this chapter, I will explore some of the broader "rules of play" that apply to both writers, before delving more deeply into the staging of individual plays.

Pinter himself was notoriously wary of making any theoretical pronouncements about his plays; as he said in a 1970 speech upon winning the German Shakespeare Prize:

> If I am to talk at all, I prefer to talk practically about practical matters, but that's no more than a pious hope, since one invariably slips into theorizing, almost without noticing it. And I distrust theory. In whatever capacity I have worked in the theatre, and apart from writing I have done quite a bit of acting and a certain amount of directing for the stage, I have found that theory, as such, has never been helpful, either to myself or, I have noticed, to few of my colleagues. The best sort of collaborative working relationship in the theatre, in my view, consists in a kind of stumbling erratic shorthand, through which facts are lost, collided with, fumbled, found again. One excellent director I know has never been known to complete a sentence.

I was reminded of a comment by Richard Hoggart in a chapter entitled "The 'Real' World of People," in which he articulates that the working class "has little or no training in the handling of ideas or in analysis. Those who show a talent for such activities have, increasingly during the last forty years, been taken out of their class . . . most people, of whatever social class, are simply not, at any time, going to be interested in general ideas."[1] Pinter had certainly been "taken out of his class" by the potency of his creative ideas, but his characters, at least in the early work, remain firmly rooted in their working-class background, and their attention to the "specific" over the "general" or "theoretical" is noticeable. It constantly annoyed Pinter that his work was read through the lens of arcane theories; perhaps because he had never been an academic, this approach to the mysteries of creative writing seemed suspect and reductive to him, and profoundly unhelpful in the rehearsal room. In an interview with Nick Hern on the occasion of *One for the Road* in 1985, he remarked that "Kenneth Tynan, for instance, discussed (*The Birthday Party*) in terms of its supposed debt to T.S. Eliot, to be specific, to *Sweeney Agonistes*. He was clearly considering the play for its formal properties. It never occurred to him that it was actually *about* anything."

Perhaps this is why, despite the reams of scholarship on Pinter, surprisingly little that I have read over the years has actually helped unlock the moment-to-moment life of the plays in rehearsal. A notable exception is Austin Quigley's 1975 *The Pinter Problem*, which brilliantly demonstrates the way in which Pinter's characters function as *doubles*, existing primarily in relationship to each other. The action of the plays demonstrates the complex and dangerous power dynamics between pairs of aggressors, between predator and prey. Quigley helped me to understand that the language of a Pinter play serves a precise function at each juncture, from reinforcement of the status quo to negotiation to subversion. It is not about an abstract "truth," nor is it about confession. As Quigley points out, the characters in Pinter use language to confirm a mutual sense of reality; conflict erupts when the demands of what that reality means are incompatible. "Look at Pinter's language from exactly the same point of view that we should adopt in approaching all language use," Quigley counsels. "We must begin with Wittgenstein's suggestion that we 'look at the sentence as an instrument, and its sense as its employment.'"[2] If the life of the play happens between two antagonists in real time, the past is a weapon or a tool to gain ground in a present conflict. Pinter never pretends to know more about his characters than they tell him: "Where a writer sets out a blueprint for his characters, and keeps them rigidly to it, where they do not at any time upset his applecart, where he has mastered them, he has also killed them, or rather terminated their birth, and he has a dead play on his hands." In other words, one must permit a theatrical character to be as complicated, contradictory, and elusive as a real human being, and accept the premise that much about a character's history will be unknowable or unverifiable.

The clues to inner life are in behavior and exact locution. Which is why each choice on stage must be meticulous; Pinter's world is one of formality and precision. It is unforgiving of sloppiness, physically or emotionally. "I am not interested in theatre used simply as a means of self-expression on the part of the people engaged in it," he insisted. "I find in so much group theatre, under the sweat and assault and noise, nothing but valueless generalizations, naïve and quite unfruitful."[3] For a playwright labeled "absurdist" early on in his career and still considered to be part of the avant garde, Pinter has always been an anomaly: the plays are both realistic and surreal, requiring a delicate and complex emotional negotiation on the part of every actor, maximum feeling coupled with maximum control. Pinter seemed to understand *in his body* what it felt like to play these remarkable roles; when the actors got stuck, he tried as hard as he could to release them with the "information" or intuition available to him. Often, watching him in rehearsal, it was hard to remember that he had actually *written* these characters, because he viewed them with a kind of objectivity and compassion as an outsider might. It was as if he were meeting them for the first time at rehearsal, and he was as open and curious about their behavior as the rest of us were.

He was also, like Stoppard, almost fanatical about how the actors attacked his language. Words are weapons, not to be deployed lightly. Comedy comes from routine and exactitude. In rehearsal, his head moved like a hawk, hearing every separate sound and holding the silences with his fierce gaze, listening, evaluating what had landed. When I directed the American premiere of *Mountain Language,* we spent hours on the phone together trying to figure out whether we should replace certain British expressions in the text with American equivalents, so that the American audience might not feel distanced from the work. Ultimately, we decided against this approach, because it was clear that the play required the specific musicality of Pinter's English to accomplish its intentions. For example, the sonic impact of the word "bloke" is completely different from that of the word "guy," even if the meaning of the two words is the same; the same holds true of "Joseph Dokes" as opposed to the American equivalent "John Doe." The sound of an exploding "k" is one Pinter treasured (as we shall see later in his appetite for the words "fuck" and "duck"); when deployed by the right actor, that "k" goes off like the sound of a gun. We had to trust that Pinter's graphic sonic poetry would give *Mountain Language* both a specific and a universal potency, without adjusting anything for an American ear. The task instead was to activate every consonant, to attack every word ending, to refrain from swallowing a single syllable.

The process of developing a character in Pinter demands unfamiliar tools, which we will examine in detail in Chapter 4, in reference to *The Birthday Party.* It is hard to "prepare" for an entrance in a Pinter play: the actor steps onto the stage, the clock starts, and action erupts. Character is revealed by what the people on stage *do,* and what they *hide.* This is not because Pinter wanted to tease us or withhold information about his characters. On the contrary, it is because he did not believe that knowledge about a character's "past" was reliable or even possible, it was only a tool to gain some advantage in the current moment. In his famous 1966 speech "Writing for the Theatre," Pinter explained:

Apart from any other consideration, we are faced with the immense difficulty, if not the impossibility, of verifying the past. I don't mean merely years ago, but yesterday, this morning. What took place, what was the nature of what took place, what happened? If one can speak of the difficulty of knowing what in fact took place yesterday, one can I think treat the present in the same way. What's happening now? We won't know until tomorrow or six months' time, and we won't know then, we'll have forgotten, or our imagination will have attributed quite false characteristics to today. A moment is sucked away and distorted, often even at the time of its birth.

Pinter had spent his twenties acting in plays in which the motives of his character were, for the most part, articulated, explained and tied up by the end of the evening, but his own radical dramaturgy refuses to traffic in that kind of certainty, which is what makes it so electrifying in performance. We watch moments getting "sucked away and distorted," right before our eyes.

This is not to say that Pinter's work does not require extreme psychological acuity. But it also requires a respect for the mysteries that every character holds within his or her heart, mysteries that are often hidden even from the playwright. When the actor Roger Davidson first worked with Pinter on *Hothouse*, he was eager to understand the biographical details of his character, Lamb. "So I was standing there wearing my Stanislavski hat, and Harold basically knocked it off my head very quickly! He looked at me and he said, 'I don't think you need to know any of that. I think . . . when the door opens and he walks through the door, that's when you start to exist."[4] Like an athlete arriving on the cricket pitch.

The athlete metaphor is also useful for a director to consider when approaching the *casting* of a Pinter play. As an actor, Pinter came of age in a rep system that invited stars to hold center stage, while supporting players were expected to get out of their way. In the universe of Pinter's plays, by contrast, no actor is there to simply "support"; each must be able to sustain his or her moment in the sun (or in the hot seat). Because the status of a Pinter character keeps changing in relation to the other members of the team, morphing from victim to aggressor to ally, the plays demand a supple company of actors who can move from offense to defense on the turn of a dime. Like a jazz musician, each performer has to be ready to step forward and shine in his or her solo, and then to retreat back into the ensemble. The person in power inevitably becomes victim to the character who seemed vanquished the moment before, just as a soloist gives way to another instrument in the band. It is rare in the theater to have a whole room full of "leading actors" whose energy and power must be sculpted into a coherent ensemble, but that is what Pinter requires. Each actor must possess the kind of vivid energy and precision that Pinter's language demands, and must intuit when to deploy that energy and when to recede or to sustain silence. Actors who have the muscle to hold their energy coiled tightly inside are able to walk Pinter's tightrope most effectively.

Over and over again, I have been reminded of the central importance of Shakespeare and Shakespearean acting to Pinter's dramaturgy. As the director Peter Hall commented when asked about whom to cast in Pinter, "They have got to have enormous verbal dexterity, and enormously good breath control, because Pinter doesn't allow you to take ordinary breaths, you know. You can't colloquialize it. Experience in Shakespeare is a help."[5] There is no "fat" in a Pinter script, no time to relax or regroup or let down one's guard. Everything matters. Every word, every gesture, every pause. Each moment is as if for the first time; judgment is useless and surprise is all. As Peter Hall implied, Pinter may have gleaned this approach from his years as a classical actor, reveling in "Shakespeare's refusal to codify or categorize intransigent individuals and judge people according to abstract precepts."[6] Each Pinter character lives and dies according to his or her own unique circumstance. This fierce "present tense" quality makes the rehearsal process of a Pinter play exhausting, demanding a unique kind of concentration. The standard "rehearsal day" for most plays is seven hours, but with Pinter I have consistently found that five hours is the maximum that even the most energetic actors can sustain before their concentration lags and diminishing returns set in. I will never forget the first run-through we did of *The Birthday Party* at CSC; although the play is relatively short, by the end the actors were barely standing, and as soon as the run ended, Peter Reigert lay on the ground and refused to budge. Pinter the athlete seemed to enjoy the demands that Pinter the playwright placed on his performers, and insisted on their being in peak shape to perform his plays.

Central to an understanding of what is "at stake" in Pinter is the slippery nature of *memory*. Pinter's characters long to fix crucial memories in their minds only to find them contradicted by other people's recollections. Memory is a tool to be deployed for present advantage, but it is rarely reliable or consistent. Indeed, conflicting memories can reveal intense tension and longing. For example, early on in *Betrayal*, Emma and her ex-lover Jerry recall a past event involving Emma's daughter, Charlotte: "Do you remember that time . . . oh god it was . . . when you picked her up and threw her up and caught her?" Emma asks. Jerry is immediately anxious that Charlotte might know about their long infidelity, but Emma assures him of her ignorance. "Yes, everyone was there that day," Jerry recalls, "standing around, your husband, my wife, all the kids, I remember." "What day?" Emma asks. "When I threw her up. It was in your kitchen." To which Emma quickly replies, "It was in your kitchen." *Silence*. Later in the play, when we have gone backward in time to a moment of great intimacy between Jerry and Emma, the same event is recalled. Immediately our antennae are out: we have heard this memory and its corrected form before. Now, in Scene 6, when Emma knows her husband has discovered her affair with Jerry, but Jerry is unaware of this fact, Jerry once again asks: "Do you remember, when was it, a few years ago, we were all in your kitchen, must have been Christmas or something, do you remember, all the kids were running about and suddenly I picked Charlotte up and lifted her high up, high up, and then down and up," to which Emma first replies, "Everyone laughed," but then, finally, "It was your kitchen, actually." This time, the correction breaks our heart; in the midst of a seemingly happy reunion, the fragile narrative of this affair is clearly unravelling. Although the characters may not be aware of it on a conscious level, the contradiction in their mutual memories is a vivid warning sign that the relationship is not going to cohere.

Pinter once told me, while we were rehearsing *Old Times*, that he did not believe one could be nostalgic until one turned forty, at which point it was possible to remember "old times." He intuitively understood that memory is necessarily subjective, hurtling into our present consciousness when we least expect it, like the Proustian moment of tasting the madeleine. And of course, Proust was an obsession of Pinter's for many years. In his highly original screenplay of *A La Recherche du Temps Perdu* (1977), Pinter returns to key moments of Marcel's past over and over again in an endless reel, accompanied by the ringing of the tiny bell on the gate at Combray. Only when the narrator suddenly sees, when walking into a party of grotesque old fools, how his memories might be transmuted into art, is he able to say, "It was time to begin." Memories (like the "ghosts" in Ibsen) can change the dynamic of a room and open up areas of acute feeling that destabilize the present moment. In that sense, each memory is always "true" because it carries its own freight, even if objectively it is suspect. It is thus a waste of rehearsal time to try to "fix" which past events "really happened"—that is never the point in Pinterland, despite the fact that actors constantly long to do so. It is far more useful to try to understand what role the memory is playing at the current moment.

Pinter's characters are often as desperate to know more about their own identities as are the actors who play them. For example, Davies in *The Caretaker* spends the entire play wishing he could get down to Sidcup "to get my papers" so that he will finally be able to articulate who he is. But knowledge of self is as hard to come by as knowledge of another person, and the search can prompt dangerous revelations. This is why Pinter's characters hold tight to their "masks"; care must be taken to sustain the façade so as not to be found out or exposed by the wrong person. Yet paradoxically, the longing to *connect*, to be part of a community of other human beings, remains strong in Pinter's universe. That tension (between cover-up and connection) is the source of Pinter's drama and is crucial to explore in rehearsal. Like the Waiter in *Celebration*, "interjection" is a way of throwing out a lifeline from within a great sea of solitude. "To speak in a Pinter play, to engage or refuse to engage in that most hazardous of forms of interaction, is not just to participate in a community but to engage in a process of community reinforcement, community contestation and community reorganization in which the precarious status of the self is constantly mediated through its precarious and conflicting allegiances to others," Quigley explains. "Speaking is a means of consolidating the status quo, exploring the status quo and altering the status quo and it involves attempts to exert control that always put the speaker at risk of being controlled."[7]

As the playwright himself reiterated, without access to the kind of extensive "backstory" other plays provide, a character in a Pinter play only begins to exist when he or she steps onto the stage. Thus, *scenography* is a key to determining behavior. Before one can understand, for example, the behavior of a man who cannot leave his room, one must understand precisely what that room looks like and how it functions to entrap him. A production process usually begins with a conversation between director and designer about the set, a conversation that helps encapsulate the director's understanding of how the play will actually work "on its feet." One would think the task with Pinter would be simple, since his plays almost always take place in a single room with relatively little adornment. But Pinter's rooms are minefields in which the characters fight to survive. If Brecht's stage was a boxing ring and Sophocles' a jury box, Pinter's room is a platform where predator meets prey, where human beings compete through wit, sexual dominance, latent and not-so-latent violence, and the power of suggestion. Because there is no literal world "outside" the play, the set is basically a zone of attention upon which dangerous encounters may occur. It cannot be muddied with extraneous details. It is a space for games, for conflict, for combat, and for verbal jousting. It is often a fortress that keeps the threat of external invasion at bay.

Pinter's description of scenery is minimal compared to that of most contemporary playwrights; in this sense he is the opposite of Stoppard, who delights in providing details about the visual demands of his work (down to a priceless note in the text of *Rock 'n' Roll* that begins "Hair ... is a problem," and proceeds to describe exactly what length of hair each actor must have in each scene as the play moves forward in time.) Pinter's writing process was different: he never launched a play knowing how it was going to evolve, and thus rarely began with a full visualization of its universe, unlike, for example, Tennessee Williams, whose detailed and poetic description of the neighborhood surrounding his "two-story corner building on a street in New Orleans" precedes the text of *A Streetcar Named Desire,* or August Wilson who visualized in great detail the back gardens of the Hill District in Pittsburgh. Pinter's process began with an almost blank slate: in his famous 1962 speech to the National Student Drama Festival in Bristol he said, "I have usually begun a play in quite a simple manner: found a couple of characters in a particular context, thrown them together and listened to what they said, keeping my nose to the ground." Over time, he came to understand "where we were." The envelope that ultimately contained his characters was crucial, but it was never literal or embellished.

Since Pinter plays are about power and about the relational dynamics between competing individuals, if two actors are sitting across from each other at a table and one suddenly rises, the world is upended. The choreography of bodies in space ("They were there, they sat, they stood, they bent, they turned"[8]) is crucial to Pinter's storytelling, and the set design must allow for each movement to read clearly and without encumbrance. Every piece of furniture and each prop is of the utmost importance and must be carefully selected. The same applies to the floor plan. In a dangerous game, it is crucial to know where the exits are. What interested Pinter was *action*, behavior, physical life; the actors themselves are scenic elements, and the architecture of their physical life must be precisely attended to in rehearsal.

In this regard, Pinter is similar to Beckett. But whereas directors of Beckett tend to respect the severe limitations (and invitations) of Beckett's stage instructions, Pinter's interpreters often design his rooms as if they were exemplars of American realism, replete with knickknacks on the mantelpiece and family pictures on the wall. This makes it difficult for an audience to pluck out and de-familiarize objects and physical behavior that are going to be central to the storytelling. Pinter's objects can take on a kind of magical anthropomorphic life when they are freed from the mundane world of set decoration. Describing his early rehearsal process with director Peter Hall, Pinter tellingly said that they discovered through trial and error that "the image must be pursued with the greatest vigilance, calmly, and once found must be sharpened, graded, accurately focused and maintained, and that the key word is economy, economy of movement and gesture, of emotion and its expression, both the internal and the external in specific and exact relation to each other, so that there is no wastage and no mess."[9] Embedded in his texts, Pinter created his own complete "scenography,"[10] like Ibsen, who "succeeded in transforming the apparently neutral trappings of the realistic stage into highly charged ingredients in a spiritual action, to which no element of the mise en scene is finally unrelated. . . . Thus the costumes, properties, lighting and décor become the diction of a new kind of dramatic poetry, the vocabulary of a vision of the human situation."[11]

Pinter's "vision of the human situation" has its own shape and palette; the first rule I discovered in staging his work was that *while everything on stage has to be real, everything that is real does not have to be on stage*. It is not that the real world is absent from the plays, merely that only very particular elements of that world are allowed in. As he so clearly stated, "the key word is economy." My process in staging Pinter is to start with what you absolutely must have on stage to further the action of the play. Remove everything else. And then see what you have got. There is no necessity and indeed nothing remotely useful about filling the interior space in Pinter with naturalistic details. Just as the physical moves of the actors need clear space to "land," so do the crucial objects or props. Interestingly, critic David Thompson speculates that Pinter's appreciation for the magical power of props stemmed in part from his early collaboration with the legendary actor-manager Donald Wolfit, who treasured and performed with props from actors who came before him, such as Lear's whip, believing that such talismans gave off a mysterious aura. Through harnessing the magic of a well-chosen prop, Wolfit was able to tap into the power of earlier performances to give his own work depth and scope. The actress Eva Le Gallienne, heir to the theatrical legacy of Eleanora Duse, had a similar reverence for the aura of important props: on her desk, as if on a sacred altar, "she arranged Juliet's dagger, L'Aiglon's riding crop, and Masha's snuff box."[12] Pinter deploys props as if they were the tools a magician might use to hold his audience in thrall. The specific objects may look simple, but if they are not meticulously conceived, the catharsis and indeed the comedy of the play will be blunted, like a magic show gone wrong.

"I have referred to facts, by which I mean theatrical facts," Pinter commented in the 1970 speech quoted above. "It is true to say that theatrical facts do not easily disclose their secrets, and it is very easy when they prove stubborn, to distort them, to make them into something else, or to pretend they never existed. This happens more often in the theater than we care to recognize and is proof either of the incompetence or fundamental contempt for the work at hand." It is not only *we* who invest in the specificity of objects, it is Pinter's characters themselves. In *No Man's Land*, as Hirst begins to cultivate a relationship with Spooner, he says to him, "I shall show you my library. I might even show you my study. I might even show you my pen, and my blottingpad. I might even show you my footstool." As we zero in from the macro to the micro, each of these objects is endowed by Hirst with a deep personal significance that he hopes might be equally meaningful to Spooner, one magical prop at a time.

Even more crucially, Pinter was aware that theatrical props are not static objects but exist in *time*. The writer and then the director must fully consider how long it takes to activate a certain prop, and how that activation becomes part of the rising action of the play. In an interview with Mel Gussow during rehearsals for *Old Times*, Pinter said, "There are problems with coffee cups. You'd be surprised the problems you can run into with coffee cups. . . . In this play, the lifting of a coffee cup at the wrong moment can damage the next five minutes. As for the *sipping* of coffee, that can ruin the act."[13] So, to borrow a phrase from Arthur Miller, "attention must be paid" to each specific prop and to how and when it is deployed, if one is to achieve the luminous effect required.

Pinter's Joycean ability to engineer epiphanies by defamiliarizing ordinary objects creates unique challenges for prop masters and set designers. For example, in his 1961 television play *The Collection* (which starred Pinter's then-wife Vivien Merchant as Stella), the heightened objects are a "pouffe" (with all the intended punning on homosexuality), two little knives (a cheese knife and a fruit knife), and some olives. James, the husband who suspects his wife Stella of infidelity with Bill, makes a "sudden move" at Bill such that "*Bill starts back, and falls over a pouffe on the floor.*" That pouffe becomes the battleground between rivals; when Bill wants to regain status vis a vis James, he "*props himself up on the pouffe*" and says, "The rest of it didn't happen. I mean, I wouldn't do that sort of thing." Over the course of the play, the placement and use of that pouffe will establish territory and determine who has control of the room. When I directed *The Collection* at the Mark Taper Forum in 1990, we could not locate an American "pouffe" that had the requisite shape, height, and padding to fulfill all of the many duties the play demanded of it. I distinctly remember a budget meeting in which, in spite of the demands of the repertory of which *The Collection* was a part (a whole spectrum of short plays from the 1950s and 1960s), I had to make the case for a bespoke pouffe, without which the requisite territorial battles would not succeed.

In a similar way, *The Homecoming* (which we will explore more fully in Chapter 6) is filled with battles involving seemingly simple objects; in Act 1, for example, the sexual tension between Ruth and Lenny is played out around and through a glass of water placed on the table between them. That glass of water becomes weaponized in Ruth and Lenny's battle for domination. One would think it contained the most expensive of elixirs instead of simply tap water. Where you place Ruth's hand in relation to that glass of water and to the ashtray, and how you light that glass of water such that its glow helps build mystery and tension, will determine the outcome of the sexual standoff between Lenny and Ruth. Pinter's dialogue bespeaks a masterful understanding of the choreography of prop and gesture:

Lenny   Excuse me, shall I take this ashtray out of your way?

Ruth   It's not in my way.

Lenny   It seems to be in the way of your glass. The glass was about to fall. Or the ashtray. I'm rather worried about the carpet. It's not me, it's my father. He's obsessed with order and clarity. He doesn't like mess. So, as I don't believe you're smoking at the moment, I'm sure you won't object if I move the ashtray.

He does so.

And now perhaps I'll relieve you of your glass.

This is followed a few moments later by:

Lenny   Just give me the glass.

Ruth   No.

Pause.

Lenny   I'll take it then.

Ruth   If you take the glass . . . I'll take you.

In staging that verbal striptease, an extreme selectivity of visual and physical cues is necessary. It is Ruth's "magic trick" to take an ordinary glass of water, turn it into a dangerous beacon of sexual allure, drain it of its power, and then, finally, restore it to its perch, such that it becomes nothing more than an ordinary glass again. Weeks of rehearsal can be spent experimenting with which is the right glass, and exactly how much water it should contain to fulfill its multiple magic tricks.

Just as visual choices and physical behavior in Pinter operate by extreme selectivity and economy, so too does language. The absence of speech in Pinter is as crucial to observe as the words themselves. Volumes have been written about Pinter's use of "pause" and "silence" to underscore his texts. He has explained on many occasions that a *pause* is a bridge between thoughts—a moment of rupture before a resumption of activity, and that a *silence* is where the true bottom drops out. One thing he insisted upon in rehearsal was to honor the music of those rhythmic indications even before understanding how they functioned or how they should be filled. He asked us to trust that if you leave space where a pause is indicated, over time in rehearsal that space will be filled—with menace, with sexuality, with need, with fear, with the whole subterranean world beneath the comic surface of the plays. Room must be left for the unknown to creep in, and for the audience to clock whether a line has "landed" on its intended recipient. From the first day, Pinter could sit and watch a scene be played without holding the script, and say at the end of it, "I believe you missed the pauses here, here and here." They were that much part of the text. He referred us back to a statement he had made in his speech "Writing for the Theatre" in which he had said:

There are two silences. One when no word is spoken. The other when perhaps a torrent of language is being employed. This speech is speaking of a language locked beneath it. . . . It is a necessary avoidance, a violent, sly, anguished or mocking smoke screen which keeps the other in its place. When true silence falls we are still left with echo but are nearer nakedness. One way of looking at speech is to say that it is a constant stratagem to cover nakedness.

What does this actually mean in practice? A simple example can be found in *Old Times*, a play about two women, Anna and Kate (who may or may not have been lovers in their younger days), and Kate's husband Deeley, who may or may not know about that past. In the opening scene between Kate and Deeley, in which he interrogates her about Anna, the pauses nearly always come after Kate has spoken. Deeley is unnerved by her insinuations but keeps the mask up; he has no desire for her to see that she is unsettling him. "Did you think of her as your best friend?" he asks. Kate replies: "She was my only friend." Deeley: "Your best and only." Kate: "My one and only." *Pause.* In that pause, Deeley realizes that the word game he and Kate have been playing has led her to a backdoor (and, from Deeley's point of view, unwelcome) confession that Anna was her "one and only." What is he to make of this? In the pause, we have just enough time to let our eyes travel to Deeley's face and then back to Kate's, impassive and inscrutable. We need the pause in order to realize that what she said has *landed* on him. And then she, taking the ball back into her own court, replies: "If you have only one of something you can't say it's the best of anything." Deeley: "Because you have nothing to compare it to?" Kate: "Mmnn." *Pause.* Again, our eyes travel to Deeley's face. He longs to ask, to demand, to get clarity about his wife's past, but he does not dare. Nor does he offer a clue about his own possible history with the woman his wife has described as "her only friend." That discovery is yet to come, but the pause lets us wonder for a moment what Deeley's relationship to Anna might be. The mystery hangs in the air, as we experience Deeley's growing anxiety and subterfuge.

A *silence* is a much more radical moment, a moment in which a crisis happens that cannot easily be recovered from. A moment "closer to nakedness." A character in Pinter is never entirely the same after such a silence. Often, it exposes him or her to the terrifying absence of any belief, any word or sound that could prevent exposure. Sometimes the silence happens while a physical move is made (such as sitting down), sometimes it happens while a character is frozen. In silence, the protective mask is suddenly gone. The terror of emptiness fills the space. This is a frightening and powerful thing for an audience to witness. But sometimes, in a world in which language is particularly vicious and aggressive, silence can also be a respite, a zone of intimacy and love. Such is the case in *Mountain Language*, in which a group of people have been forbidden to speak their own language. In such an oppressive environment, human connection can only come from the *absence* of speech, from two people looking into each other's eyes and imagining what is being thought and felt. There are times when silence is the only remaining option.

One of the reasons silence can carry such weight in Pinter is that *nature* is kept resolutely at bay. There are no open windows in Pinter, no moments when you hear the cherry trees being cut down as in Chekhov or a woman singing a spiritual outside as in Williams. It is almost as if, when you enter the enclosed universe of Pinterland, the outside world ceases to exist. If a landscape *does* exist outside the windowpane, it is usually filled with death. Davies asks Aston whether there are fish in the pond he can see through the window in *The Caretaker*, to which Aston replies, "No. There isn't anything in there." Nourishment is not to be found beyond the room. That is what makes Pinter's interior spaces so potent: they are salient as much for what they keep out as what they contain. David Jones' brilliant film version of *Betrayal* opens with a shot taken outside the window of Robert and Emma's house; through the glass, one sees a couple arguing, but we are sealed off from what they are saying. When the film premiered, audiences were said to have called out "turn up the sound!" only to realize that the deadening silence on the screen was deliberate: people were speaking but we were allowed to hear nothing. What is said inside a Pinter room stays inside the room.

Every time Pinter described his enforced stay in Cornwall during the war, it was clear that he felt none of the passion for the countryside that some of his peers claim to have felt during their escapes from London, he only longed to return to the urban environment in which he had been raised. (In this regard, he is quite different from Stoppard.) When nature *is* described in his plays, it is often a locus of decay and destruction, like the lake in Hirst's dream in which a body seems to be drowning, or the dark and dangerous park of Anna's memory in *Old Times*. If the enclosed room can contain absolute silence, it can also register the slightest noise, which is why the sound of McCann tearing newspaper strips in *The Birthday Party* feels so monumental, or why the opening of a door can make Ruth jump out of her chair in *The Room*. The absence of naturalistic ambient sound creates a unique tension in Pinter's plays, inviting each word to occupy physical space in a way language is rarely allowed to do. This is why sound designers must be so careful with Pinter's work: the addition of any naturalistic noise to "underscore" a scene can be disastrous.

The rehearsal studio for a Pinter play has to follow suit. So that he could ascertain whether key moments were registering, Pinter demanded complete quiet in the room; any extraneous noise drove him mad and had to be dealt with immediately. His own concentration was fierce, and he expected the same of everyone around him, including, ultimately, the audience. He knew that, in performance, if the carefully shaped pauses and silences onstage were marred by coughing or by candy being opened in the house, the impact of the moment would be destroyed. In his memoir *Let Me Set the Scene*, one of Pinter's longtime stage managers, Michael Hallifax, tells a wonderful story about the first revival in London of *The Birthday Party* by the RSC at the Aldwych in 1962: "Harold, strongly backed by Peter Hall, told me that I must ensure absolute silence once the play had started. This meant that the practice of letting latecomers stand at the back of the circle behind the glass screen until (as stated in the programme) 'a suitable break in the performance' would not be allowed. 'It won't be easy,' I started. But Harold cut in with, 'Easy or not, that is what has to happen.'"[14] Hallifax goes on to describe nightly altercations on the part of angry audience members who had paid for their seats and wanted to enter (noisily) whenever they chose. But Pinter's sanctity of silence was maintained, and no one was allowed in until the interval. Only then could the integrity of the theatrical event be assured.

If the focus in rehearsing Pinter is on the epiphany of the object, the economy of movement, the sculpting of sound and silence and the dangerous power dynamics of each active moment, a Stoppard rehearsal begins with "wanting to know." The scholar Hannah says it best in a gorgeous passage toward the end of *Arcadia*, when she confronts Valentine, who is in despair that his research has failed. "Comparing what we're looking for misses the point. It's wanting to know that makes us matter. Otherwise we're going out the way we came in. That's why you can't believe in the afterlife, Valentine. Believe in the after, by all means, but not the life . . . If the answers are all in the back of the book I can wait, but what a drag. Better to struggle on knowing the failure is final." In every Stoppard play, there is a hunger to know. To understand. To make sense of something seemingly random, or contradictory, or opaque. As I articulated in Chapter 1, this may be connected to Stoppard's own innate Talmudic appetite for "arguing with himself," for questioning every proposition. It is certainly connected to his belief that knowledge *matters*, that nuanced thought is a bulwark against tyranny. The struggle to "know" is not cerebral, it is deeply personal and deeply *felt*. The longing to "know" is what gives his characters passion, vitality, and desire. "People do awful things to each other," says the war photographer Guthrie in *Night and Day*. "But it's worse in places where everybody is kept in the dark. Information is light. Information, in itself, about anything, is light."

That appetite for knowledge and "light" is evinced right from his first theatrical success, *Rosencrantz and Guildenstern are Dead*, in which two nobodies from the court of Elsinore desperately try to figure out who they are and what they are meant to be doing with their lives. Knowledge is elusive and mortality is near, but the quest is life-giving nonetheless. As AEH (Alfred Housman) reminds us in *The Invention of Love*:

> A scholar's business is to add to what is already known. That is all. But it is capable of giving the greatest satisfaction, because knowledge is good. It does not have to look good or sound good or even do good. It is good just by being knowledge. And the only thing that makes it knowledge is that it is true. You can't have too much of it and there is no little too little to be worth having. There is truth and falsehood in a comma.

The quest for knowledge shapes the structure of nearly every Stoppard play in active and playable ways that inform how one rehearses and stages the work. Understanding that quest helps actors play what is at *stake*, and connects us to Stoppard's sense of the value and function of art. Unfashionable as it may seem, Stoppard has (as I have argued in Chapter 1) something of the Austrian and German Jews' reverence for "*bildung*," the quest for self-betterment through an appreciation of, and knowledge about, culture. Again and again, he talks about art as what remains when all else has disappeared or become irrelevant: "An artist is the magician put among men to gratify—capriciously—their desire for immortality," James Joyce says to Tristan Tzara in *Travesties*:

> If there is any meaning in any of it, it is in what survives as art, yes even in the celebration of tyrants, yes even in the celebration of nonentities. What now of the Trojan War if it had been passed over by the artist's touch? Dust. A forgotten expedition prompted by Greek merchants looking for new markets. A minor redistribution of broken pots. But it is we who stand enriched, by a tale of heroes, of a golden apple, a wooden horse, a face that launched a thousand ships—and above all, of Ulysses, the wanderer, the most human, the most complete of all heroes.

One could argue that art, and the quest for the meaning of art, is life's organizing principle, not only for Stoppard himself but for many of his characters; it is what makes sense of the chaos of human existence. Indeed, the conflict between order and chaos, and the value of art as the moral center of a life, manifests itself constantly in Stoppard's work. In *Arcadia*, this theme appears in the collision of Classicism and Romanticism as reflected in the gardens of Lady Croom and the divergent research projects of the two main scholars; in *Travesties*, in the aesthetic disagreement between Tristan Tzara's anarchic Dadaism and James Joyce's linguistic precision. If Stoppard plays can occasionally seem too "clever" in performance, it may be because actors fail to understand how high the stakes are in these central arguments about art and culture, and how *personal* the arguments must be. These arguments are not intellectual pronouncements meant to stand as elegant epigrams inside the life of the play or to make an audience feel stupid for lack of knowledge, they are the weapons that Stoppard's characters hurl at each other in order to fight for what matters the most to them.

In another example from *Arcadia*, the pompous Byron critic Bernard Nightingale debates with Valentine (the young scientist who is also his host and heir to the elegant Croom estate) about what kind of knowledge matters the most. As we have seen in Stoppard, each argument has sexual/romantic overtones as well: Bernard wants to bed Chloe, and Valentine wants to impress Hannah, to whom he has already proposed and been rebuffed. "Oh, you're going to zap me with penicillin and pesticides!" exclaims Bernard. "Spare me that and I'll spare you the bomb and aerosols. But don't confuse progress with perfectability. A great poet is always timely. A great philosopher is an urgent need. There's no rush for Isaac Newton. We were quite happy with Aristotle's cosmos. Personally I preferred it." He finishes by waxing rhapsodic about Byron: "I can expand my knowledge without you," he asserts. "'She walks in beauty, like the night of cloudless climes and starry skies, and all that's best of dark and bright meet in her aspect and her eyes.' There you are, he wrote it after coming home from a party." At which point Valentine stands up close to tears and runs out the door, deeply humiliated at the thought that Hannah would find him a philistine for disagreeing with Bernard's thesis. Arguments about art are life and death in Stoppard's universe. Or, at the very least, sex and death.

Love is often the cog in the wheel, the surprising and unexpected stealth agent that upends rational choice and sets his characters in new directions. In exploring a Stoppard play, it is always worth looking for the *reversals*, the illogical elements in a universe of logic, the moments when the set up gets clearly undercut. These twists are what cut against the intellectual grain of the plays and give them their anarchic humanity. Even in a play as cerebral and often hard to follow as the spy-thriller *Hapgood*, everything comes down to *feeling*. The Russian double agent Kerner pretends to explain why he first came to the West: "We were using computers which you had in museums. I wasn't seeking asylum, I was seeking an IBM 195." But his

British colleague Blair knows the truth: "No. They put you up to it and Elizabeth turned you. You were her joe." And Kerner has to agree: "Yes, I was. There's something terrible about love. It uses up all one's moral judgment. Afterwards it is like returning to a system of values, or at least to the attempt." Over and over again in Stoppard's work, one is confronted with a character of impeccable intellectual and moral credentials who suddenly starts behaving in a completely unexpected manner, a manner which cannot be rationalized and is often very difficult for actors to parse. Precisely because they are so radical, those internal contradictions must be trusted and mined, rather than smoothed over. Emotional reversals collide inside Annie in *The Real Thing* when she betrays Henry for Billie, or inside the brilliant scholar Housman when he deliberately fails his Oxford finals in the hopes of staying close to his love Mo Jackson. Watching those events on stage, we can barely catch up to what has happened, because in Stoppard's universe, the human heart is subversive and illogical, and love is always without precedent. Rather than gradually acquainting the audience with a character's inner struggle, Stoppard employs a shock of discovery in which we discover something about a character that we have been totally unprepared for. Trust in that process of reversal would prove to be crucial when we rehearsed *Indian Ink*.

Stoppard's fascination with upending emotional expectations is connected to his appetite for theatrical structures and devices that defy audience expectations. Along these lines, both Pinter's and Stoppard's work is filled with an abiding passion for the playing of *games*. I have found (in all my years of marriage to a British man) that games are a particularly English obsession. Perhaps because they are an island people, the English are (in general) more naturally reticent than Americans, and their use of language is markedly different from ours. If Americans tend to believe in the transparency of language and the efficacy of confession, the English use language to tease, to cover, to distract, and to avoid emotional exposure; "taking the piss" is an English art form for which we have no exact equivalent in America. Director Giles Havergal has speculated that for the English, the playing of games (from chess to cards to charades) is a platform for interaction that permits a modicum of communication without too much emotional exposure.[15] British theater scholar and practitioner Clive Barker was one of the first to articulate the relationship of games to the theatrical enterprise in his 1987 book *Theatre Games* and in articles for the *New Theatre Quarterly*, quoting director Ed Berman's assertion that "locked within all of us is a social language learned in childhood. This is a language of behavior based on the rules of children's games . . . the language remains within us . . . as a major formative influence and touchstone in our adult intellectual, social and emotional relationships."[16] Being avid cricketers, it is perhaps not surprising that both Pinter and Stoppard traffic so often in the world of games, but games in their work need not involve sport, just strategy and surprise.

In staging these plays, it helps if the director begins by figuring out what game is being played within the "super-structure" of the play. The rules often change midstream, which is part of the fun (and the terror); the characters are forced to constantly recalibrate to ascertain how to "win." Pinter's games tend toward entrapment and latent violence. At the startling conclusion of Act 1 of *The Caretaker*, Mick confronts Davies with the curtain line, "What's the game?" Blackout. In the midst of Stanley's "party" in *The Birthday Party*, Meg leaps up and announces, "I want to play a game!"; within seconds, we find ourselves watching a terrifying round of "Blind Man's Buff." Even the simplest children's game can be dangerous in the extreme: status is upended, the weak are assaulted, and power determines survival. On the surface, the many interrogations in *The Birthday Party* are just games, but the stakes are life and death. "All my life I've said the same. Play up, play up and play the game," Goldberg exhorts McCann in *The Birthday Party*. Poor McCann. It is hard to follow those instructions when you have no idea what the game is to begin with.

Stoppard has an almost mathematical fascination with probability, with logic, with luck, and with the irrational. With each play, he has to find a structure that will best epitomize and activate the ideas he is interested in exploring. Put another way, Stoppard delights in setting up theatrical games that he then has to play out. "Drama is a series of reversals," Stoppard told the cast of *The Hard Problem*. "That's what makes it interesting. So Scene 6 of the play ends with 'no way!', in reference to Hilary sleeping with Leo, and at the top of Scene 7, there's a naked man in bed with Hilary, but it's not Leo! It's Spike!" Surprise! In the *The Real Thing*, the game is that the first scene is actually the fictional creation of a playwright who appears in the second scene. Thus, we first seem to be witnessing a painful break-up between a man and a woman in a real living room, but as soon as Scene 2 begins and we are in a second living room, we discover that the first scene was happening between actors on a stage. The play moves back and forth from "reality" to "theatricality"; the audience is invited to parse which is which. In *Hapgood*, Stoppard encased Heisenberg's principle of uncertainty in a Russian spy thriller that, underneath it all, is a love story about two very mismatched individuals. Asked to write a television film about Lech Walesa and Solidarity in 1982 (*Squaring the Circle*), Stoppard realized that no "bio-pic" or fictional documentary could ever evoke the terrifying separation of language and truth that pertained to Cold War politics, so he created a structure (another kind of game) in which a fallible Narrator is constantly interrupted by anonymous Witnesses subverting and commenting on what the Narrator asserts. In writing the film, Stoppard set himself the task of answering a single question: "Was freedom as defined by the free trade union Solidarity reconcilable with socialism as defined by the Eastern European Communist bloc?" he wrote in his "Introduction" to the published screenplay. "My position is that the two concepts cannot coexist and are irreconcilable in an absolute sense, in the sense understood by a logician or a mathematician . . ."[17] This logical irreconcilability determined the structure of the film.

Sometimes, structure comes before story in Stoppard. While ideas and emotions have always come easily to Stoppard, plot does not. He agonizes about the plots of his plays long after he has come up with the characters and their arguments. "Incidents. All we get are incidents," Rosencrantz sighs in *Rosencrantz and Guildenstern*. "Promise without fulfillment. Dear me, is it too much to ask for a little sustained action?" This self-critique of his own work is poignant. With each play, a story and a structure must be found to encase the undercurrent of feeling and the conflicts about world view that lie at the heart of the enterprise. But once that is achieved, the ideas begin to take on an organic life of their own. It is crucial for the actors to remember that there is an erotic energy to Stoppard's ideas that carries the story forward, an energy that must be mined if the plays are to have life on stage.

It can take a long time to master the relevant details in a Stoppard text, which means "table work" (the time the cast spends at the table dissecting the text) is supremely important (more so than with Pinter, for whom too much talk can be futile, while discovering the physical life reveals all), because the dialectic of ideas is complex, the references are often obscure, and the subject matter not always familiar to the average theater artist. If it requires forensic and careful excavation to understand the arguments of a Stoppard play and to become fluent in whatever world view is being expressed, from Byron to Dadaism to artificial intelligence to Heisenberg's principle of uncertainty, it helps to begin by locating the central *dialectic*. Stoppard has said that his plays are really about him arguing with himself ("I write plays because writing dialogue is the only respectable way of contradicting yourself," he told Mel Gussow in 1972), and in each play there is a clear and specific collision of ideas. What makes his plays dramatically satisfying events rather than diatribes is the way in which the dialectic shifts and changes over the course of the story. Often, like Shaw and Granville-Barker, Stoppard gives the strongest argument to the side he actually disagrees with, so, for example, in *Travesties*, the Dadaist Tristan Tzara gets far more stage time than James Joyce to argue his view of art, even though Joyce's view is much closer to Stoppard's own. In *Rock 'n' Roll*, Jan's resistance to dissent creates a dialectic with the "activist" Ferdinand that, surprisingly, reverses itself in Act 2: "I had worked out that, in my play, Tomas (later Jan) would need a foil who would be taking Havel's viewpoint in the dialectic," Stoppard wrote in the "Introduction" to *Rock 'n' Roll*. "I didn't know, when I began, that in the second half of my play, it would be Jan, not Ferdinand, who would be Havel's spirit."[18] What is exhilarating about the dialectical nature of Stoppard's plays is that the conflict is so human and thus often inconsistent or filled with doubt. One must always be alert in rehearsal to the moments in which the speaker shifts course or re-evaluates the argument; this is where the drama lies. Stoppard has no interest in advancing an agenda or demanding allegiance to a point of view, although it is indisputable that on some fundamental level he believes in beauty, in the necessity of humanistic thought, and in the moral compass evidenced in great literature. In nearly every Stoppard play, there is at some point a passionate defense of the role of art in sustaining civilization and defeating philistinism. And then someone contradicts it.

If the first week of rehearsal invites intensive work on the text to understand the dialectic that is happening, the bulk of the next three or four weeks requires teasing out the undercurrents of the play, where the secrets of the characters are hiding. Finding vulnerability is a complex task in the face of a writer who treasures reticence and the restraint of buried emotion. Each time Stoppard came to San Francisco to work on a production, he graciously spent time with the graduate students in our accredited Masters of Fine Arts program. (Stoppard has always been interested in the perspective of youth and writes with great compassion for young actors, so our M.F.A. students often had the opportunity to play small roles or, in the case of *Arcadia*, *The Real Thing*, and *The Hard Problem*, substantial roles, in the productions.) On one such occasion, the students were studying Chekhov and were thus immersed in the vast array of emotional experiences that Chekhov provides. They breathlessly asked Stoppard what he most valued in an actor. "Clarity of utterance," he instantly replied. This initially disappointed our young actors-in-training, who were hoping Stoppard would expound upon something more psychological and profound. But the truth is that Stoppard, who is full of feeling, rarely speaks about it. He trusts that if you actually get the text right, absolutely right, the wellspring of emotion from which it sprang will reveal itself. The muscle and precision it takes to get Stoppard's language right is connected to what Shaw described as "audible intelligibility" and it is the key to a successful production of his plays. If the language is precise, the feelings will have a form to support them. As the Inspector opines in *Cahoot's Macbeth*, "The way I see it, life is lived off the record. It's altogether too human for the written word."

Stoppardian "clarity of utterance" takes time and training to achieve, and requires an understanding of how the writer structures his language. When he watches a run-through of one of his plays, Stoppard sits quietly with the text, making little marks by certain words. Upon closer viewing, those marks are usually the letters "L.A.," meaning "look after." This is his way of reminding an actor to "look after" or "lift" a key word or expression that will carry the thought forward. It is not always obvious. Sometimes it is a way of setting up a joke—for the right word to be highlighted or "looked after," one has to think of it as pitching a ball that the other actor can cleanly "hit." If the ball is not thrown with energy and clarity (i.e. if the "set up" is not precise), it is impossible for the other actor to land the joke. "It's not a big deal, and yet it's an instance of a point I try to make about my stuff as a whole," Stoppard told the *Rock 'n' Roll* cast in London. "It works best when it's very clean and (except where stipulated otherwise) edge-to-edge."[19] This is the philosophy he puts into the mouth of his surrogate Henry in

The Real Thing when he gives his famous speech comparing effective language to using a well-sprung cricket bat: "What we're trying to do is write cricket bats, so that when we throw up an idea and give it a little knock, it might . . . travel."

In some cases, the word that requires "looking after" is a clue to a future revelation, or a subtle signaler of erotic desire, something that when first mentioned seems to carry less freight, but which ultimately generates significant heat. For example, early on in *Indian Ink*, the painter Nirad Das tells Flora that the *rasa* of erotic love is aroused by "the moon, the scent of sandalwood, or being in an empty house," to which she replies, "I see. Thank you. Empty house is very good." Much later in the play, a weeping Flora tells Das, "Your handkerchief smells faintly of . . . something nice." She deliberately does not say the most important word: "*sandalwood*." Nor does she point out that at that precise moment, they are standing in an empty house. But the conditions for love prevail. It is not incumbent upon her to say "sandalwood" or to point out the moonlight to acknowledge that she can sense the potential for erotic love; if the actor playing Das has clearly set up both the word "sandalwood" and the image of the "empty house" in the first act of the play, we will remember that in the universe of *Indian Ink*, those elements provide the conditions for the erotic. The unsaid word at this vulnerable moment in the play makes Flora's comment all the more sensual, but if the actor playing Das has failed to "look after" the word "sandalwood" earlier on, Flora's discovery will lose its charge. Nothing in Stoppard can be glossed over. He counts on his audience to pay attention. His words may jettison like billiard balls across the stage, but each word counts, and the actors must take responsibility for the whole game if the play is to cohere.

Sometimes it is difficult for actors to determine which key words need to be "looked after." During *Night and Day* rehearsals, Stoppard mused about the way actors tend to salivate over multi-syllabic words but usually ignore the lowly "if." He would remind them that, often, "if" is the set up that makes the whole subsequent proposition clear. "If" is a word particularly at risk when it starts the sentence, as in this exchange from *The Hard Problem*: "HILARY: Is your doctorate in psychology? AMAL: If necessary." The "if" tells us everything we need to know about Amal's intellectual arrogance—he is even willing to pretend he is interested in psychology *if* that will gain him access to the Krohl Institute. Stoppard repeatedly gave Romola Garai the note, during run-throughs of *Indian Ink* in New York, that she was under-powering the catalyzing "if" from her sentence "If you're going to be Indian, I won't tell you." Without the launch of the "if," the argument of the sentence is lost. The same note prevailed during *Night and Day* rehearsals: "A lady, *if* surprised by melancholy, might go to bed with a chap, once; or a thousand times *if* consumed by passion," Ruth tells Wagner. Stoppard insisted that those two "ifs" were far more important to emphasize than either "melancholy" or "passion," despite the fact that "actors always gravitate to the words they think are juicier."

Stoppard also feels strongly that actors not "naturalize" his speech by inventing pauses or hidden commas. "Don't add punctuation where it's not indicated. It only confuses everything," he begged the cast during rehearsals for *The Hard Problem*. For example, when the scientist Leo, in love with Hilary, confronts her after an encounter in Venice at which he tried to go to bed with her, he says, "Welcome back, I think. Sorry about my language. (*pause*) Also me in Venice." Anthony Fusco, the actor playing Leo, wanted to put a breath after "me" to help explain the line: "Also me, in Venice." To Stoppard, this confused a simple thought by over-explaining it, and he courteously requested that the unseen but clearly heard comma be removed. (Stoppard, like Pinter, can hear unnecessary punctuation a mile away. As AEH says so eloquently in *The Invention of Love*, "there is truth or falsehood in a comma.") On repeated occasions, I have listened to Stoppard explain to a cast that approaching his language is like driving a car with a clutch: you have to change gears quite deftly if you are to control the flow of meaning and not go completely off the rails.

"You can't just speed up or turn left," he reminded the company of *Indian Ink*, "there are key markers like 'oh' and 'you see' which help the gears to shift and must be attended to." He referred to a moment when the Indian painter Das is upset with Flora, and she cannot understand what she has done to insult him. He asks Flora if she has looked at his painting-in-progress. "DAS: You have looked at the portrait, Miss Crewe?" FLORA: "Oh, I see. Yes, yes . . . I did look." In eight monosyllabic words, Flora travels from discovery ("Oh, I see") to acknowledgment ("Yes, yes . . .") to confession ("I did look"). Each phrase has to be made distinct if the emotional current is to incrementally move forward. First, she discovers what he is upset about, she then switches gears and affirms what he is most afraid of, and finally she makes a simple assertion, about which she is not ashamed. Of course, it turns out, in typical Stoppardian fashion, that what is upsetting Das is not at all that she has looked, but that she has chosen to say nothing afterward.

Although or perhaps because the language moves very quickly in Stoppard, the sculpting of visual and verbal cues is key. Everything in the text is crafted so that actors do not race blindly forward or make a sudden turn that cannot be followed; the speeches may seem dizzying in their complexity but are always shaped for maximum clarity if you pay attention to the minute transitions embedded in the language. "My biggest interest is how things *sound*," Stoppard commented in an interview with Patrick Leahey of the *New York Times* in January 2016. Perhaps this obsession with how words sound is connected to the fact that English is not Stoppard's first language—there is a sense that he can *hear* the music of English in a way that a native speaker might not. When tasked with translating Chekhov's *The Seagull*, he struggled with how to put Konstantin's play-within-a-play into English, until he made a discovery that he addressed in his "Introduction." "I don't think all is quite as it seems in English," he writes. "In Russian,

'Men, lions' is *liudi, l'vi,* which makes it instantly clear that Chekhov didn't give a fig for which animal Konstantin evokes. The *sound* of the names is what matters to Konstantin." And so, in his translation, Stoppard focuses on alliteration and assonance ("Mankind and monkeys, ostriches and partridges") rather than a literal translation of the Russian. His desire in translating Chekhov was to try to convey the *sound* the play made as well as the meaning. Thus, Stoppard greatly admired the word choice Michael Frayn had selected for a line in his own version of *Seagull:* "You keep asking me about people who came out of the Ark." This filled Stoppard with admiration because of Frayn's three "k" sounds which he considered "a treat."[20] (Like Pinter, Stoppard relishes the sound of a good "k.")

Stoppard once commented:

> My plays for me—in my head, before anyone gets hold of a text—make a certain quality of noise, which rises or falls at certain places, and slows or speeds up at certain spaces, and much of our rehearsal time consists of me trying to explain what this noise is like, and trying to make the actors make this noise; and then Peter (Wood) and the actors, from the other end, show me how the action can speed up in a different place, and not get loud there but very quiet, and it's my turn to be shown an alternative orchestration for those voices.[21]

It is entirely to Stoppard's credit that he is generous enough in the room to allow for "an alternative orchestration," although I have witnessed hilarious verbal contortions in which he has tried to explain how a line should be read without just demonstrating it himself. "One is constantly on the point of saying the line for the actor," Stoppard told Hermione Lee. "Occasionally as I stumble through my complicated exegesis about the insides of a sentence and its multiple meanings, I am tempted just to scream, 'Say it like *this!*'." It is hard for Stoppard to explain that while the emotional content of the play is ultimately what compels an audience to watch, the structure in which that emotion is contained requires as much attention as the excavation of feeling. During *Indian Ink* rehearsals he became frustrated at American actors' insistence on facing the other character in the scene as one would in life (thus playing in profile to the audience), rather than opening their faces out to include those watching. "About my plays," he patiently tried to explain, "they're as artificial as Restoration comedy. They have absolutely nothing in common with Arthur Miller, they are more like Sheridan. Don't do it for the other actor only, you must always be aware that the audience is listening and needs to be included."

Stoppard is entirely unapologetic about the level of articulation and verbal dexterity his scripts demand. In life and in art, he is passionate about people who speak well; in particular, again perhaps because English is his second language, he is passionate about people who speak *English* well. As he once said to Mel Gussow, "In *Night and Day,* the African dictator is the only African dictator, as far as I was concerned, who went to the London School of Economics. He has to, because he had to say all the things I wanted him to say ... Doolittle (in Shaw's *Pygmalion*) is a dustman but he's an exceptional dustman, because he would have to be in order to say what he has to say."[22] While I do not actually believe, as Stoppard has occasionally averred, that all his characters sound alike, and while I have come to realize what an acute instinct for psychology and human behavior Stoppard possesses, I have to admit that it is an enormous pleasure to sit in a rehearsal room for eight hours a day with characters who speak so beautifully, assuming that you have cast actors who can make that language come alive.

It is not that "surface" is all that matters in Stoppard's work. On the contrary, the emotion lies buried beneath words that exist to help the characters control and navigate their strongest feelings without losing their composure. In this sense, the idea of "masking" which is so crucial to Pinter's work is germane to Stoppard as well, but unlike in Pinter's universe, where characters sustain their masks to prevent being devoured by rapacious predators, in Stoppard's world the mask preserves a certain decorum and shyness, which the playwright himself reflects. "Confession is an act of violence against the unoffending," says AEH in *The Invention of Love* in order to defend his own reticence, and one cannot help but think he is speaking on the author's behalf. Vulnerability must, for the most part, be kept to oneself.

In my experience, Stoppard generally finds it unseemly to unburden himself to anyone, and he certainly finds it unseemly in his characters, for whom the masking of emotion or deployment of wit helps further a strategy of flirtation or supply a cover for erotic desire. Different people have different ways of wrestling with their own "inner life"; Ruth in *Night and Day* copes by talking to herself, breaking the "fourth wall" to share outrageous things with the audience that she would never utter in the room. At times, this makes her seem slightly mad, until one realizes that we all have inner monologues, Ruth simply expresses hers aloud. In reference to his characters, Stoppard is always careful not to force a crisis or to assume a level of emotional chaos that does not exist. When I was staging *Night and Day* at A.C.T. in 2002, I asked him what he felt about Ruth and Carson's marriage. In particular, I wondered what to make of a moment in which Carson (a rich ex-pat mining engineer in an unnamed African country) remonstrates with his wife about being so snide to Wagner (with whom she has just had a quick affair in London) and then asks her, "Do you want a change?" That question seemed quite significant for such a buttoned-down man to ask his (second) wife. Did Carson intuit that something had happened between Ruth and Wagner, I asked? Was he concerned that Ruth was getting restless in their marriage? What did his question imply?

Stoppard laughed and said that my "psychological key was more complicated than the lock," assuring us that Carson does not think his wife is crazy, just a bit extreme. When, in Act 2 of the play, danger presents itself in the form of meeting the volatile African President, and Carson offers Ruth a chance to escape, "she stays because she wants a seat at the show, not because she's trying to be a good wife," he explained, insisting that there was not much self-examination going on. "A way of life has established itself which is better than what they had before for both of them, and that's enough." Be careful, he seemed to imply, of making every character as self-reflective and introspective as performers always wish them to be or as they often are in conventional plays. Keep your equanimity, he urged the actors. For many of his characters, the status quo is hard won and worth preserving. He has been known to say about himself that he is "culpably self-sufficient," and that is frequently true of the people he creates as well.

Thus, when a character finally *does* erupt with emotion in a Stoppard play, it is a startling event. "The outburst which escapes one is the real truth about one's character," he told us during *Indian Ink* rehearsals; in order for that outburst to surprise, it has to come out of emotional balance, and perhaps even surprise the character. This balance can be tricky to get right. For example, Stoppard was relentless in urging first Romola Garai and then Brenda Meaney (who played Flora in *Indian Ink* at A.C.T.) never to get sulky or to make it appear that she is masking anger or despair when initially dealing with Das and India; as with Ruth, he believed that Flora had found a balanced way of moving through the world, until those key moments when something triggered a moment of desire, rage, humiliation, or sorrow. For a man whose life had been violently uprooted at age two and who had made his own fate at every step of the way, Stoppard had clearly learned that it did not pay to lose control or to over-react except in extreme circumstances. This shaping of emotion can be frustrating for American actors, who are encouraged to look for the emotional spine and reveal it as frequently as possible. What Stoppard admired so much about his frequent "muse" (and lover) Felicity Kendal was that she was not a "Method actor," she was a disciplined comedienne with remarkable timing and an uncanny ability to keep her emotions in check until given the moment of release. Best of all, "clarity of utterance" was her native instinct.

Balancing Stoppard's dialectical arguments with the undercurrent of longing and loss that usually suffuses them is never easy: focus too much on the "thought" and the plays become brittle, expose the emotion too obviously and they become sentimental and melodramatic. Striking this balance is a key part of directing a Stoppard play. "Happiness is equilibrium," Henry says in *The Real Thing*. "Change your weight." Dramatically, it is when equilibrium is impossible to maintain that the pain leaches out and something changes. With the arrival of *The Real Thing*, critics suddenly began exclaiming, "Stoppard has a heart!", but in truth, his writing had always been filled with feeling, it was just a matter of deciding where and how to expose it. (Stoppard seemed to mock that critical reaction when it came time to write *The Invention of Love*, in which AEH's sister Kate, having read his love poetry, exclaims, "We're all proud and astonished. Clem said, 'Alfred has a heart!'")

In an interview in 1983, Stoppard mused, "Love is a very interesting subject to write about. I've been aware of the process this last 25 years, of shedding inhibition about self-revelation. I wouldn't have dreamed of writing it 10 years ago, but as you get older, you think, who cares?"[23]

Scenery in Stoppard often follows the same logic of romance and reversal as the characters' inner lives. As with Pinter, Stoppard's scenography is emotional and metaphoric rather than naturalistic, but unlike Pinter, Stoppard views scenery as a kind of magical puzzle which a director and designer must "solve." Some of the most wonderful writing in a Stoppard play is to be found in his descriptions of the physical space, the lighting, the sound and the "world" of the play. For example, *Night and Day* begins thus: "An empty stage with a cyclorama, representing the open air, and a living room share the stage in various proportions, including total occupancy by the one or the other. Thus, the living room is mobile. Herewith, a few dogmatic statements tentatively offered." He then goes on to describe, in great detail, a possible visual world for the play. His self-effacing comment "tentatively offered" is key; Stoppard is never prescriptive about how his plays should be designed. On the contrary, it is much more important to understand the "theatrical playground" he is proposing than to follow exact instructions for realizing it. He is interested in surprise, transformation, and theatricality. Even with *Arcadia*, his simplest play to design as it all occurs in a single room, the challenges that present themselves when two time periods occupy the same space are delightful and difficult to get right, requiring color-coded letters, props in different stages of "distress," and lighting that can take us instantly from past to present and back. The subtle interplay of nineteenth- and twentieth-century props and costumes, coexisting in the same space and often used across time, requires the same vigilance and precision as we discovered with Pinter. Constructing a credible "Plautus the tortoise" consumed weeks of our prop master's life.

What is remarkable about Stoppard's oeuvre is that each of his plays creates its own unique world, and the set often requires extreme sleight of hand to achieve the kinds of effects the playwright imagines. In *Hapgood*, the description of the initial spy *lazzi* in a swimming pool changing room covers three pages of text and took us a week of rehearsal to unravel. If the language of the plays were not so resolutely theatrical, one would think Stoppard was always yearning to write for film: for example, the opening of *Night and Day* involves an elaborate dream sequence in which a photographer imagines someone shooting at him from a jeep. We see the whole explosion happening in real time, and assume he has been killed. Jump cut to a woman walking across the yard toward the sleeping photographer, who suddenly wakes, shaken. We discover retrospectively that the sound of a telex machine inside the house has triggered his violent nightmare. Thus, Stoppard establishes the dangers of life as a foreign correspondent and the human cost of covering war before a single line of dialogue is spoken. The event has to feel utterly real for the reversal to work, which requires a lot of smoke and mirrors onstage, and many hours of technical rehearsals.

A play such as *Indian Ink* is complex to design not only because there are a multitude of times and places to reveal but because the play is about beauty; hence, the visual world of the production needs to suggest the kind of *rasa* the play's characters seek to find in their work. The opening of *Indian Ink* involves a train arriving in Jummapur and a large convocation of Indians with marigolds gathering to greet it. In a beautiful example of Stoppard's innate theatrical sense, the images in the first scene of *Indian Ink* keep moving forward, almost as if we are on a magical conveyer belt: Flora arrives at the train station and the scenery evolves around her until she ultimately arrives at her "dak bungalow" and begins to speak. The visual and the verbal unfold together; both are contained in a letter being read by a woman far away in time and space. Many images must be sustained at the same time for the story to be seamlessly told, and often that takes extensive trial and error. In my experience, Stoppard is always cognizant of the fact that the exigencies of live theater require constant recalibration. For example, when we did *Indian Ink* at the Roundabout Theater in New York in 2014, the stage at the Laura Pels Theater was shallow, with almost no wing space. It was thus impossible to recreate the gorgeous effect of the opening moment that we had created years ago on the Geary stage at A.C.T., in which a large pair of lights had travelled from upstage to downstage surrounded by smoke in a *tromp l'oeil* effect that truly looked like a train chugging into the station. As we began technical rehearsals in New York and reckoned with the spatial limitations of the stage, we came up with a new and simpler idea for the opening: instead of launching the play with a dramatic train effect, we began with a light glowing on Eleanor Swan, sitting in her garden chair. She plucked a letter out of a box; as she opened it, the sounds of India began to magically emerge as if released by its contents, a layer of smoke drifted in from the wings, and Flora appeared right behind her sister, as if having just stepped off the train. This provided a different "sleight of hand" in which both time periods were instantly established; the proximity between the two sisters, so far apart in time, pleased Stoppard very much. The point is, there is never a single answer to his design requirements and Stoppard leaves plenty of room for a director and designers to find their own solutions; his copious descriptions serve to stimulate the imaginations of the creative team to discover and then re-invent the metaphor he is pursuing. With every play we have worked on together, Stoppard has eagerly waited for me to forward the set designs, and then sent back informed and exuberant responses. What excites him the most is when the design can morph and flow in concert with the language.

Stoppard is a romantic at heart—he loves color and shape and beauty. That is partly why he is so obsessed with how his plays are lit. It is inside the world of light that *rasa* can emerge, and Stoppard can often be found sitting at the lighting table beside the designer, silently and happily watching the magic that can be created when the right light hits an outstretched arm or a delicate piece of scenery and instantly transports us to another place.

FIGURE 6 *Brenda Meaney and Roberta Maxwell in* Indian Ink, *A.C.T. 2015. Scenery by Neil Patel, Lighting by Robert Wierzel, Costumes by Candice Donnelly. Photo courtesy of Kevin Berne.*

Following the logic of light, the designs for his plays need never be realistic, but it helps if the surfaces can be beautifully lit. For *The Real Thing* we created a series of sliding panels painted like Rothkos, with evocative deep colors that concealed and revealed, so that the entire Geary stage was in some way inside Henry's messy heart. For *Rock 'n' Roll*, we tipped a Czech building on its side and looked inside its courtyard; everything that happened in the play was within that canted lens, which was full of windows to spy from and depths to imagine (see Figure 15). *The Invention of Love* invited us to design a world in which stacks of books magically glided into view and boats could float past the green lawns of Oxford like the memories of love. The most important thing is to meet the text with a sense of play that releases it from naturalism and encourages a kind of beauty to emerge. "You have to bow down before the true god of theater, who is merciless and is saying, 'This is not a text, this is an event happening in a room at this time in front of people who are under no obligation to remain,'" Stoppard commented once in an interview in *Harper's Bazaar*. His respect for the way actors, director, and designers sustain and nurture that event is immense.

I have noted that Pinter's plays are encased in a world of silence, a silence waiting to be filled by the language of his characters. Stoppard's plays, by contrast, revel in music and ambient sound; indeed, Stoppard has often remarked that he writes every play while compulsively listening to a single song. While that is not necessarily the "sound" one wants to attach to the play, and while Stoppard himself claims to be musically illiterate, it is clear that music and sound are extremely important in the world of Stoppard's plays. He knew intimately the sounds of India that he longed to hear in *Indian Ink*. He delighted in the electronic beats we created for *The Hard Problem*. He meticulously described every single song cue in *Rock 'n' Roll* and from which section of each song the cuts should come. He imagined the extraordinary blend of waltz music and contemporary dance tunes that merged into the final moments of heat and love in *Arcadia*, a musical sequence that took our composer Michael Roth many weeks to get exactly right. He knew how the bells of Oxford could underscore the buried heartbeat of his heartsick poet in *The Invention of Love*. Sound designers and composers have found enormous pleasure in trying to score the world of Stoppard's plays in ways that lift the mystery and open our ears to new locations without getting in the way of the torrent of words.

The most challenging design experience I have had in my collaborations with Stoppard revolved around *The Hard Problem*, not because it was difficult to deliver all the scenes (although that was certainly a challenge, since in ninety minutes we travel to eight different locations) but because, in my conversations with Stoppard, we both felt that the hard edges of the scientific arguments called for a counterpoint visually. In its initial London production, on the thrust Dorfman Stage at the National Theatre, the relatively bare set was covered by a floating wire sculpture that lit up like neurons during each scene change. Perhaps because I knew that ultimately Stoppard believed more deeply in consciousness than in artificial intelligence, I was looking for something more "natural," perhaps more spiritual, to anchor our set. One day, designer Andrew Boyce brought in a photograph that captivated me: inside the courtyard of a sleek and high-tech building, a tree was growing, slightly angled against the sharp lines of the walls. It was absurd, in a sense, but it was clear that an insistent force of nature had pushed its way inside a place it did not belong. In *Rock 'n' Roll*, Lenka says to Max, "we have to discover our human mystery in the age of technology." The image of the tree seemed to follow the same logic; it was the mystery of nature in an age of technology. Ultimately, Boyce designed a gorgeous white box with lots of sliding pallets and a huge open screen at the back that could project everything from equations to faces to clouds. And center left, he placed two trees, rising up as if they were growing right there in the lobby of the Krohl Center for Brain Research. The critic from the *San Francisco Chronicle* hated those trees and could not fathom why they belonged in that office. But to us they helped mitigate the potential dryness of the play. "Nature is deeper than reason, and stranger," Lenka had told us. Our trees were an act of rebellion against an increasingly mechanized world, and we loved to imagine that high above the set, their leaves were turning green.

4

Excavating "Rules of Play" in Pinter's *The Birthday Party*

Learning how to realize Pinter's unique aesthetic in performance began for me with *The Birthday Party,* Pinter's first full-length play. I have directed *The Birthday Party* on three occasions: first in 1988 at the Classic Stage Company in New York, then again at CSC in 1989 on a double bill with *Mountain Language,* and finally at A.C.T. in 2018. It was during the second CSC production that I collaborated directly with Pinter in rehearsal for the first time; this chapter focuses on how his notes and ideas helped open up the world of the play.

The Creation of the Play

Pinter wrote *The Birthday Party* while performing in rep in 1958 ("I finished *The Birthday Party* while I was touring in some kind of farce, I don't remember the name," he related[1]) staying in seedy bedsits along the east coast of England and acting in two plays a week for months on end. In the same *Paris Review* interview, he described how the squalor of his theatrical digs inspired the play:

> *The Birthday Party* had also been on my mind for a long time. It was sparked off from a very distinct situation in digs when I was on tour. In fact the other day a friend of mine gave me a letter I wrote to him in nineteen fifty something, Christ knows when it was. This is what it says, "I have filthy insane digs, a great bulging scrag of a woman, with breasts rolling at her belly, an obscene household, cats, dogs, filth, tea-strainers, mess, oh bollocks, talk, chat rubbish shit scratch dung poison, infantility, deficient order in the upper fretwork, fucking roll on." Now the thing about this is *that* was *The Birthday Party*—I was in those digs, and this woman was Meg in the play, and there was a fellow staying there in Eastbourne, on the coast. The whole thing remained with me, and three years later I wrote the play.

At the time of writing, Pinter was nearly broke, already married (to actress Vivien Merchant) and in need of an additional source of income. The play emerged miraculously whole and totally *sui generis*. "The first image of this play, the first thing that about a year ago was put on paper, was a kitchen, Meg, Stanley, cornflakes and sour milk," he wrote in a letter to director Peter Wood in 1958. "They were there, they sat, they stood, they bent, they turned, they were incontravertable, or perhaps I should say incontravertible. Not long before Goldberg and McCann turned up. They had come with a purpose, a job at hand—to take Stanley away. This they did. Meg unknowing, Petey hapless, Stanley sucked in. Play over."[2] *The Birthday Party* played successfully at the Arts Club in Cambridge, but when it came to London it received mostly scathing reviews, lasted a mere six performances, and closed ignominiously after the Sunday matinee. In a speech given in 1995, Pinter related with chagrin, "I decided to pop in to the Thursday matinee. I was a few minutes late and the curtain had gone up. I ran up the stairs to the dress circle. An usherette stopped me. 'Where are you going?' she said. 'To the dress circle', I said. 'I'm the author.' Her eyes, as I recall, misted over. 'Oh, are you?' she said. 'Oh, you poor chap.'" But Harold Hobson famously reviewed the play in the *Sunday Times*, finding in Pinter's writing a level of originality and theatrical brilliance that rescued *The Birthday Party* from obscurity and set it on its path to becoming a modern classic. Its language is meticulous, precise, without any kind of "fat," and demands that audiences listen in a way that may seem extreme today but was less unusual in a post-war period accustomed to radio drama. "As with a lot of people who grew up during the war, that was their only theatre," Michael Billington noted. "People were *extremely good listeners*" (my italics).[3]

The play opens in the boarding house of Meg and Petey Bowles; Meg is a somewhat scattered working-class housewife who can barely hold together her daily routine, and Petey is a deck chair attendant, out "in all weathers," as Meg proudly proclaims. The third resident of the house is a mysterious guest named Stanley Webber, who claims to have once been a concert pianist but is now hiding out upstairs. Pinter never reveals what it is Stanley is hiding from or why, although there are hints throughout: he is an artist, a rebel, possibly a Jew. (In a letter to his director Peter Wood before the first rehearsals in April 1958, Pinter wrote, "Stanley is the king of his castle and loses his kingdom because he assessed it and himself inaccurately. We all have to be very careful. The boot is itching to squash and very efficient.") Something cataclysmic has happened in his life that has caused him to leave all contact with his past behind. Meg dotes on Stanley as if he were both her son and her lover, and he torments, teases, and disparages her in equal measure.

Meg's house purports to be a boarding house. Not only that, it is "on the list." What list it is on is not clear (more on this anon), but the fact that such a list exists, at least in Meg's mind, is a source of great pride for her. The breakfast routine between Meg and Petey that launches the play is a master class in comic *non sequitur*, but also importantly sets up the "rules of play" that hold Meg's life together. The meal starts with a bowl of Cornflakes, which she proudly offers as if they are a culinary delicacy. The second course is fried bread, which Petey accepts gratefully and Stanley disdains. The fried bread is presented as a massive surprise ("I bet you don't know what it is!" "Oh yes I do." "What is it, then?" "Fried bread." "That's right!") in a brilliant comic exchange that tells us it is fried bread most mornings at the Bowles household.

The catalyzing event of the play is the arrival of two men, who evidently came up to Petey on the beach asking if he could "put them up for a couple of nights." Petey is excited; the Bowles household could use the money. Meg is equally delighted—they have not had visitors in this supposed "boarding house" since Stanley's been there. But Stanley is terrified. Goldberg and McCann initially appear to be something out of a vaudeville routine ("A Jew and an Irishman walk into a pub . . .") but there is something lethal beneath their veneer of bonhomie. Goldberg probes Meg about her "lodger"; when she reveals that today is Stanley's birthday (a fact which seems to be her own invention), Goldberg proposes a party. This idea thrills Meg: "I wanted to have a party, but you must have people for a party." After she has escorted the gentlemen upstairs to their room, Stanley slips back in and interrogates Meg about the purpose of the two men's visit. His anxiety prompts Meg to calm the waters by giving Stanley the gift she's bought him: a boy's drum. The act ends with Stanley marching around the table, banging the drum, first with a certain degree of childish acceptance but slowly becoming more and more savage and possessed as the curtain falls.

Act 2 takes place in the evening and culminates in the lethal birthday party that destroys Stanley. Goldberg and McCann begin the evening by interrogating Stanley in two virtuoso sequences that lay out nearly every possible crime he could have committed. "If you accuse a man of enough things," Pinter told us in rehearsal, "he will be guilty of one of them." At the party, which includes Goldberg, McCann, the ebullient young neighbor Lulu, and Meg in her party finery but not Petey (it is his "chess night"), the group plays a seemingly innocuous game of Blind Man's Buff, which ends with Stanley's spectacles being snapped, his drum being destroyed, and, in a chilling moment after the lights have gone out, an attempted assault by Stanley on Lulu. When the dawn rises on Act 3, the house seems to have returned to a state of calm. But Meg appears at the kitchen hatch and we discover the worst has happened: she has run out of Cornflakes. So begins the terrifying dissolution of Stanley's safe place. Eventually, while Meg is out shopping, Goldberg and McCann bring Stanley downstairs, destroyed and no longer capable of speech, and cart him off. There is a seminal moment of resistance from Petey ("Stan, don't let them tell you what to do!") and then a buckling under Goldberg's cold intimidation ("Why don't you come with us, Mr. Bowles? Come with us to Monte. There's plenty of room in the car.") The final scene between Meg and Petey is a heartbreaking demonstration of denial, as Petey resists telling Meg what has happened to Stanley and Meg retreats into blissful memories of last night's party. "I was the belle of the ball," she reminisces. "I was. I know I was."

Launching the Production

What is *The Birthday Party* actually about? Who are these mysterious characters, and what is their "real" relationship to each other? Why are they so intent upon destroying Stanley? As one begins to prepare the play for production, there are questions one can ask of this play that will yield fertile theatrical results, and questions that are absolute dead ends. Needless to say, there have been innumerable analyses of *The Birthday Party* since that first production in 1959; it has been read as a drama about fascism, about the oppressive grip of organized religion, about Britain's delusions after the war, about incestuous sexuality between a mother and a son; it has been interpreted as Pinter's homage to Beckett, it has been parsed psychoanalytically, it has been placed in the context of mythic fertility rituals and post-war economics. Where should a director begin?

Our collaboration on *The Birthday Party* was informed by the fact that it was sharing an evening, on its second outing at CSC, with Pinter's recent one-act *Mountain Language*. While *The Birthday Party* needs no curtain-raiser, the producing challenge for *Mountain Language* is that it is only twenty minutes long. The idea of combining the two plays on a double-bill excited Pinter, in part because, while he had always stressed the political overtones of the earlier play and its insistence on individual expression in the face of tyranny, audiences and critics rarely read it that way. By pairing his early play with the more overtly political *Mountain Language*, Pinter believed that undercurrents of both plays could be foregrounded in interesting new ways.

We also believed it would be a remarkable exercise for the actors to play opposite types across the two plays (as would occur again in 2001 when we paired *Celebration* and *The Room* at A.C.T.); thus, we decided that the actor playing the terrorized Stanley in *The Birthday Party* would play the vicious Officer in *Mountain Language*, while voluble and ditzy Meg would be doubled with the Elderly Woman whose hand has been bitten, aggressive Goldberg would become the beaten-down Prisoner, and flirtatious Lulu would portray the tough and intelligent Young Woman fighting to save her wrongfully imprisoned husband. Well-trained in repertory theater of this kind, the actor in Pinter relished the possibilities inherent in such a scheme, as did those in our company (although the extreme contrasts were not without their difficulties in rehearsal). We were intrigued that both plays dealt with terror, with the removal of or loss of language, with mothers and sons, and with political resistance, while employing radically different theatrical vocabularies. And we believed that the challenge of linking them in a single evening would provide a strong platform for *Mountain Language*'s debut in New York.

Over a long and boozy lunch in Islington in the winter of 1988, Pinter and I discussed the project in great detail and made plans to work on it together. His enthusiasm during that lunch belied what I had heard about his laconic and taciturn behavior. It was clear to me that he lived to work, that he relished the process of making theater and talking about theater, that he sought not deference but passion and commitment, and that no theatrical detail was too small to consider. His eyes lit up and his baritone voice filled the restaurant as we made our plans, like co-conspirators at work. Pinter's conversation that day was matched by his appetite, and we got through quite a few bottles of white wine over the course of the afternoon. By the end of the lunch, he had agreed to come to New York for several weeks in the fall of 1989 to be with us in rehearsal at CSC.

The autumn of 1989 turned out to be a remarkable moment in world history: the Soviet Union was collapsing, the Berlin wall was finally breeched, the Velvet Revolution brought down Communism in Czechoslovakia, and, as it would happen, on September 2, my daughter Lexie was born. When I had first agreed to mount the Pinter double bill, I had not yet known I was going to give birth ten days before the first rehearsal, but such is life. Pinter's agent Judy Daish was somewhat concerned about my pregnant state and rang me occasionally over that long hot summer to ask, "Have you had that child yet?" As it happened, Lexie arrived past her due date, timing her appearance for the aptly named Labor Day, which gave me just over a week to organize my life before diving into rehearsals. When I look back now, I wonder what on earth I was thinking. Collaborating with Harold Pinter would have been unnerving at the best of times, and looking after a ten-day-old infant is not necessarily the best of times. But perhaps that is why I was relatively unfazed by the prospect of Pinter: when a child is waiting to be fed, it is easy to remember that the rest of it is just theater. Furthermore, I quickly discovered that having a child in the rehearsal room provides a useful reality check; it is amazing the way extraneous "white noise" disappears when you have to make strong choices and move forward expeditiously before the baby wakes up. As I noted in the "Introduction," Lexie slept in a carrycot in the dressing room behind the stage, and Jean Stapleton, our Meg, used to sidle up to me every few hours or so with the coded missive, "The princess needs you now." Years later, Peter Riegert claimed that he knew which act we were on by which breast Lexie was attached to on rehearsal breaks.

Given that the cast and I had met with Pinter over the summer when he was in New York on a visit, there was some degree of familiarity by the time he arrived in mid-September to join us in the studio. I have rarely seen an artist so eager to get to work. He paced the rehearsal room, took in the atmosphere, eyed the actors, and was ready to dive in with no preliminaries or gradual introductions. We had initially intended to focus on *The Birthday Party* in the morning and *Mountain Language* after lunch (a good long lunch was always important to Pinter) but ended up spending a good deal more time on the former than the latter, because the demands are so much greater. From the first session of work, Pinter's approach was singular. Despite the fact that by 1989, *The Birthday Party* was thirty years old and he had worked on the play innumerable times, Pinter approached it with the vigor and curiosity with which one might approach a new play. It was a rehearsal full of discoveries and short on prescription or dogma. Whenever we brought up an issue, no matter how trivial, Pinter considered it with the full force of his formidable intellect and imagination. He always paused, *really* paused, until he had a plausible answer. He studied his characters as one would real people, never presuming to know more about them than they were willing to divulge. We showered him with questions. "Was Stanley Jewish?" we asked. Long pause. "Perhaps," Pinter replied. Because that was the truest answer he could muster. Pinter intuitively understood that human beings are essentially unknowable and that the past is another country, which means that the only way to understand a person is to examine how they are behaving in present tense. When asked a specific character question, Pinter considered it exactly as if he were considering a problem in a play written by someone else; the answer could only come from the evidence at hand. Resisting any attempt to theorize about his plays, he considered the situations about which he wrote to be *true* in some fundamental way, but never abstract.

If Pinter was suspicious about the verifiability of individual biography, he nonetheless viewed his characters as credible individuals with a life of their own, and was thus surprisingly open to what he could learn about their impulses by watching their behavior. In rehearsal, he offered both his characters and the actors portraying them a measure of respect and a latitude that I have almost never encountered with a playwright; while he was meticulous about the language and the sound of the play, he was open to what tactics could be employed to best bring the action of the play to life on stage. There is nothing extraneous in a Pinter play and no "warm up"—every move and every word counts, so rehearsal has to proceed with specificity and precision. Early, on, he urged us to keep the "façade" tight but also to look for the cracks, for those moments where the humanity or the danger lurking behind the façade of language and drinking of tea finally leached out. "A character on the stage who can present no convincing argument or information as to his past experience, his present behavior or his aspirations, nor give a comprehensive analysis of his motives is as legitimate and worthy of attention as one who, alarmingly, can do all these things," Pinter had insisted. "The more acute the experience the less articulate its expression."[4]

Casting and Character

When I first solicited the rights to direct *The Birthday Party* in 1988, Pinter's agent Judy Daish asked us to forward the resumes and headshots of all the actors in contention so that Pinter could vet them in advance. He was renowned in terms of his own directing for his intuitive sense of which actors would be successful in his work. In the first round, his agent wrote back, "F. Murray Abraham and David Strathairn are approved but we require biographies of David Warrilow and Olympia Dukakis." In the end, Strathairn did indeed play Stanley in both outings of *The Birthday Party* at CSC, but the rest of the cast evolved somewhat differently. It was clear to me that in order to make the production as muscular and as humorous as possible, we had to be on alert to find American actors with a highly developed ear for rhythm and language, and with an ability to hold the "mask" and play a powerful subtext. As I said in the "Introduction", the ability to use language as a smoke screen, distraction and defense is not native to all Americans, nor is the kind of irony Pinter routinely requires.

One of the most interesting of all the auditions was with Peter Riegert, who came down to the apartment of my Casting Director Ellen Novack to read for us one afternoon in early 1988. I had never worked with Peter, but I knew that aside from his sexy and subtle performances in the films *Delancey Street* and *Local Hero*, he was a favorite actor of David Mamet. This seemed propitious, since Mamet's tough clipped menacing language derives so much from Pinter. (Indeed, in the early days, Mamet sent his scripts to Pinter for notes just as Pinter had sent his to Beckett.) Riegert began reading from the first act of the play, when Goldberg has to reassure McCann that this hit job is going to go smoothly. Within a few moments, we knew he was our man— he trusted the language absolutely, understood the Cockney charm Goldberg must possess, and displayed a kind of full-throated comic appetite that aligned with Pinter's comments that theater above all required energy and a deep appetite for the spoken word. Most of all, Riegert had a sense of *play*. That quality turned out to be crucial in a Pinter rehearsal—the moment-to-moment sense of *being in the game*. Watching Riegert create his Goldberg over those two productions, and then in *Celebration* at A.C.T. (in which he played the vile and vigorous Lambert), was like experiencing a master class in menace, manipulation, and mayhem. Peter grew up a non-observant Jew in Hartsdale, New York, steeped in the rhythms of Catskill comedy. Because his training was in improvisation, he knows how to stay resolutely "in the moment," how to say "yes" to whatever choice is handed to him by his scene partner, and how to avoid the trap of over-thinking or over-analyzing a moment on stage. No symbols where none intended. Riegert played for keeps, his jaunty stance belying a quick intelligence and an innate desire to "win." Riegert's Goldberg transformed completely depending upon who was across the table from him, from *bon vivant* to family man to killer to faceless bureaucrat. He once said to me, "Never work with an actor who can't keep time." His own sense of rhythm meshed perfectly with Pinter's.

David Strathairn also came to acting from an intensely physical and intuitive place. His Stanley may have seemed disheveled and disorganized, but his behavior was meticulous, precise, and almost dance-like in its

economy of gesture and movement. He is that unusual actor who never
wants to occupy center stage; rather, he watches carefully from the sidelines
and then makes his move. His Stanley was hunted, horny, sexy, and scared,
but also dignified enough to almost make the audience believe he could take
on the fearsome duo of McCann and Goldberg. Both Riegert and Strathairn
are capable of sustaining extreme *stillness*, which is something Pinter
consistently encouraged. He himself was capable of great economy of gesture
and facial response as an actor, and he encouraged the cast to trust the power
of holding one's position, as well as holding one's *gaze*. In fact, I learned a
great deal from Pinter about how to watch for where the gaze of an actor
either heightened the tension or gave away the game. Often in a scripted
pause, Pinter would watch to see whether the eyes of an actor shifted, and
how that might give us a clue as to who was covering up or hiding something.

Resistance was a central part of the journey for Strathairn. Pinter urged
us to consider Stanley's reticence as a source of strength rather than
weakness, exploring the energy it took to put up even the smallest resistance
in the face of Goldberg's relentless assault. This active choice was extremely
useful, helping Strathairn avoid the kind of passivity that often entraps
actors playing Stanley. In collaboration with Pinter, Strathairn felt able to go
further into the dark well of that tormented character over the course of our
second attempt at the play. In an interview he explained:

> Rehearsals were very exhausting, to get back into Stanley, because that's
> a dangerous place to go, when someone tries to break down everything
> that you have chosen, or not chosen to be, when somebody just breaks
> you down, and I was letting that happen. . . And I realized that I had to
> have a different quality of strength for Stanley (this time around) because
> of what Peter was developing with Goldberg. They had to be foes. Stanley
> had to be a formidable opposition for Goldberg, so Goldberg could *crack*.
> If Stanley's already a victim when they get there, there's no work to be
> done.[5]

This brings us back to Austin Quigley's perception that Pinter characters
never exist in absolute terms, but only in relation to each other. When an
actor makes a choice, his scene partner must immediately decide whether to
advance or retreat, confront or evade. Perhaps this is why performing Pinter
is such catnip for actors. The role changes moment to moment depending
upon the behavior of one's fellow actors; nothing is pre-ordained and every
moment is for the first time.

Pinter's response to Bill Moor, who played Petey in our second *Birthday
Party* at CSC, was revelatory. In an interview in *The Pinter Review* (1989),
Bill Moor describes it thus:

> He did a *fascinating* thing with me. He called me aside, it was during a
> break, he called me aside—Carey was there—and he said, "You're doing

two things that I see." He said, "The first is you're playing a man, I see a man that is sort of feeble, slightly depressed, and also, rather hesitant, but also I see another man too, that you do on occasion, that is very much in love with his work, is very vigorous, is very fit, has a lot of energy, loves his work, loves his newspaper . . . I'm much more interested in your developing that . . . you see, the trap in him is to play him feeble, or unable to hold his own. I want him to be very vital, very positive."[6]

Here and so many times, Pinter spoke about his own creation with deference and respect; he was never prescriptive, always curious, almost scientific in his analysis. The idea was, what would happen to the motor of the play if you played Petey like *this* as opposed to like *that*? Clearly, a vital and active Petey immediately poses a greater obstacle to Goldberg and McCann, generating a more dangerous conflict and more active engagement between them. So it is a useful choice. *Class* is crucial here; Pinter did not spell it out in so many words, but in Petey he had created a working man who is proud of his job and uncomplaining about his life, characteristics Richard Hoggart beautifully articulates when exploring his own roots: "More than vigour, there is a clear dignity in that reaction to the pressures of the outside world which takes the form of insisting on 'keeping y'self-respect' . . . which itself spread outwards and upwards . . . through the pride of a skilled workman, to the integrity of those who have practically nothing except a determination not to allow themselves to be dragged down by circumstances."[7] Furthermore, Pinter reminded us over and over again in rehearsals that Petey is a chess player. He is always on to the next move. Pinter's notes released Bill Moor to focus on what Petey actually *did* in the play rather than what he *felt*. This paved the way for his final devastating encounter with Goldberg.

As I have noted in Chapter 3, the ideal Pinter cast must be both an ensemble as tight as a cricket team, and a group of individual personalities with unique capabilities. While Petey would seem to be a minor player in *The Birthday Party*, the last ten minutes of the play reveal how crucial it is to cast a "leading man" in the role. When Goldberg tells Petey that they are taking Stanley "to Monty," Petey, with surprising presence of mind, says: "He can stay here." GOLDBERG: "Don't be silly." PETEY: "We can look after him here." GOLDBERG: "Why do you want to look after him?" PETEY: "He's my guest." That simple statement of human decency is one of the most poignant lines in the play. It was for this reason that Pinter encouraged Bill Moor to find the strength in his character—Petey may be a man of few words but he is not stupid, neither is he immoral, in spite of his inability to tell Meg the truth at the end of the play. He tries to face off against Stanley's abductors. "Leave him alone!" he cries. Ultimately, he is not powerful enough to make a stand, but he tries. Much has been written about Petey as a "collaborator," as the kind of German who stood by and watched Jews getting taken to the camps. But I do not believe Pinter ever judged him so harshly; indeed, he gave him a line which he later claimed was the dictum by which he had tried to live his own life: "Stan, don't let them tell you what to do!" Petey is no hero. But for a brief moment, he attempts to stand up to evil. That is the most he can do. And what is left of that stance by the end of the play? A flutter of torn newspaper strips blowing to the ground, memories of a life that has been snuffed out.

When I cast Jean Stapleton, the famous comedienne, as Meg, she was initially anxious that she had never performed language like Pinter's, but she ultimately trusted that her innate sense of musicality would carry her through. What Pinter loved about Stapleton was her sense of innocence: Jean was able to play every moment without anticipating the next, so her Meg was in a constant state of suspended surprise. Her natural sense of humor was also an enormous boon. "It was the strength of the form that was absolute protection, for you to grow in," she remarked after working on *The Birthday Party*. Since there was never the security of a known biography to ground the character, everything had to be learned from a close observation of behavior, and from the actual rhythm of Meg's speech. Jean Stapleton had to accept that, as a character, Meg exists purely in the present, in the vivid relational world of the boarding house over which she presides. While there may be a feeling of *loss* that pervades her being, a loss perhaps attributable to the death of a child or to a frightening wartime experience, we can verify very little about Meg's past except for the unreliable fantasies she shares with us when drunk. We must watch her build her reality cornflake by cornflake to understand what is at stake when the cornflakes run out. Pinter encouraged Stapleton to take Meg seriously; his own mother, he assured us, had been an immaculate housekeeper, and Meg aspires to nothing less. The fact that she is consistently failing only makes the stakes higher for her, particularly because she lives in dread of Stanley's judgment. It happened that Stapleton was extremely myopic, and Pinter delighted in the way that life seemed to sneak up on her when least expected. Stapleton was also a natural flirt, which gave her encounters with Stanley and Goldberg an endless undercurrent of both charm and dread.

It is always interesting to observe the profound effect that casting decisions can have on a production. Again, this is one of the key areas of directorial interpretation. Although Pinter never rewrote his texts to suit the occasion as Stoppard has been known to do, he was completely open to re-imagining production choices depending upon the specific attributes of the artists in the room. One of the fascinations of working on a great play is how differently it reveals its secrets depending upon the context in which it is produced. Twenty-five years after working with Pinter at CSC, I began the process of casting Stanley in a new production of *The Birthday Party*; by then, 9/11 had happened and the world was radically different. America had woken up to the reality of terror (and Islamophobia) on our own shores. As we discovered when we produced Pinter's *The Room* and *Celebration* in the days right after 9/11 (see Chapter 7), the "knock on the door" was no longer an abstract fear; domestic terrorism was a real possibility, and a sense of surveillance was pervasive. It occurred to me that having an actor of color play Stanley could illuminate the story of that hunted and complex character in a vital way, and I offered the role to Firdous Bamji (with whom I had done Stoppard's *Indian Ink* twice, as well as Schiller's *Mary Stuart*). Firdous brought both an openness and paranoia to the role that were palpable and deeply disturbing; he also projected a refined intellect. He and Judith Ivey were closer in age as Stanley and Meg, so the heat and banter between them felt extremely charged. During the interrogation sequences, with Marco Barricelli (McCann) and Scott Wentworth (Goldberg) standing over Firdous and verbally assaulting him, the sight of a South Asian man caught in a vise between two powerful white bullies was horrifying and immediate. Firdous is also relatively small in stature, which made for some wonderful comedy when paired with Julie Adamo, the actress playing Lulu. A tall girl made taller by extreme high heels, Adamo's Lulu towered over the terrified Stanley with well-meaning domination, before settling happily onto Goldberg's lap. The physical contours of individual actors always become central to the choreographic "scene painting" of a Pinter production, and this was no exception. The casting of our 2018 production also reminded me of Pinter's deep roots in Elizabethan drama, since it featured two consummate Shakespeareans (Scott Wentworth and Marco Barricelli) playing Goldberg

FIGURE 7 *Scott Wentworth, Marco Barricelli, and Firdous Bamji in* The Birthday Party, *A.C.T. 2018. Scenery by Nina Ball, Lighting by Robert Hand, Costumes by Candice Donnelly. Photo courtesy of Carey Perloff.*

and McCann. Wentworth and Barricelli brought classical scale to the interrogation scenes; their presence and sense of language heightened the mythic combat of the play.

Fortuitously, we discovered a fascinating historical thread when Firdous Bamji played Stanley. His partner Hayley Mills came to the dress rehearsal and told us afterwards that her mother Mary Hayley Bell had written a play many years before called *The Uninvited Guest*; in the first production of that play, an actor named "David Baron" had starred as the mentally-ill Candy who had recently been released from an institution. David Thompson quotes a review of the performance as follows, "Candy is the elder son of Lady Lannion. He was certified at the age of fourteen and twenty years afterwards by his own efforts is released from the institution ... David Baron is this uninvited guest. He ... keeps our interest very effectively and fully exploits the mystery and strangeness of the part; ... he conveys well the movements and attitude of a man who has been set free after being imprisoned in this way."[8] Furthermore, the critic notes that, "It is a good idea to have him (David Baron) stand with his back to the audience while the other characters question him," exactly the posture Pinter indicates for Stanley in the Act 2 interrogation scene in *The Birthday Party*: "*sitting, his back to the audience.*" Hayley Mills vividly remembered the experience of seeing her mother's work, and it moved her to watch her partner Firdous perform a role which had undoubtedly been inspired by Pinter's own performance all those years before.

Scenery and Staircases

If *The Birthday Party* is a play about a fortress being breeched, it is crucial to be as specific as possible about what that fortress looks like and how it functions to contain and shape the dramatic action. We are told that the play takes place in "the living room of a house in a seaside town." What kind of house? What are its components? There are three doors, one leading to the outside, one to a hallway, and one to a kitchen, which is made visible in the center wall through a kitchen hatch, where much of Meg's action takes place. This hatch is the vortex; it functions as a sort of "puppet stage" onto which Meg's wide-eyed face appears as she ministers to her husband or her beloved Stanley. Early on in the play, we are told that the house is a "boarding house"; as soon as Petey informs Meg that two men have come up to him on the beach and asked to be put up for a couple of nights, Meg asks, "Had they heard about us, Petey?" and when Petey affirms "They must have done," Meg trumpets, "Yes, they must have done. They must have heard this was a very good boarding house. It is. This house is on the list." Later in Act 1, her "boarder," Stanley, implies the opposite to McCann: "This is a ridiculous house to pick on. . . . It's not a boarding house. It never was." But Meg repeatedly insists that her house "is on the list." That assertion will return repeatedly during the course of the play, and each time, it becomes more mysterious. What does it mean for Meg's house to be "on the list"? How does that inform our decisions about what this house looks like on stage? What is the list, anyway? Who keeps it? Who put the house on the list? Does being "on the list" mean the house is desirable, or condemned? A target? A landmine? A welcoming "bed and breakfast"? Stanley tries to discredit Meg by asking, "Do you know how many visitors you've had since I've been here?" "How many?" asks Meg breathlessly. "Me! I'm your visitor!" exclaims Stanley. If a boarding house has never had any real visitors, can it claim to be called a boarding house? And if Meg's house is not a boarding house, what is it?

These are the questions facing the director and designer as they begin the process of designing *The Birthday Party*. In order to get closer to a solution, the designer might at this point begin to do research on "bed-sits" and boarding houses in small seaside towns on the east coast of England, where the play ostensibly takes place, to see what that inspires. He or she might look at places Pinter himself had stayed while he was on tour with the various minor rep companies in which he acted in his twenties. The designer and director would have to ask whether it is important to retain the period in which the play was written (1959) or to move it to the present, whether its "Englishness" matters or whether it could reasonably be re-set elsewhere, and so on. But none of these questions matters as much as the fundamental necessity of designing a floorplan on which the verbal action of the play can detonate.

The scenic challenge in my initial two productions of *The Birthday Party* was that CSC's theater was a "thrust" stage, meaning that the audience sat on three sides, with the performance space in the middle. This configuration was not how Pinter had originally imagined his work. The singularity of focus that a proscenium stage provides, with its enclosed box of the three walls, was something Pinter had always counted on to keep the muscle of his plays taut. This was also the stage configuration he had trained on as an actor. But the possibilities of CSC's thrust stage fascinated him. For a start, the play sets up a palpable division between upstairs and downstairs: downstairs is the reassuring world of cornflakes and conversation, upstairs is the threatening world of bedrooms, sexuality and mystery ("I've had some lovely afternoons in that room," Meg says seductively about Stanley's bedroom in Act 1). In the stage directions to the play, there is an implied off-stage staircase on stage left which takes characters upstairs to the bedrooms (*"a door leading to the hall down left"*) but there is no indication that we see the staircase, that conduit to the world above.

However, in order for the actors to exit as if going upstairs at CSC, given that there were no walls on either side to mask a hall and stairway, the staircase had to be brought out into the open. The visible staircase eventually became a central part of our staging. (Interestingly, as we shall see in Chapter 6, by the time Pinter wrote *The Homecoming*, the self-contained room had already been breached and the staircase was front and center, the liminal space between civilization and barbarism: "*In the hall a staircase, ascending up left, well in view,*" the stage directions for that play indicate.) The onstage staircase at CSC allowed us to calibrate Stanley's three descents in the play, from insouciance in Act 1 to anxiety in Act 2 to complete brokenness in Act 3. It highlighted Meg's triumphant arrival with the drum in the party scene, and McCann's determined march upstairs at the end of the play after insisting "I'm not going up there again." It proved so immensely useful that even when I restaged *The Birthday Party* at the Geary Theater (a proscenium) in 2016, I made sure to retain the onstage staircase.

In rehearsal at CSC, Pinter watched the use of the staircase like a hawk. *Status* is everything in Pinter—at each moment, one needs to gauge who is "up" and who is "down." He sets up that tension right from the top of the play:

Meg   Is Stanley up yet?

Petey   I don't know. Is he?

Meg   I don't know. I haven't seen him down yet.

Petey   Well then, he can't be up.

Pinter was understandably fascinated by how much the physical presence of the staircase in this *Birthday Party* highlighted the mystery, comedy and, ultimately, horror of what was happening upstairs, and the characters' relationship to that reality. One afternoon, he was watching us work on the end of Act 1. McCann anxiously asks, "Could I go up to my room?" to which Meg replies flirtatiously, "I'll show you. If you don't mind coming upstairs." Goldberg, having won the day, enthuses, "With a tulip? It's a pleasure." Pinter was captivated watching Jean Stapleton sashay up those stairs with Peter Riegert right behind her. He was intrigued by how unnerved the socially-awkward McCann was about putting even a single foot on that staircase (thus committing to the destruction that was to follow). Suddenly he stopped rehearsal and said, "Peter, I wonder if you could add a line for me at that moment?" Riegert (his jaw dropping with excitement) nodded his assent, and Pinter went on, "As you walk up those stairs, I wonder if you could stop, turn around, look at the stairs and say to the world at large, 'What a lovely flight of stairs!'" Peter did this with alacrity. The new "stairs line" became part of our *Birthday Party* script from that time forward.

Epiphanic Props

I sometimes think of a Pinter set functioning like a Joseph Cornell box: the seemingly ordinary objects (or props) that they contain take on a kind of luminosity by virtue of their precise arrangement and placement. As I mentioned in Chapter 3, Pinter learned from Donald Wolfit, among others, how central the deployment of objects is to the "magic show" of the theater. Each prop must be built so as to accomplish the necessary sleight of hand. This is an aspect of Pinter's work that does not reveal itself clearly when the plays are merely read; one must experience it live to understand the magic. In exploring the design of these crucial props in *The Birthday Party*, I would like to look at five specific examples, beginning with the all-important box of *Cornflakes*.

There are few plays in Western drama in which breakfast cereal plays as crucial a role as in *The Birthday Party*; one could argue that the whole story of Meg and Petey's marriage is contained in that box of cereal. As soon as Meg hears Petey return from the beach in the morning, she rushes into the kitchen, grabs the box of *Cornflakes*, pours the flakes into a bowl for Petey, adds (sour) milk, and brings him his breakfast. She takes this task extremely seriously, and Petey responds in kind. "I've got your cornflakes ready!" she exclaims. "Are they nice?" she nervously enquires, as if she had made them herself. "Very nice," he assures her. "I thought they'd be nice," she breathes with relief. This seemingly banal opening exchange establishes the daily routine that holds Meg's fragile psyche together. As long as the day begins with her husband entering the house from his morning deck chair duties and eating his cornflakes with equanimity, the horrors of the world can be kept at bay. We must remember that the play was written in England after the war, when rationing was still in force and the daily anxieties of the Blitz were not forgotten. The constant danger of the war years, a profound memory for Pinter, gave way to the release of the post-war period, a period characterized by a veneer of peace and plenty, accompanied by American foreign aid and American packaged food, including items like breakfast cereal.

From a design point of view, this means that the box of *Cornflakes* sitting on the sill of the kitchen hatch must have as much immanence as does a Campbell's soup can in an Andy Warhol lithograph. If there is other clutter on the ledge or on the table, or if the box is wrongly placed, too small or not the right color, the strange defamiliarization required to make those *Cornflakes* detonate will be obscured. The white box with the red and green rooster is an anchor that will tether us throughout the play; thus, it must be freed from competing with a field of other objects. And because, as with all consumables, the covers of cereal boxes have changed in fifty years, it may be necessary to create a bespoke cornflake box in productions today so as to approximate the immanence of the original item. The actress Susan Engel (who was a student actress in Pinter's first play *The Room* in Bristol) describes taking *The Birthday Party* on tour to Morocco in 1970: "We had to take a box of *Cornflakes*, because they wouldn't have known what a box of *Cornflakes* was for. So we had these props, commonplace to us but strange to them. And it was a bit like we were creatures from outer space." What a perfect way to think about props in Pinter: iconic objects so defamiliarized as to appear from outer space.

Meg's investment in that numinous prop must have the highest possible stakes and precision, as with any vaudeville routine. Only then will the *Cornflakes* box begin to take on the required resonance and prepare us for intimations of disaster in Act 3, when the box is found to be empty. "I've run out of cornflakes," a hung-over Meg says in despair to Petey the morning after the disastrous birthday party. "What else have you got?" asks Petey. "Nothing," Meg moans. That empty box is a potent warning that the safety of the house has been breached. The morning routine has been destroyed. There is nothing to stand between Stanley and destruction, not a single cornflake.

Let us expand the lens from the *Cornflake* box to four other significant props in *The Birthday Party*: the toy drum, Petey's newspaper (and the strips into which it gets torn by McCann), Stanley's eyeglasses, and Meg's stool. Each one has its own precise role to play and must be conceived and designed for maximum impact. The toy drum is, ostensibly, Stanley's birthday present from Meg; over the course of the play, the drum becomes a proxy for Meg's deep personal feelings for Stanley, and for Stanley's acute fragility in the face of coercion. It is also a comically diminished reminder of Stanley's musical past. Although he has been hiding out upstairs at Meg and Petey's house for "about a year now," Stanley claims to have been a concert pianist at one time: "I've played the piano all over the world. All over the country. (*pause*) I once gave a concert." While it is, of course, impossible to ever prove the veracity of Stanley's tales about his past, it cannot be coincidental that Pinter made his central character an artist who could no longer perform. As someone who loved to write, Pinter vividly understood the despair of being blocked from one's own work, whether by internal or external forces. In his 1970 speech upon having received the German Shakespeare Prize, Pinter ended by saying,

> I find it ironic that I have come here to receive this distinguished award as a writer, and that at the moment I am writing nothing and can write nothing. I don't know why. It's a very bad feeling, I know that, but I must say I want more than anything else to fill up a blank page again, and to feel that strange thing happen, birth through fingertips. When you can't write you feel you've been banished from yourself.

The image of self-banishment applies beautifully to Stanley, an educated and articulate man who has clearly been exiled from himself. He hates his neediness for Meg, yet he is utterly dependent upon her to protect him from intruders and keep him safe. When Meg casually announces that "two gentlemen asked Petey if they could come stay for a couple of nights. I'm expecting them," Stanley intuits that the men are coming for *him*. (This takes us back to Pinter's early obsession with the work of Kafka, and particularly with *The Trial*, which he adapted for film, and whose first line is, "Someone must have been telling lies about Josef K., for without having done anything wrong he was arrested one fine morning.") In her love and devotion for Stanley, Meg longs to heal all that is broken in him, and so, in order to cheer him up, she concocts the fiction that today is his birthday. Not only that, but she has got him a present: a boy's drum. This prop, a fragile and pathetic children's toy, will play a crucial role in Stanley's demise.

The drum first appears at the house wrapped in brown paper, "a solid round parcel," in the arms of Meg's friend Lulu. The excitement of the two women transforms this ordinary object into a source of mystery and potential danger. "Oh, has it come?" Meg asks. "Yes, it's just come," replies a delighted Lulu, who then tiptoes into the house with the wrapped parcel. Stanley trains his eyes on the package. "That's a bulky object," he comments. "You're not to touch it!" Lulu replies breathlessly. "Why would I want to touch it?" asks Stanley, mystified. Lulu cannot answer that without giving away her big secret, so she just says, "Well, you're not to, anyway," and places it on the sideboard. Initially, the drum seems to be an object full of promise. Lulu believes it is a worthy gift, and her banter with Stanley about it is flirtatious and charming. But by the end of Act 1, the wrapped drum begins to feel like a bomb waiting to be detonated. Stanley is so visibly distraught at the thought of the "two men" arriving at his "safe house" that night, Meg feels the need to comfort him: "You mustn't be sad today. It's your birthday." Stanley is flummoxed—he denies it is his birthday. "It is," insists Meg. And she's got proof: "I've brought you a present." She grabs the bulky brown parcel. "Here it is. Go on. Open it."

Stanley tears the paper apart, revealing a child's toy. "It's a drum. A boy's drum," says Stanley flatly. For a moment we relax, we laugh even, relieved. "It's because you haven't got a piano," Meg tells him tenderly. The exiled pianist will have to make do with an alternative and much diminished musical instrument. "Shall I put it round my neck?" asks the defeated Stanley, trying to please her. He does so, and begins banging on it with the toy sticks that come in the package. Meg is delighted; she has longed to reactivate Stanley's musical talents. At first, as Stanley marches around the table beating his little toy drum, there is something clownish and almost charming about the situation, but slowly his despair and terror start to erupt. The rhythm of his drumming becomes more and more savage, erratic, and wild. It builds to a violent peak, Meg reacts in horror, and then the lights black out. In this thrilling denouement, an ordinary prop has been transformed into the occasion for ritualistic violence akin to that in Greek tragedy, as we watch the epic battle of a man fighting for his life. Meg's offering of love has gone horribly wrong. A children's toy has become a battleground.

By Act 2, the drum seems to have been rehabilitated. When Meg descends in her party outfit, her arrival is announced by that crucial sound: "*A loud drumbeat off left, descending the stairs . . . Enter MEG, in evening dress, holding sticks and drum.*" She happily surveys the landscape of her sitting room, announcing "I've brought the drum down. I'm dressed for the party"

(Figure 8). Placing the drum on the table, she beams: "Doesn't it make a beautiful noise?" But her precious gift quickly becomes a stand-in for the complete crushing of Stanley's spirit. Halfway through the party, in the midst of a game of Blind Man's Buff, "*McCANN picks up the drum and places it sideways in Stanley's path. STANLEY walks into the drum and falls over with his foot caught in it.*" While Meg's beloved toy is being destroyed by its recipient, she is too drunk and preoccupied to notice. Here is where the prop construction becomes complicated. While it might seem like an ordinary object one could buy at the corner store, Stanley's drum (like most props in Pinter) has to be specially built so as to function in the way Pinter intends. We went through a dozen drums in rehearsal until we figured out how to structure the drum to accomplish everything it needs to do. At first appearance, it must look innocent and unthreatening, completely childlike. Perhaps its sides are striped, or patterned, setting off a comic collision with Stanley's pajamas and with Meg's dress in Act 2. But it must be rigged to hang flat as the strap goes around Stanley's neck, a challenge in and of itself. More importantly, the drumhead must be robust enough not to get destroyed when Stanley savagely beats it in Act 1, yet it must be capable of being broken when Stanley steps on it during the party in Act 2. We quickly discovered that this necessitated replacing the solid drumhead with a paper one at intermission, so that when pushed, Stanley's foot can tear right through it. But it must not *sound* like paper: thus, an alternative drum must be played offstage for Meg's arrival in Act 2 so that the fanfare of her arrival can register in volume. The construction and destruction of the drum is one of the hardest effects to get right in the whole show.

By the morning of Act 3, the drum is lying on the floor like a corpse, its fragile head ripped open just like Stanley's mind, a tragic reminder of last night's party. When Meg discovers it, she is dismayed: "Oh, look. The drum's broken. Why is it broken?" The innocuous child's toy has become an image of the gratuitous violence that Meg was not only unable to stop but oblivious to. By missing all the signs, Meg has been complicit in Stanley's destruction in spite of her overwhelming love for him; now all she can do is stare mournfully at the smashed drumhead, unable to comprehend what has happened. And of course, because this is the theater, every night that broken drum will have to be reconstituted after the curtain comes down to prepare for tomorrow's carnage.

The role of Petey's newspaper is even more complex than that of the drum. Initially, the prop appears to be an ordinary English tabloid (filled with short articles and pictures) that Petey reads to Meg in the morning and leaves on the table. The paper is a crucial part of Petey's identity, and Meg and Petey's morning routine revolves around it. "You got your paper?" asks Meg, even though she sees clearly that it is in his hands. Petey affirms. "You read me out some nice bits yesterday," she reminds Petey. "Will you tell me when you get to something good?" One of the first questions we asked Pinter in rehearsal was, "Why does Meg keep asking Petey to read her the

FIGURE 8 *Judith Ivey as Meg in* The Birthday Party, *Scenery by Nina Ball, Lighting by Robert Hand, Costumes by Candice Donnelly A.C.T. 2018. Photo courtesy of Kevin Berne.*

paper?" Were we supposed to glean clues about their marriage from this exchange? Pinter thought about the question a moment and then replied, "I believe Meg has forgotten how to read." We found this a wonderful note; instead of having to play the psychological burden of a needy woman begging her husband for attention, Jean Stapleton could play the baffled but engaged spouse who is dying for gossip and connection to the outside world but cannot remember how to access it herself.

The act of "forgetting" in Pinter means that things are always happening for the *first time*. If Meg does not remember how to read, everything she hears from Petey is new. The newspaper is Petey's bridge to the outside world, just as it is Meg's bridge to Petey. It is a tangible symbol of survival, of normalcy, of an ordered and predictable world, and it introduces Meg and Petey to people they would never encounter otherwise. In *The Uses of Literacy*, Richard Hoggart discusses how the workers he grew up amongst in Leeds are always "enormously interested in people: they have the novelist's fascination with individual behavior, with relationships—though not so as to put them into a pattern, but for their own sake. 'Isn't she queer?', 'Fancy saying a thing like that!', 'What do you think she meant by that?' they say; even the simplest anecdote is told dramatically, with a wealth of rhetorical questions, supplementary illustrations, significant pauses, and alterations of pitch."[9] Meg and Petey are perfect exemplars of this thesis, mining Petey's newspaper for gossip and excitement:

Petey   Someone's just had a baby.

Meg   Oh, they haven't! Who?

Petey   Some girl.

Meg   Who, Petey, who?

Petey   I don't think you'd know her.

Meg   What's her name?

Petey   Lady Mary Splatt.

Meg   I don't know her.

An entire detailed and enthusiastic conversation occurs about people neither of them knows and events that bear no relationship to their own lives, but which spark their imaginations and engender judgment and comment nonetheless. Such is the crucial connective role played by the local newspaper.

In Act 2, Petey's benign newspaper becomes weaponized. McCann sits at the table at the top of the act, picks up Petey's innocuous paper, and slowly begins ripping it into symmetrical strips. This strange action is one of the most unnerving events one will ever experience onstage. The directions simply say, "*McCann is sitting at the table tearing a sheet of newspaper into five equal strips.*" What does this imply? As Irving Wardle perceptively commented in his review of *The Birthday Party* in *Encore*, "This device is an extreme example of the playwright's habit of introducing an intrinsically theatrical idea and letting it find its own road back towards common sense."[10] In other words, we do not have to figure out what McCann's newspaper *lazzi* means intellectually, because as we watch a hulking killer carefully ripping newspaper into even strips, it comes to feel as if someone is being gutted. The director and designer have to carefully create the conditions by which this newspaper routine will have the most impact. In rehearsal, one quickly discovers that most newspapers do not rip into neat, straight strips the way Petey's must. One has to "score" the tabloid with invisible marks to help the actor playing McCann succeed in creating strips, and even then, it takes extensive practice to get the action right. Extensive trial and error will reveal the most amenable newspaper brands; one night during the New York run we accidentally used a copy of the *Village Voice,* and the result was a disaster—the rag on that paper went horizontally not vertically, so the paper would not rip into strips at all, and the actor struggled in vain to accomplish McCann's lethal task while only succeeding in destroying the paper completely.

If the texture of paper is crucial, the actual *sound* of the paper tearing is even more important. We would be wise to remember that Pinter's introduction to theater included acting in Agatha Christie whodunits such as *Spider's Web* and *Peril at End House*, plays which were marked by gunshots and screams that penetrated the darkness. Pinter understood how the right sound cue could unnerve an audience, particularly when unleashed in the dark. (He will employ this brilliantly in *The Caretaker* when, in the midst of a blackout, Mick starts up the "electrolux" and terrifies Davies.) When we arrive at the beginning of Act 2 of *The Birthday Party*, the audience begins to hear a distinctive sound happening on stage before the lights come up, a sound few people will be able to identify. As the stage becomes lit, we discover that it is caused by a man (McCann) methodically, one might say maniacally, tearing a newspaper into strips. For the event to have impact, the sound must be visceral. This is much easier to accomplish in an intimate space than in the thousand-seat Geary Theater, where our A.C.T. production took place. We struggled with how to make the sequence work until, after much trial and error, Sound Designer Darron West arrived at a solution: he decided to hide a tiny microphone in the jacket sleeve of the actor playing McCann, so that as McCann pulled the newspaper strip toward him, the violent sound of ripping paper would be picked up by the mic and would begin to fill the auditorium more and more. No one was aware that the sound was amplified, but the moment became appropriately heightened.

These kinds of details contribute significantly to the overall storytelling of a Pinter production. The right action without the right sound will be impotent. Each decision takes hours of a rehearsal and consideration to achieve success. Lest you think I am exaggerating, I should note how fixated Pinter's own theatrical hero, Samuel Beckett, became when trying to create the perfect sound created by Clov's slippers dragging across the floor in *Endgame*. Actor Ron Cluchey, who played Hamm in Beckett's Dublin production of the play, describes it thus: "Sam was obsessed with the sound of the slippers," he explained. "First we tried sandpapering the soles, then layering them with pieces of metal, then brand-new solid leather soles. Finally, still not satisfied, he appeared one day with his own slippers. 'I've been wearing these for twenty years,' he said. 'If they don't do it, nothing will.'"[11]

Assuming one makes McCann's newspaper action "work" theatrically, what exactly is it meant to signify? We do not know. Neither does Stanley. That is what makes it so frightening. As Tynan pointed out early on, "Where most playwrights devote their technical efforts to making us wonder what will happen next, Mr. Pinter focuses our wonder on what is happening *now*."[12] When Stanley enters and sees what McCann is doing, McCann simply clocks him and continues to rip the paper. Soon there is a pile of strips spread carefully on the table. As Stanley tries to touch one, McCann "moves in." "Mind that," he snaps. "What is it?" Stanley inquires. "Mind it. Leave it." McCann demands violently. Stanley quickly gathers that the paper is some kind of touchstone, a proxy for the immense violence of which McCann is capable and which McCann is trying to contain. Stanley moves toward the newspaper strips *three times* (following the rules of any good comedy routine). Each time, McCann's tension rises until finally he yells, "Your cigarette is near that paper." By unnerving McCann in reference to his sacred strips, Stanley momentarily recovers his status. In the next instant, McCann loses his cool completely and hits Stanley across the arm. The temperature in the room, which has stabilized, rises again—the conflict is now out in the open.

When order is restored, we momentarily forget about the newspaper. The party gets underway, and Act 2 builds in complexity and violence. But as the morning breaks on Act 3, the newspaper again plays a crucial role. The room seems calm, as if this is just another morning at the boarding house. Petey enters the house with a fresh newspaper. Meg has a splitting headache; she goes off to do the shopping. Petey questions Goldberg about Stanley's "breakdown" last night, and then disappears into the kitchen, just as McCann enters with the suitcases. "I'm not going up there again," McCann announces with determination. He tries to reassure himself by polishing his shoes, but ultimately sits at the table and resumes the now iconic activity of tearing newspaper into strips. This time, Goldberg cannot endure it: "Stop doing that!" Goldberg yells. "What?" asks McCann. "Why do you do that all the time?" Goldberg asks in despair. "It's childless. It's pointless. It's without a solitary point." The effect of the newspaper *lazzi* at that moment is to reveal the unraveling of even the most criminal minds. McCann's methodical game can no longer soothe or normalize. The crisis has come to a head: Lulu must be sent away, Stanley must be brought downstairs and carted off to "Monty," the killers must have a final confrontation with their host.

Finally, after Stanley is gone, Petey (who has failed to save him) goes to the table. And then something astonishing happens. When he lifts up his paper and opens it, five strips fall to the ground. Like the breath of a dead man. Like the feathers of a bird that has been shot. The bits of newspaper lie on the carpet, a brutal reminder of Goldberg and McCann's violence and of Stanley's fragility. Petey stares at them, appalled. Suddenly he hears Meg returning. He "*studies the front page of the paper.*" "What are you doing?" she asks cheerily, just as she did at the top of the play. "Reading," replies Petey, without meeting her gaze. When the surrogate mother asks if her boy is up yet, Petey does not dare tell Meg that Stanley is gone. Meg is oblivious, filled with happy memories of the birthday party the night before. She has no idea that her beloved Stanley has been torn to bits, like the remnants of newspaper on the floor.

This is another example of the meticulously orchestrated "magic tricks" Pinter deploys to create suspense and, ultimately, to unleash despair. These moments take enormous time and care to finesse. The wrong texture of paper, the wrong number of strips, the wrong air current when Petey holds up the paper for the strips to fall, and the desired effect will be ruined (indeed, we always turned off the air conditioning system for Act 3, so that the strips would fall and not float). It is all about pursuing theatrical "facts." Again, we must remember that props exist *in time*. They have to evolve and surprise, if the magic show is to be kept on track. I was again reminded of Pinter's interview with Mel Gussow in which the critic asked him whether he had done any revisions of *Old Times* for the New York production and Pinter replied, "I changed when the brandy was poured, and that altered the rhythm of the whole play." If a pause is a bridge between two thoughts and a silence is when the bottom drops out, then the length of time it takes to pour a drink or to tear a newspaper while no one is speaking is a silence that can have epic consequences if it is properly orchestrated.

Stanley's glasses are the third quotidien prop that takes on profound meaning under the collective gaze of the audience. We learn early on that Stanley is completely dependent upon his glasses to function, which is one source of his vulnerability. The specter of blindness was something Pinter worried about all his life; he himself felt he had ruined his eyes as a teenager by reading so much in the dark. He understood the need to control his own glasses and to determine when and how he took them on and off. "You have to remember Harold is a master of maintaining finesse and etiquette," remarked actor Douglas Hodge in an interview. "But that's something that could change violently any moment. He once said to me, 'I can take off my glasses faster than anyone.'"[13] Blindness is strongly featured in other Pinter plays as well: for example, at the end of his one-act *The Room*, after Riley is knocked over and beaten by Rose's husband Bert, Rose "stands clutching her eyes" and exclaims, as the last lines of the play, "Can't see. I can't see. I can't see." It is as if the horror of her husband's brutality to Riley has rendered Rose blind.

In *The Birthday Party*, Stanley too seems to be all but blind without spectacles. "Do you have to wear those glasses?" asks Lulu tartly. He does, much to his humiliation. "You're a bit of a washout," she concludes. The *"glasses lazzi"* moves into full gear in Act 2, as the prelude to McCann and Goldberg's brutal interrogation of Stanley. "What can you see without your glasses?" demands McCann. "Anything," Stanley quickly replies, but they know he is lying. "Take off his glasses," instructs Goldberg, and McCann does so, grabbing them off Stanley's face. The first interrogation thus happens to a nearly blind Stanley, and his debilitation is palpable. "Could I have my glasses?" Stanley begs McCann plaintively as Meg enters to save the day. "Ah yes. Here they are," taunts Goldberg before holding them at a distance and making Stanley fight to retrieve them.

We are thus alerted early on to pay attention to Stanley's glasses as a locus of conflict between him and the two killers who arrive to destroy him. Like the *Cornflakes* box, the drum and the newspaper, the glasses as a prop will require finesse. It might be assumed that in production, one could simply buy a few pairs of ordinary black frames at the local drugstore, but it turns out that the detonation of that particular prop is going to demand greater attention. As previously noted, Act 2 of *The Birthday Party* culminates in a seemingly innocuous game of Blind Man's Buff. When it is Stanley's turn to be the victim, he panics, fearing that this is the moment he will lose his sight in front of his two tormentors. McCann says, "I'll take his glasses" and removes them from Stanley's face, leaving space for Meg to tie a scarf over his eyes. She then spins Stanley around to get ready for the game. Just as he becomes completely disoriented, McCann "*breaks Stanley's glasses, snapping the frames*." It is an act of terrible cruelty, akin to breaking his neck. The sound of the glasses snapping, like the string breaking in the final act of Chekhov's *The Cherry Orchard*, signals doom. As with the tearing of the newspaper, the moment of the broken glasses must have hyper-intentionality both for the audience and for the other characters, and sound is a large part of the effect. But alas, as soon as you try the action in rehearsal, you discover that the frames of glasses rarely snap in a clean way, and when they do, they do not make a sharp enough sound to cause the requisite shock. A creative solution must be found.

When we performed *The Birthday Party* at CSC, David Strathairn, the actor playing Stanley, came up with an ingenious workaround for the "glasses problem": he sawed the frames in two at the bridge, drilled a tiny hole in each piece, inserted a toothpick into the hole and glued the two halves of the spectacles back together. Thus, when McCann broke the glasses, the toothpick itself provided a sharp snapping sound that highlighted the violence of the gesture. When Pinter discovered this trick (prepared meticulously night after night by Strathairn in his dressing room as part of his pre-production routine), he was delighted. These were exactly the kind of details that mattered most to him; he reveled in creative, practical solutions that allowed his theatrical ideas to resonate, and his admiration for Strathairn's DIY trick was boundless.

By Act 3, all that is left of Stanley's spectacles are two pieces of cracked shards in Stanley's shaking hands. Quietly, McCann tells Goldberg, "I gave him . . ." "What?" "I gave him his glasses." "Wasn't he glad to get them back?" Goldberg asks. "The frames are bust," McCann replies. "How did that happen?" Goldberg asks. "He tried to fit the eyeholes into his eyes. I left him doing it." Like the drum and the newspaper strips, the broken glasses are a visceral reminder of the wanton destruction of Stanley's mind. He can no longer see straight. He can no longer be put back together. This theatrical image is much more potent for being visual and unspoken; in order to lift it to the level of metaphor, the spectacles must be given their full weight from the beginning of the play, and it is the job of the creative team to look after the prop and its use with extreme care.

The final prop in *The Birthday Party* worth spending a moment upon is Meg's stool. Once again, this was the focus of endless experimentation during rehearsal. Pinter is devoted to the lowly footstool—it appears in *No Man's Land* ("I might even show you my footstool," Hirst offers provocatively) and, in its grander form as a "pouffe," in *The Collection*. In *The Birthday Party*, Meg's stool seems innocuous enough in Act 1; we hardly notice it. But it becomes crucial during the party, in Act 2. "Sit down on this stool," Meg invites McCann after having drunk a toast and feeling the happy effects of the liquor. "This?" he asks uncertainly. McCann is a killer, full of violence but also of trepidation. What is the significance of Meg inviting him to sit near her on that tiny stool? It is clearly awkward for a man like McCann to land on such a small perch, and the action of sitting on it makes McCann feel weak and unnerved. It also looks hilarious. (This visual effect can be augmented by casting a large actor to play McCann.) We know that McCann is not one to enjoy a party or social occasion of any kind; Goldberg has teased him about this in Act 1 when he first suggests the birthday party to Meg. After she gushes, "I wanted to have a party. But you must have people for a party," Goldberg replies winningly, "And now you've got McCann and me. McCann's the life and soul of any party." Poor McCann. His need to remain in control is stymied at every turn by a boss who refuses to divulge the game plan and constantly leaves his subordinate guessing. It is McCann who has been sent out for the bottles. And now, since Goldberg is preoccupied with the lusty Lulu and Stanley is silent at the table, it falls to McCann to make small talk with his ebullient hostess, a task for which he is ill-equipped.

The "game" of this moment is akin to musical chairs: because the seats around the table are all occupied, McCann cannot find a place to land. Thus, it is all the more painful, and amusing, when Meg invites McCann to perch on the little stool, while she sits on the shoebox. "It's comfortable," he tells her, cautiously. "Where did you get it?" "My father gave it to me," she avers happily. This comment repeats what Meg has already asserted about her party dress ("You like my dress?" GOLDBERG: "Wonderful. Out of this world." MEG: "I know. My father gave it to me."), casting doubt on both statements, since her father would have to have given her that dress thirty or forty years ago, which is of course unlikely. Nevertheless, Meg appears at the party ready to conjure the happier days of her "past"; as the scene goes on and the alcohol starts to flow, Meg's "memories" become increasingly fantastical and sentimental, triggering a similar journey into nostalgia for the discomfited and displaced Irishman. On parallel tracks, the two characters call forth moments of friendship, happiness, and care from their nebulous personal histories: "My little room was pink," Meg rhapsodizes, "I had a pink carpet and pink curtains, and I had musical boxes all over the room. And they played me to sleep. And my father was a very big doctor. That's why I never had any complaints. I was cared for, and I had little sisters and brothers in other rooms, all different colors."

The tiny stool containing the drunk thug, set beside the small shoebox supporting the over-dressed old woman, creates a visual landscape that is both grotesque and hilarious. We see a lost man-child and a doddering, somewhat infantilized woman suspended like giant dolls in a toy house. Seated respectively on a tiny stool and a shoebox, Meg and McCann are able to fantasize without fear about a time when they had a community, a connection to other people, a time when a father would give his daughter a little stool and a friend would "stay there all night with the boys. Singing and drinking all night." As McCann weeps about Roscrea and Mother Nolan's, the places of his youth, Meg concocts a perfect childhood for herself. The more reassuring their memories are, the more they will be shattered by what is about to happen. The stool and the shoebox will continue to carry freight in Act 3: after the destruction of Stanley, McCann deflects Petey from his line of questioning by pulling out the shoebox and brushing his shoes. As he does so, we will remember the platform it provided for fantasy in Act 2. A tiny island of safety has returned, by the end of the play, to being just another piece of expendable furniture.

Stage Movement

If the props and ground plan are meticulously conceived in Pinter's mind, so is the physical life of his characters. The ability of the actors to occupy their physical space as *territory to be taken* is key. This brings me to the second epiphany I had when working with Pinter in rehearsal: the language and menace of his plays work best *if the characters do not walk and talk at the same time*. Pinter insisted upon "economy of movement and gesture, of emotion and expression." He quickly made it clear to us that the language of *words* is only one kind of language. Even more fundamental is the language of the *body*. And when the language of the body is restricted or entrapped, the language of the *eyes* becomes crucial. The less one muddies these distinct languages, the more potent the moments of drama will be.

This is why, on the first day of rehearsal for *The Birthday Party* in San Francisco, I asked Judith Ivey (who was playing Meg) to experiment with the idea of separating the movement from the words. "Either talk or do an action, but not at the same time." A stage direction (*"he sits"*) can thus take the place of a "pause," because the sitting is done without speaking. Initially this way of working felt artificial to Ivey, but she came to love the constriction and, by following that precept, to understand the force of Pinter's language in a new way. With most contemporary realism, it does not matter precisely when or where you move as long as the behavior feels "natural." In rehearsal, an actor usually moves on impulse, finding what Stanislavski calls a "secondary action" such as lighting a cigarette or looking out the window, to fill out the time in a scene while the psychological objective is being played. But in the predatory world of a Pinter play, every inch of the space is territory to be won; turning one's back or moving the wrong way can be death. "Random" movement will not suffice. I am reminded of a review of Pinter's own physically-nuanced performance (as "David Baron") in a play by Ian Main called *Subway in the Sky*: "The outstanding acting success in the play is David Baron's plain-clothes 'dick'. With his half-ingratiating, half-cynical smile, his lazy, or suddenly swift, cat-like movement, he is beautifully in character every moment and suggests all the possibilities of a coiled spring."[14] Since a word can carry the same freight as a physical blow or a caress, it's useful if the verbal action and the physical action are made distinct so that each can do its work.

Pinter's tasks are active, specific, and designed to land on their target. Everyone is playing to win, and the room is there to be conquered or escaped. Obviously if this is taken to an extreme, the performance can become brittle or almost too mechanical. It interested me that in his memoir *An Unnatural Pursuit*, playwright Simon Gray had that caveat about Pinter's own production of *One for the Road*: "It's a concussive twenty-five minutes. Harold's direction is impeccable, every movement of the actors informed with meaning, not a detail left loose, not a gesture haphazard or lacking in eloquence. I wonder, though, my reaction to the play on the page being what it was, whether the director hasn't slightly straightjacketed the writer."[15] The balance between precision and spontaneity is a difficult one, but choreography is always a primary focus when rehearsing a Pinter play.

Two examples might help reveal this process at work. In *The Birthday Party*, one of Meg's greatest vulnerabilities, as we learn in her initial scene with Stanley, is her inability to manage the tiny universe that is her household. "You're a bad wife," Stanley accuses her early on. "I'm not. Who says I am?" Meg pants. "Not to make your husband a cup of tea. Terrible," admonishes Stanley. Meg panics at hearing this and defends herself vigorously: "You won't find many better wives than me, I can tell you. I keep a very nice house and I keep it clean." Petey has learned the necessity of managing Meg's anxiety. Early on in the play, after the *Cornflakes* ritual, Meg offers Petey his "second course." "I've got something else for you," she announces. "Good," he replies. The stage directions then state: *She rises, takes his plate and exits into the kitchen. She then appears at the hatch with two pieces of fried bread on a plate.* "Here you are, Petey." In the next moments, she holds out the bread, her head and arms appearing through the hatch like a little puppet on a stage, until he takes it. The boundaries of Meg and Petey's relationship are defined by the fried bread *lazzi* that ensues. We quickly understand that these are poor people; this offering is all she has got to give him. For the couple's well-being to be sustained, Petey must (a) pretend to be surprised and (b) pretend to enjoy the fried bread and thus to appreciate Meg's housekeeping.

Meg holds the plate out to him with touching vulnerability. Her pleading eyes invite his participation. Petey rises to fetch the plate. After she hands it off and disappears (the puppet disappearing from the little stage), Petey, alone for a moment, looks down at the bread. His gaze reveals the whole history of their marriage. How many sad pieces of fried bread has this man eaten in order to please his anxious wife? How many times has he had to

pretend to be surprised, to sustain the myth of her culinary bounty? Petey
looks down. He looks up. Then he crosses to the table and sits. He waits for
Meg to re-emerge. She arrives and stands over him at the table, expectantly.
The stakes rise. She asks, "Is it nice?" The tension is rising. She does not dare
move, or sit down, until the approbation for her fried bread has been won.
When he replies he has not tasted it yet, she sets up a guessing game, one
that has surely been played in this household a thousand times: "I bet you
don't know what it is?" "Yes, I do." "What is it, then?" "Fried bread," "That's
right." With the game completed, Petey takes a bite of the fried bread. Meg
watches, holding her breath. Only then does he *finally* speak: "Very nice."

If Meg holds absolutely still until Petey delivers his verdict, the *stakes* of
the moment will be clear and precise. Any movement before that will break
the tension and diminish Meg's immense anxiety and vulnerability. The
actress must be rigorous. If she walks and talks at the same time, or if she is
moving while he is looking down at the bread, the key events in their
exchange (and the comedy that accompanies it) will be muddied. When she
ultimately releases the tension with "I knew it was," the rickety bridge of
domestic worthiness has been successfully crossed. At the other side is safety,
which is why Petey can now proceed to test out his big news about the "two
men," knowing that Meg will be receptive to hearing it.

Over and over again, what might seem a simple naturalistic event in the
hands of another playwright becomes a tense and hilarious set of hurdles in
Pinter's universe. The precision required to make such moments concrete is
not abstract choreography, it is an active demonstration of the real landmines
confronting this couple every day. At risk is their very survival. The outside
world holds little comfort, and the thin walls of the household can be breeched
at any time. "Let me—just make this clear," Stanley warns Goldberg. "You
don't bother me. To me, you're nothing but a dirty joke. But I have a
responsibility towards the people in this house. They've been down here too
long. They've lost their sense of smell. I haven't. And nobody's going to take
advantage of them while I'm here." The "emergency" of this particular day is
that two men are coming to the house. Stanley is on high alert. He sees the
fragility of Meg's coping mechanism, and the disaster that could occur if her
routines are interrupted. But alas he is incapable of saving her.

If the actors follow the overall "do not move and talk at the same time"
dictum, even if at first it feels artificial and "unnatural," they will usually
make exciting discoveries about the scene. Let us look at a second example,
when the two strangers breech the walls of the Bowles house and invite
themselves in. "*Enter, by the back door, GOLDBERG and McCANN.
McCANN carries two suitcases, GOLDBERG a briefcase. They halt inside
the door, then walk downstage. Stanley, wiping his face, glimpses their backs
through the hatch. GOLDBERG and McCANN look round the room.
STANLEY slips on his glasses, sidles through the kitchen door and out the
back door.*" In early productions of *The Birthday Party*, Goldberg and
McCann were both presented in bowler hats as a pair of comic villains. By

the time we rehearsed the play with Pinter in New York, his advice was, "Forget the bowler hats. Imagine that they're ordinary men who've arrived selling dictionaries. The menace will reveal itself." So here come the two men about whom we have heard so much. The way they enter Stanley's domain only serves to unnerve him further. How can we tell, just by observing their behavior, who these two men are? In a letter to Peter Wood written just before rehearsals began for *The Birthday Party* in 1958, Pinter described them thus: "Goldberg and McCann? Dying, rotting, scabrous, decayed spiders, the flower of our society. They know their way round. Our mentors. Our ancestry. Them. Fuck 'em." They enter silently and by the back door. They occupy the space. They stand completely still. We are thus allowed to watch these two "decayed spiders" for quite a few moments before a word is spoken. Suspense builds! Then comes the language, terse and staccato, like bullets: "Is this it?" "This is it." "Are you sure?" "Sure I'm sure." *Pause.* The tension rises as neither of them moves a muscle. That gives us the chance to wonder, is *what* it? Who are these men and what are they doing here? In those four tiny exchanges, we learn that the Irishman is anxious, and that the other, a Jew, is in charge.

Goldberg tells McCann to take a seat. But in this game of three-dimensional chess, McCann does not dare sit until Goldberg does so himself. Sitting is too powerful a statement. "Are you going to take a seat?" McCann asks nervously. "We'll both take a seat," says Goldberg reassuringly. Now watch the action. McCann puts down the suitcases and then carefully sits at the table. But Goldberg has tricked McCann—he's still standing. Far from giving McCann the reassurance he craves, Goldberg keeps putting him off his game by promising things he does not deliver. He tells McCann to relax, to "take a holiday," to "learn to relax," all the while standing over him to remind him who is boss. Only when he has sufficiently humiliated McCann does Goldberg finally pull out a chair and take a seat. One step at a time.

The power politics of sitting and standing are like war moves in Pinter, so it helps if the shift from one position to the other is articulated as cleanly as possible and without other distractions. Stillness is the physical equivalence of silence. And within stillness, there are many varieties. Pinter himself loved to demonstrate the power of acting with one's back to the audience—that too is a kind of "silence," an erasure, in which the face is hidden and expression masked by the back of the actor's head. David Thompson believes Pinter learned this trick from close observation of his mentor, Donald Wolfit (he of the *Lear* whip). "One image of Wolfit remains with me strongly," Pinter described, speaking about Wolfit's *Oedipus at Colonus.*

He was standing high up on a rostrum with the light on him . . . he stood with his back to the audience with a cloak round him and there came a moment when the man downstage finished his speech and we all knew, the play demanded it, the audience knew, that Wolfit or Oedipus was going to speak, was going to turn and speak. He held the moment until one's stomach was truly trembling and the cloak came round; a tremendous swish that no one else has been able to achieve I think. And the savagery and power that emerged from such a moment was extraordinary.[16]

Pinter made sure his characters had similar opportunities to both hold and unleash emotion; Stanley's eruption with the drum at the end of Act 1 is such a moment. Audience members do not have to understand *why* something is happening if they can intuitively feel *what* is happening. As Beckett said about Joyce, "It is not about the thing, it is the thing itself."

Spatial relationships between characters are another key. In the second week of rehearsal for *The Birthday Party*, when we had gotten the whole play on its feet, I kept watching the beginning of the party scene with dissatisfaction—it was clear to me that we had not yet achieved the tension the scene needed, but I could not figure out what adjustment to make. When I asked Pinter for his thoughts, he paused and then said, "I believe Irishmen prefer to drink alone." That was the key. I had put McCann too physically close to the other characters. Goldberg and Lulu were having a splendid time together on one side of the table, Stanley was trapped silently behind, and Meg was fluttering about trying to play hostess. What ultimately gave the scene its tension was a hulking Irishman sitting in the far corner of the space with his "bottle of Irish," drinking alone, capable of erupting at any moment. His brooding eyes, staring out into the void, became all the more powerful when the character was isolated.

Further Rules of Play: Masking and Forgetting

I came to find that in working on Pinter, my years of directing Greek tragedy were useful. Greek drama was, of course, *masked* —the actors faced the audience and argued their points without ever being able to share the nuances of their facial expressions with the audience or the other characters. In a similar vein, Pinter's characters mask their behavior so as not to betray to an opponent where their vulnerabilities lie. That mask must only be allowed to slip on rare and explosive occasions. Tip your hand and you leave yourself open to dangerous emotional blackmail. One has to understand what is at stake *beneath* the mask and how much terror these characters are carrying, but then one must trust that *covering* that anxiety is the most useful strategy to deploy. Peter Hall, the seminal director of many of Pinter's early works, wrote eloquently about this idea of "masking" in his essay "Directing Pinter."

One of the greatest epiphanies we had in this regard came in the Act 3 scene between Lulu and Goldberg. Something terrible has occurred in the bedroom the night before, something approximating torture. We never get the details, but when Lulu compares Goldberg to her first love, Eddie, she exclaims, "He didn't come into my room at night with a briefcase!" The next morning even Goldberg seems shaken by the events of the previous night. When Lulu finally appears, this is what gets said:

Goldberg Come over here.

Lulu What's going to happen?

Goldberg Come over here.

Lulu No thank you.

Goldberg What's the matter? You got the needle to Uncle Natey?

Lulu I'm going.

But she does not go. She stands her ground until she can confront this man who has so utterly degraded her. In our production, we put Lulu on the landing for the first part of the scene so that she was higher than Goldberg; this gave her a little "stage" on which to enact her outrage. But of course, no matter how hard the character tries, she ultimately gets sucked back into the orbit of the predator. "You took me for a night, a passing fancy," she wails. "You made use of me by cunning when my defenses were down. . . . That's what you did! You quenched your ugly thirst. You taught me things a girl shouldn't know until she's been married at least three times. . . . You didn't appreciate me for myself. You took all those liberties only to satisfy your appetite. Oh, Nat, why did you do it?" This scene is extremely difficult to get right, even more so in 2016 than it had been in 1989, since as a culture we have become so much more attuned to the reality of sexual assault. It is not that Lulu is not devastated by what has happened to her, or that we as audience members should not take her pain seriously. It is that her phrases about abuse are clichéd expressions she has clearly overheard elsewhere ("You didn't appreciate me for myself," "You quenched your ugly thirst") and are thus, to some extent, laughable.

How should it be played? What seems most salient about the scene is the gap between the banality of Lulu's locutions and the horror of what happened upstairs. That dislocation is key. If the actress tries to invest her language with the heat of "emotional truth," the scene degenerates into crude melodrama, which surely cannot have been Pinter's intention. But if the lines are played as premeditated speech, Lulu seems too in control of her situation, and we fail to glimpse the broken human being underneath the clichés. What we learned after much trial and error is that the actress has to reveal both Lulu's true devastation and her desperate need to maintain her dignity. Her action is thus to *keep up the mask*. She may be spouting language right out of a Harlequin romance, yet the more clichéd it becomes, the more she breaks our heart because she is constantly fighting (and failing) to sustain her status. Finally, she forces Goldberg to show his teeth: "You wanted me to do it, Lulula, so I did it." Watching a destroyed human being trying to maintain a mask of dignity is infinitely more moving than watching that person "lose it" on stage; once we had understood the central "action" of the scene, it played effectively every night.

Here is another "rule of play" which proved helpful in cracking open difficult scenes like the final Lulu/Goldberg encounter: unlike with more naturalistic plays, it is not generally useful for actors in Pinter to attempt to find a single "spine," or to try to make each scene line up along a single axis. When David Strathairn was asked how he crafted the "arc" of Stanley's character, he mused, "From my point of view, you could look for any number of backbones to *The Birthday Party* . . . I find that you'll choose one spine, and you'll build and build and build and all of a sudden there'll be a gap— three or four vertebrae missing—and then you'll have to find another one, and you build again." Pinter confirmed that this was absolutely the case with his work, encouraging us always to "Let go of one scene, and begin clean with the next scene." The importance of starting each scene anew, rather than carrying a concept or an impulse over from a previous scene, is a unique challenge in his work. We like to think that experience is sequential and that one choice leads to another, but in Pinterland, life is never that predictable and one must always be alert to new dangers. "The echoes that carry on through the play are just those specific spines," Strathairn explained. "The danger I think is that if you play any *one* of those, you'll derail somewhere down the line, and it won't be complete and descriptive if you play one big idea all the way through."[17]

It is hard to overestimate what a radical idea this is for most American actors trained in psychological realism. Actor training in America, based on a variety of psychological techniques from Strasberg and Meisner to Uta Hagen and Stanislavski, usually asks an actor to craft a logical beginning, middle, and end to a character's "arc" so that the audience can watch the distance that character travels in the course of the story. For Pinter to instruct actors to start each scene from a clean slate seemed counterintuitive and frightening. But Peter Riegert quickly reminded us what he had learned from years of doing improvisation: you stay in the moment, you do not plan ahead, you do not carry a lot of baggage (such as "biography"), and you do not hold on to "mood" from one moment to the next. You play the beat and move on. In Pinter, this means you land on the deck with the tools that you have got and you engage with the language and the oppositional energy with your scene partner, trusting that an event will occur which has a certain kind of impact. That impact is its meaning. When it is over, the next "bout" begins. The play is the accretion of all of those encounters. The fact that they do not all "add up" neatly is what gives the play life and surprise.

This technique is connected to Pinter's fascination with active "forgetting," and with the disturbing but genuine way characters can experience something frightening and then reset completely in the next minute. For the character of Meg, Pinter's note that she had "forgotten how to read" meant that every encounter with Petey was a new experience—one moment she has learned something about the light in winter, or about a local event such as a birth or a death, and the next moment that knowledge has vanished. Life for Meg is thus one surprise after another. The actress need not carry certain emotions or knowledge over from one scene to the next because the character of Meg is not capable of doing that. Pinter even speculated that Meg and Petey "may have forgotten that they run a boarding house," which we found to be a hilarious and disturbing thought. But it makes sense: Meg is so bound up in day-to-day life with her beloved surrogate son Stanley that she loses all thought of renting out rooms, until the "two gentlemen" appear asking if there is space. Stanley feels immediately betrayed—why has Meg not talked about renting the rooms before? Possibly because she has forgotten. Or because she longs to keep Stanley to herself. Or because the house is too run-down to be desirable to visitors. Or because the whole boarding house idea is merely a product of Meg's fertile imagination. This is up to the interpretative decisions of the director and the actress playing Meg. Regardless of the reason, the threat to Stanley of his "womb" becoming a boarding house again suddenly becomes real.

Line-Learning

If language in Pinter is a constant improvisation to control power and status in the room, memorizing that language can be punishingly difficult for an actor, partly because the speech is full of *non sequiturs* and blind alleys. As I mentioned in Chapter 1, Pinter's ear for the outrageous contradictions of ordinary conversation was impeccable, and he never "filled in" the logic in order to make a line easier to parse. This is connected to Pinter's love of games and to his appetite for surprise; he rarely wants an audience to know what is going to come next. But as an actor himself, Pinter was deeply sympathetic to the challenges of memorizing his text, particularly when it came to the two long interrogation scenes in *The Birthday Party* which involve a rapid-fire sequence of unrelated attacks and accusations. At the final dress rehearsal at CSC, when Peter Riegert and Richard Riehle were facing off, trying to woo Stanley with what they will do for him, Riegert went completely dry and could not for the life of him remember the next line. The text goes:

McCann   We'll provide the skipping rope.

Goldberg   The vest and pants.

McCann   The ointment.

Goldberg   The hot poultice.

McCann   The fingerstall.

Goldberg   The abdomen belt.

Riegert got to the "vest and pants" and it was as if the record hit a scratch. McCann fed him "the skipping rope," but nothing came. Goldberg was silent; he could not come up with the line. Riegert stared at his scene partner, blank and panicking. Riehle did not know how to help. He kept repeating "the skipping rope! The skipping rope!" over and over as if to dislodge Riegert from his paralysis. I turned around and looked at Pinter who was sitting behind me, and realized he was convulsed with laughter.

Afterwards, he told Riegert that when he himself had played Goldberg across from the great Irish actor Patrick McGee, the same thing had happened. He could not for the life of him remember the next phrase. He recalled pleading silently for some help from McGee, only to be met with McGee's grinning face which seemed to say, "you wrote the bloody thing, you think of the next line!" But no amount of logic will produce "the vest and pants" if the lines are not there. Pinter never forgot that particular actor's nightmare, and his sympathy with the pair of interrogators was immense. As Ian Smith has commented,

> There is, in the nicest possible way, undoubtedly something of the old ham in Harold. He understands the nature of the craft of acting in weekly rep, and of simply standing there, being able to tough it out when basically you hardly know what you're going to say next! Sometimes you see his own plays or read them and at first sight it's almost like the rep actor's worst nightmare—as if they've *all* forgotten their lines and *nobody* knows what's going to happen next.[18]

This is probably what makes watching a Pinter play so electric and unnerving.

If Pinter could not mitigate the challenge of learning his outrageous text, he was quick to display his gratitude to the actors who performed his work. His deep and abiding affection for the company was on full display on our opening night in April 1988, when the following telegram arrived: "SORRY I CAN'T BE AT THE PARTY BUT I'LL BE WAITING OUTSIDE IN THE CAR. GOOD LUCK. MONTY PINTER." And then, as if he felt the need to diffuse the horror with something lighter the second time, came his opening night missive on October 23, 1989; "LOVE AND GOOD LUCK FROM STANLEY'S DAD ALL MEG'S LITTLE BROTHERS AND SISTERS, PETEY'S CHESS MATES, THE LADS AT MOTHER NOLAN'S, GOLDBERG'S OLD MUM AND ALL AT THE ETHICAL HALL BAYSWATER, LULU'S MUM, DAD, GRANNIE, GRANPA. EDDIE, MONTY, JOHN DOAKES AND HAROLD."

Pauses and Silence

I have spoken in Chapter 3 about the theatrical imperatives of the "pause" and "silence" in Pinter, and two occasions in *The Birthday Party* helped us to understand exactly how Pinter wished those lacunae to be deployed. In Act 3 of *The Birthday Party*, a moment of utter verbal vacancy happens to Goldberg. This silence is particularly frightening coming from one who is loquacious to a fault: from his first appearance, we have watched Goldberg articulate his world view in a rush of words that never seems to stop. He is the life of the party. He relates stories about his mother, he waxes sentimental about his childhood, he tells jokes, he gives advice, he pontificates, he reassures, he threatens, he invents. And then, suddenly, he hits the wall of his own hollowness. The morning after the party, Goldberg comes downstairs exhausted. This "job" has been much harder than he had anticipated. He is set on edge by Petey, who seems to have an intuition that something has gone terribly wrong (PETEY: "I think I'll see how my peas are getting on, in the meantime." GOLDBERG: "The meantime?" PETEY: "While we're waiting." GOLDBERG: "Waiting for what?"). Goldberg feels caught. The atmosphere is tense. To make matters worse, as we have noted earlier, McCann reverts to his activity of choice when trying to stay calm: he begins ripping the newspaper into strips. This sends Goldberg right over the edge. McCann begs Goldberg to tell him what to do about Stanley, but Goldberg does not answer. In desperation, McCann addresses him as "Simey," the forbidden name, the name his mother called him. Goldberg replies *murderously*, "Don't call me that! (*he seizes McCann by the throat*) NEVER CALL ME THAT!"

Goldberg has erupted, and in doing so, has dropped his mask of civility. Underneath, the raw murderous face of an angry killer is exposed, a face Goldberg has worked so hard to hide beneath charm and bonhomie. In order to recover, to be able to move forward at all, Goldberg needs to talk himself back into coherence. Thus, he launches into a speech full of truisms and clichés, the kind of speech that has proved so successful for him before: "All my life I've said the same. Play up, play up and play the game. Honour thy father and mother. All along the line. Follow the line, the line, McCann, and you can't go wrong." He gears himself up until he can arrive at the conclusion that will rescue him from terror and exposure:

And you'll find—that what I say is true.

Because I believe that the world ... (*Vacant.*) ...

Because I believe that the world ... (*Desperate.*) ...

BECAUSE I BELIEVE THAT THE WORLD ... (*Lost.*) ...

He sits in a chair.

This is a wonderful example of a physical move creating the requisite silence. Goldberg has reached the end of his belief system; he simply cannot go on. His mouth is open, ready to finish the sentence, but in his moral vacancy, there are no words at his disposal. He stands in gaping silence, suspended in time, unable to continue. Pinter encouraged us to hold on to that moment as long as we could, before allowing Goldberg to sink into a chair. The silence was terrifying. This is, after all, the same man who declined to sit in Act 1, who exercised his dominance by *standing*, the man who heretofore has been utterly in charge of his own loquacious world view. Suddenly his façade has crumbled, and inside, we see that the cupboard is bare. When Goldberg runs out of words and sits in front of McCann, we witness an empire collapsing. Such is the significance of the silence. McCann knows what has happened, and is afraid.

One other "silence" worth remarking upon occurs in the last moments of *The Birthday Party*. The cocky Goldberg who entered the house in Act 1 told McCann, "At all events, McCann, I can assure you that the assignment will be carried out and the mission accomplished with no excessive aggravation to you or myself." But surprisingly, Goldberg ends up being confronted by an antagonist who is far more of an obstacle than he had expected, and the result is considerable "aggravation" for all concerned. Petey, quiet chess-playing Petey, turns out to be the voice of conscience that nearly succeeds in rescuing Stanley from the clutches of his tormentors. After a final round of torture, Goldberg and McCann are ready to get Stanley into the car: GOLDBERG: "Come with us. Come on, boy." McCANN: "Come along with us." But at that moment, Petey appears from the garden, where he has been keeping watch. "Where are you taking him?" he demands to know. "*They turn. Silence.*" This silence is particularly potent because there is no possible response; it gives us time to let our eyes travel from Petey to Goldberg to McCann and then back to Petey. In the silence, we are forced to imagine Stanley's destination. Goldberg, rarely at a loss for words, has no idea how to reply to a man who has guessed the awful truth. Goldberg is caught, and in the silence, Petey understands that Stanley's fate is sealed.

Pinter consistently encouraged us to think of silence both as an *absence* of something and as a viable choice. In a world full of words, the most courageous act might be to refuse to speak. Pinter felt this idea applied most particularly to the character of Stanley. Stanley has made a *choice* to drop out of society. It is not lassitude that keeps him upstairs at Meg's, it is both terror and active resistance. We never know precisely why he made the choice to "drop out," but clearly it is a deliberate one. He is a man in hiding. If he seems "exhausted" much of the time (even though "he's in bed half the week," as Petey comments), it is because abandoning human society takes enormous psychic energy. Conformity is easy. Habit is reassuring, if deadening. But the refusal to "go along" demands constant vigilance, and that is Stanley's condition in *The Birthday Party*. Being silent is thus not giving up, Pinter insisted, it is *holding out*. Stanley must approach this behavior with energy. For much of Act 2, during the party scene, Stanley says nothing. But he is on high alert. Maintaining his silence when every "impulse" tells him to cry out is the hardest acting challenge of all for the actor playing Stanley. And having sustained that silence so vociferously in Act 2, what does Stanley finally utter in Act 3? "Caaaa ... caaaa." The world is shit. In a sense, through his silence and final broken words, Stanley is the only character in the play who actually speaks the truth.

Final Thoughts

The Birthday Party was the among the first plays I staged as a young director in my twenties at CSC, when I was juggling a baby, a bankrupt theater, and the invaluable input of the author himself in rehearsal. It was also the last play I directed in my twenty-five-year tenure at A.C.T., at a moment in which I was leaving the leadership of an institution I adored in order to set out on my own path. As with all great plays, *The Birthday Party* revealed itself to me differently as a middle-aged woman than as a twenty-something. In its first outing, my sympathies lay primarily with Stanley, the alienated and misunderstood artist at the center of the play; by 2018, I had grown to have a deep affection for, and understanding of, Meg, the mother manqué whose only desire is to make her "son" happy and to keep the ship of life from crashing against the rocks. The A.C.T. production of *The Birthday Party* also occurred at the height of the Trump era, which meant that my antennae were more alert to the toxic falsities spouted by the smiling bully at the center of the play. Perhaps this is why, in 2018, it seemed more important than ever to give Petey his dedicated if futile moment of resistance at the end.

My familiarity with Pinter's universe by 2018 meant that the A.C.T. rehearsals of *The Birthday Party* could be risk-taking and vigorous because we did not spend time asking the wrong questions and attempting to solve unsolvable problems. Returning to the play gave me a strong sense of my own evolution as an artist and helped me understand how my encounters with Pinter had shaped my aesthetic and practice. Most importantly, by 2018, I felt a deep sense of belief in the material. I knew that if I followed the "rules of play" and trusted my own instincts about the text, the play would lift off, even in that cavernous theater. When you decide to go to "Pinterland," as his friend Henry Woolf affectionately called it, you cannot dip your toes into the water. You have to (as Joey says about sex in *The Homecoming*) "go the whole hog." This was particularly important post 9/11: plays which dared to take on the reality of terror and the necessity of human connection were rare. What had seemed abstract or unfamiliar had become urgent and immediate. Nothing felt as perfect a way to culminate twenty-five years at A.C.T. as putting six thoroughbreds onstage in *The Birthday Party* without apology or explanation, and letting them rip.

5

"Wanting to Know" and the Rehearsal Process of Stoppard's *Indian Ink*

Having explored some of the salient aspects of interpreting and staging Pinter, I would like to do the same with the work of Stoppard by focusing on my rehearsal experiences with *Indian Ink* (1996). I have directed *Indian Ink* twice in collaboration with Stoppard, first for its American premiere in 1998 and then for the first New York production at the Roundabout Theater in 2014. The "rules of play" that revealed themselves in those processes proved applicable to all the work I have done on Stoppard plays, as those found during *The Birthday Party* rehearsals guided my subsequent work on Pinter.

Indian Ink began its life as a radio play called *In the Native State*, commissioned by BBC Radio in 1989 and completed in October 1991. It draws upon the affection for India that Stoppard has felt since he spent his childhood there during the war: "My first memories are of India," he told Publications Manager Elizabeth Brodersen in an interview for the A.C.T. program in 1998. "I loved India when I was there, and I loved it still when I returned." He developed this particular story over a number of years; the play starred Felicity Kendal as Flora Crewe in both the radio and stage premieres and is dedicated to the memory of her mother Laura Kendal, who was part of a traveling Shakespeare company called "The Firm" that toured India in the 1930s, the era in which the play is set. *In the Native State* also grew out of a tragedy in Felicity Kendal's own life, the early death of her sister Jennifer, also an actress. Thus the play responded to personal memories that were intensely felt by them both. The structural "game" Stoppard set himself was to write a play about a poet posing for a painter while writing a poem about being painted. That theatrical notion became a work which focuses on empire, colonialism, intercultural love and "who is doing what to whom." Several years after *In the Native State* was recorded for radio, he rewrote it completely for the stage; while Felicity Kendal felt that some of its magic disappeared in that process of transformation, much of its mystery and sensuality deepened and grew.

Indian Ink is set in the fictional town of Jummapur in the north of India, the area where the young Straussler family lived during the war before emigrating to England. Stoppard has repeatedly stressed his belief that India saved him, even though he was acutely aware of being a complete outsider while he was living there. As Czech refugees in Darjeeling, the Strausslers were certainly a liminal family, neither "native" nor "Raj"; they were white, but they were refugees. Stoppard and his brother Peter went to the Mount Hermon School, a multiracial establishment run by American Methodists in Darjeeling, rather than a school for children of the Raj. In early 1991, Stoppard traveled back to India for the first time, writing a piece about the experience called "Going Back" for the *Independent Magazine* of March 1991, in which he describes searching in vain for the tree outside his school where he and his brother Peter used to sit every Sunday, waiting for their mother to appear over the crest of the hill, carrying treats for her boys. Alas the tree had long since disappeared, but in *Indian Ink*, through the wonders of theater, it makes a welcome return as the tree Flora sits beneath and Dilip later photographs in service to Eldon Pike's biography. While *Indian Ink* exposes many painful fault lines in the Anglo-Indian relationship during the years leading to Independence, it is not a play focusing primarily on anticolonial activism; for this lack, Stoppard received (predictably, by the late 1990s) a certain degree of heat. But he defended it. "It's a much more intimate play than a polemical play," Stoppard told us in 1998. "There are no villains in it. I really enjoy its lack of radical fierceness. It has its checks and balances. There's no ranting or storming around; there are no long monologues." But there is much heartache and misunderstanding, and many quests for a sense of self in a rapidly shifting universe.

Indian Ink revolves around an English poet named Flora Crewe who travels to India in 1930 on doctor's orders to help ease an acute pulmonary condition. She is the sister of Eleanor Swan, a leftwing journalist whom we meet fifty years later as an old lady in Shepperton, England. The play travels back and forth in both time and place, from 1930s India to the 1980s in both the Shepperton garden and India, and is structured as a kind of reverse mystery. If, as we discovered, *The Birthday Party* is built upon a set of seemingly ordinary props from eyeglasses to newspapers, *Indian Ink* could be said to be a play about four portraits (all echoes of Flora) and some letters. Having spent untold hours during *Arcadia* rehearsals color-coding the various letters in the play so that the audience could track the ongoing plot twists, my production team was prepared by *Indian Ink* for the task of meticulously creating a series of paintings and sketches, some of which had to endure physical fights and nightly destruction onstage.

In 1930s Jummapur, Flora meets a painter named Nirad Das who spontaneously draws a sketch of her at a public meeting, a sketch which he later tears into pieces right in front of her (this is *Portrait 1*). Das then proceeds to paint an oil portrait of Flora, using a Westernized approach ("It's fairly ghastly, like an Indian cinema poster" according to Eleanor) that bewilders Flora ("I thought you'd be an *Indian* artist") and that Das ultimately abandons after a dramatic fight between the two of them (this is *Portrait 2*). Meanwhile in England in the 1980s, Eleanor Swan serves tea in her garden, first to a fatuous American academic named Eldon Pike who is editing "The Collected Letters of Flora Crewe" and is on the hunt for the nude portrait referred to in her letters, and then to a young painter of Indian extraction named Anish who turns out to be Nirad's son, and who is the possessor of the nude Eldon is looking for (but never gets to see): a watercolor miniature of a naked English woman whom Anish believes to be Eleanor's sister ("Perhaps my soul will stay behind/As a smudge of paint on paper," writes Flora about this third portrait, which we shall call *Portrait 3*).

Just to complicate things even further, there is a second nude miniature that surfaces in the play: in Act 2, a Rajah who entertains Flora in Jummapur gives her a copy of an image from the *Gita Govinda* of the nude herdswoman Radha, lover of Krishna, the original of which Eleanor has found in Flora's suitcase after her death (this is *Portrait 4*). The bewildered biographer Eldon Pike confuses Portraits 3 and 4 and (satisfyingly) fails to make the discovery about the real nude of Flora, which Anish gives to Eleanor and which they agree to keep as a private matter between the two of them. Such are the pitfalls of biography. As we discovered with Pinter, the precision of props will prove to be all-important if the audience is to follow the erotic secrets of the play.

If the broad mystery of *Indian Ink* is whom Flora Crewe actually had an affair with in India (the candidates being, so far, Nirad Das and the Rajah), a third romantic entanglement emerges in the person of a young English military man named Durance who falls instantly in love with Flora and proposes to her on horseback. He is less than sanguine about Flora's relationship with Nirad Das, since he considers fraternizing with Indians inappropriate. This infuriates Flora. The play builds to a climax as British-Indian relations grow increasingly strained, the Indians with whom Flora has been consorting are reprimanded, and their Theosophical Society is shut down; amidst the chaos and recriminations, Das comes to Flora's bungalow at night to retrieve his painting. Flora feels betrayed by Das because she believes he has spread gossip in Jummapur about her ill health; he tells her that her illness was mentioned in the letters of introduction from England that proceeded her visit, and that he has revealed nothing. In her gratitude and shame, Flora begins to weep; to cheer her up, Das gives her a gift. It is a portrait he has just made (*Portrait 3*), a "Rajput miniature" created for her in his own native Rajasthani style. Her enchantment with this gift apparently leads to a night of love with Das, after which she departs Jummapur. In examining that beautiful miniature, given to her by Das' son Anish fifty years later, Eleanor begins to understand that her sister may have had a love affair with an Indian painter, something that is equally extraordinary and meaningful to Anish, given that the Indian painter was his father.

Linking the four portraits in *Indian Ink* is a concept which is central to an understanding of the play and which, as described in Chapter 2, Stoppard discovered quite by accident: the notion of *rasa* in Indian art. As Das explains it, "*Rasa* is juice. Its taste. Its essence. A painting must have its *rasa* . . . which is not in the painting exactly. *Rasa* is what you must feel when you see a painting, or hear music; it is the emotion which the artist must arouse in you." When Flora inquires whether a poem has *rasa*, Das replies, "Oh yes! Poetry is a sentence whose soul is *rasa*." The concept of *rasa* ultimately defines the subtle but magical bond between two artists at the heart of *Indian Ink*. Toward the end of the play, when Flora sees Das' final miniature, he worries that she might be offended at his having painted her nude, but she is not:

Flora   No, I'm pleased. It has *rasa*.

Das   I think so. Yes. I hope so.

Flora   I forget its name.

Das (*pause*)   Shringara.

Flora   Yes. Shringara. The *rasa* of erotic love. Whose god is Vishnu.

Das   Yes.

Flora   Whose color is blue-black.

Das   Shyama. Yes.

Flora   It seemed a strange color for love.

Das   Krishna was often painted shyama.

Flora   Yes. I can see that now. It's the color he looked in the moonlight.

Their shared understanding of the erotic beauty of this offering finally brings the two artists together; it is what gives the play its "juice." When one observes how deeply woven into the heartbeat of the play the concept of *rasa* is, it is all the more remarkable that it was a concept Stoppard discovered when he was well into the writing of the play. (Perhaps this is what often gives Stoppard's plays such a feeling of life being lived and discoveries being made; he rarely ever plans his work out as meticulously as he would like, and it is often the "happy accidents" that show him where he's headed. "The truth is that stories don't fall into your lap, you have to edge into them and try to find them," he told Patrick Leahey. "When I'm writing a play, that's not a job. Writing a play is *life*.") In the midst of his life as he wrote *Indian Ink*, the notion of *rasa* appeared by lucky accident, and that notion helped him understand or articulate what he intuitively knew lay underneath the dialectic of the play. *Rasa* is the impulse Flora is so hungrily pursuing in the writing of poetry, and it is what she ultimately sees reflected in Das' portrait. That impulse, the sense of *rasa* or juice that makes lived experience sensual and true, is the undercurrent an actor and director must pursue as they rehearse the play.

And because *rasa* is what connects Flora and Das, much time must be spent in rehearsal negotiating the complex relationship between these two characters, and how that relates to the overall dialectic between individualism and colonialism in the play. Stoppard admits to having had a hard time writing the Indian characters in the play without making them sound like bad imitations of *The Raj Quartet*—how would he make Das a unique and three-dimensional character? Seen first through the eyes of Flora, Das is as eager as a "Labrador, knocking all the brick-a-brack off the shelf"; he is insistently enthusiastic and overly "English," using expressions like "top hole" and "red-letter day." But slowly the perspective on the character changes, as we stop seeing Das from Flora's point of view and meet him on his own terms. If Flora thinks Das is not "Indian" enough, he feels she is not really "English." Their aesthetic, political, and personal collisions build to the physical fight at the end of Act 1 that exposes the depth of Flora's illness and prompts the creation of the watercolor nude. Stoppard injects surprising reversals at every turn.

Questions of appropriation and the legacy of colonialism had, crucially, moved further to the forefront of contemporary cultural criticism from 1998 when we first collaborated on *Indian Ink* until 2014 when we revived it; thus, the second time we worked on the play, we were able to interrogate those issues more fully, although at neither time was the play able to fully satisfy those who wanted it to be a scathing attack on the Raj. We had to remain cognizant that the play was set in 1930 and that Flora, as a guest of the Indians in Jummpaur, was subject to the morés of her own time and class; she had not come to India to deliver a contemporary screed about the Raj. In our 2014 rehearsals, Stoppard was concerned that some of the actors were bending the play to fit our own contemporary attitudes, infusing it with the kind of censoriousness about colonial behavior that we would register today. He wanted to keep it full of contradictions but not didactic. In dialogue with the actress playing his heroine, Stoppard explained, "A recurrent note that Flora has is one of affectionate mockery. She believes the sincere affection in it trumps the mockery and when it doesn't, she's genuinely sorry and knows or is reminded of the limits of her understanding about India. But she's a boho not a toff" (meaning "unconventional" rather than "upper class"). He was adamant that she has not come to India to make a point or to visibly deride colonialism, much as we would wish it. Flora is ultimately interested in Das' own individual voice as an artist; it is only in that context that she becomes passionate about "who whom."

If the first task of the director is to tease out the dialectic in the play and make sure the arguments are given heat, the second is to excavate the *rasa* that lies beneath that dialectic. This is what encouraged us to rethink the ending of the play when we came back to it twenty years after its American premiere in 1998. I noted in the "Introduction" that Stoppard, unlike Pinter, never tires of revising his scripts to suit specific occasions, and *Indian Ink* is no exception. In the first version, the play ended with Flora sitting on a train reading *Up the Country*, an 1866 travelogue by an intrepid British woman named Emily Eden that concluded with a description of a Queen's Ball in Simla (heard in Voiceover):

> Twenty years ago no European had ever been here, and there we were with a band playing, and observing that St. Cloup's Potage a la Julienne was perhaps better than his other soups, and so on, and all of this in the face of those high hills, and we one hundred and five Europeans being surrounded by at least three thousand Indians, who looked on at what we call our polite amusements, and bowed to the ground if a European came near them. I sometimes wonder they do not cut all our heads off and say nothing more about it.

This is a remarkable statement, coming from a member of the Raj at the height of British power. *Up the Country* is a gift that Das gives to Flora early on in their relationship, a gift that delights her: "Oh, but this will be just my book!" she exclaims upon learning about its subject matter. It is also the locus of one of the many misunderstandings between Das and Flora; he calls it a "birthday present" and she replies that it is not her birthday; only later do we realize that it is his own birthday, and that he is marking the occasion by giving to this fascinating English woman a treasured book that had belonged to his father. I fully understood why Stoppard had initially found it effective to end the play with this quote, a lens onto what Flora has been reading that helped open her eyes to the injustices of the Raj, locating the play in its political and historic context in its final moments. Yet as a closing gesture, I found it theatrically problematic, and, as I watched it night after night in performance at A.C.T. in 1998, somewhat emotionally unsatisfying. I knew that Stoppard felt the same way.

Thus, when we returned to *Indian Ink* in 2014, in a co-production between New York's Roundabout Theater and A.C.T., we decided to try to imagine an alternative ending. As I explained in my Director's Notes at that time, "Stoppard is one of those rare writers who views a script as an evolving document amendable to change. He is aware of the whole context of a production, how changes in worldview might affect an audience's perception of a play, and how the benefit of time can reveal better ways to tell a story." Prior to rehearsals, we sat in Stoppard's London kitchen and talked for many hours about what the play ultimately wanted to evoke, both emotionally and visually. Some months later, an email arrived from Tuscany:

> Dear Carey, I feel like Flora writing to her sister, on our verandah in the hot weather—in ink, of course, for Sabrina to put in her laptop for you. I've been happily immersed in the text, and as a consequence we will need to spend some time on the phone to go through my offers of excision, clarification and correction. We return home on Sunday. Not that I'm ready for you . . . One thing I've come to think is that the plot should 'come clean' on p. 9 where Pike is 'puzzling over a letter'—I think it would help us later if the possible existence of the nude portrait is planted

without teasing . . . Peter Wood used to complain about my 'retroactive exposition' so I'm finally heeding his complaint.

From his holiday balcony in Italy, Stoppard made judicious cuts throughout the text ("Madame Blavatsky" had to go) and clarified complex plot points. But the most important changes had to do with that last section of the play. In an A.C.T. program interview, Stoppard commented:

I'd always felt conflicted about the ending. On the one hand, I loved quoting Emily Eden, because it contextualized the story of Flora Crewe historically. And I thought that was welcome and desirable. On the other hand, I always felt a loss in the sense that the last voice you heard in the play was a recorded voice . . . when we got to New York all these years later, the idea was not to end the play politically, but to end it emotionally and romantically . . . What's interesting about the new ending—and you shouldn't be shy about taking a bow for this (*he said to me*)—is that Eleanor and Flora share the stage for one long beat.

That was indeed a happy outcome of our second collaboration on the play. While the primary "story" of *Indian Ink* is the subtle love story that emerges between Flora and Das, a secondary story is the love between two sisters who have been separated in life far too early but remain devoted to each other; Flora's premature death is the great sorrow of Eleanor's life, as the death of her sister had been for Felicity Kendal. In the 1998 version, there was no opportunity for the sisters to actually share the stage, which may have diluted the moment when Eleanor finally intuited the truth about her sister's Indian romance. In 2014, we looked for a way to conclude the play with a shared moment of discovery and love between the sisters. We thus decided to remove the Emily Eden quote and to end the play with the "post-coital" letter that Flora sends to Eleanor after departing from Jummapur. In the first version of *Indian Ink* (published by Faber in 1998), this letter follows the graveyard scene in which young Eleanor (Nell) mourns her sister and is comforted by Eric, whom she will subsequently marry. The original stage directions called for Nell and Eric to exit; "*As they go, PIKE enters, looking for the right grave. He finds it, takes his hat off and stands looking at it*"; then we hear Flora's letter, before concluding with the Emily Eden quote, read by Flora on the train. We realized that if we eliminated the Emily Eden quote, we could also dispense with having to recreate the train in the last moments of the play. Instead, we could place Flora center stage, sitting on her suitcase, while Eleanor sat behind her, imagining it all as her sister spoke the letter.

Flora's letter withholds as much as it reveals about Flora's mysterious romance:

Darling, that's all from Jummapur. Because now I'm packed, portrait and all, and Mr. Coomaraswami is coming to take me to the station. I'll post this in Jaipur as soon as I get there. I'm not going to post it here because I'm not. I feel fit as two lops this morning, and happy, too, because something good happened here which made me feel halfway better about Modi and getting back to Paris too late. That was a sin I'll carry to my grave, but perhaps my soul will stay behind as a smudge of paint on paper, as if I'd always been here, like Radha who was the most beautiful of the herdswomen, undressed for love in an empty house.

In our re-examination of the ending in New York in 2014, we were able to watch Eleanor's face, as the luminous Rosemarie Harris listened to that letter being read. Time and space merged as the sisters shared the secret of Flora's love. In the course of rehearsal, with the two women so close to each other physically, we were also able to find an occasion when Flora stopped reading for a second and the two women looked up at the same time. As Flora turned, their eyes met. It was a wonderful moment of mutual recognition, the kind of discovery Stoppard treasures, in which the text at hand becomes the "event" of theater. As the two sisters caught each other's glance, the elder woman understood for the first time that, in the days before her death, her sister had experienced something filled with beauty, something connected to India and specifically to the Indian painter she had known. There was catharsis in that discovery, a catharsis that could slightly mitigate the sorrow of having lost Flora so precipitously. Eleanor, having resisted romanticizing Flora's time in Jummapur, has *changed*. The encounter she has with Anish over the course of the play has introduced her to a range of possibilities she had not even considered. That, in fact, is the *action* of the play. As Eleanor concludes to Anish, "one alters." This recalls the notion of "equilibrium" in Stoppard, as discussed in Chapter 3. If one generally pursues a life of "balance," the slightest shift in weight becomes significant. We will never know exactly what passed between Das and Flora that night, but we do know that the experienced altered them both in a deep way, and that for Eleanor is enough.

While we rehearsed this new ending, a second idea occurred to me (another happy "event"), triggered by the stage direction about Pike arriving in that faraway cemetery years after Flora's death. As in *Arcadia*, time and place become fluid by the end of the play, driven by the contemporary characters' "wanting to know" about Flora's encounters in India. In collaboration with choreographer John Carrafa, I began experimenting with bringing the "ghosts" of all the characters we have met in the play onto the stage as the final letter is read. There was already a poetic quality to the atmosphere at that point: the set was covered in blossom that had fallen on Nell and Eric at the graveyard. I invited the characters to arrive in ones and twos, from all corners, as Flora spoke, until finally the stage was fully populated with those we had met along the way, both past and present. Characters from the two periods and cultures could coexist in one collective image against a deep blue background, swirling around Flora, who glowed in the center. Flora's emotional journey thus encompassed everyone whom she had encountered on her Indian journey and everyone who would try, later on, to make sense of it.

Movingly, it occurred to me that Stoppard personally understood the sensation of discovering, after the fact, heartbreaking truths about a lost relative. The moment of grief he describes in *Talk Magazine*, when he touched the scar his father had stitched, has a similar poignancy to Eleanor's emotion in touching the "wound" of her sister's death and discovering the love Flora had felt for Nirad Das. There is, in both cases, a deep sense of loss for what might have been, and appreciation for those who have experienced it. The revised ending meant that the central emotional thread connecting Eleanor and Flora with Anish and Das had been subtly and satisfyingly completed; it had real resonance for the audience and gave us a visual coda that was both beautiful and poetic, as befitted the themes of the play. The revision, both textual and directorial, was a clear demonstration of the way in which an active playwright–director collaboration can function: we both knew where we were heading, so Stoppard looked after the necessary script changes while I created the visual world that would bring them to fruition.

This discovery brings us to the question of scenography and "visual dramaturgy" in Stoppard's work. My two outings with *Indian Ink* were shaped by two very different designers and for different spaces: 1998 was designed by Loy Arcenas for the Geary stage (a large, elegant proscenium house), whereas 2014 was designed by Neil Patel for the Laura Pels Theater at the Roundabout, a shallow, low-ceilinged space. In both cases, I started not with the actual scenic requirements but with what I believed was the central image of the play: the painting of a naked woman under a mosquito netting on a bed inside an Indian house surrounded by trees and monkeys. The painting Das makes of this event (which follows Flora's pulmonary attack at the end of Act 1) is the centerpiece not only of the complex relationship between Flora and Das but of the mystery being explored by the contemporary characters over fifty years later. As Das has explained early in the play, "There are nine *rasa*, each one a different color. I should say mood. But each mood has its color—white for laughter and fun, red for anger, pale yellow for tranquility." As a poet, this notion interests Flora enormously, particularly when Das tells her that the *rasa* of erotic love is called Shringara. "Its god is Vishnu, and its color is shayama, which is blue-black." In order to fully evoke the moment of *rasa* between Das and Flora, it seemed valuable to be able to bathe the entire stage in that deep blue-black when necessary.

But even more so, given the meta-theatricality of the play, it felt desirable to see whether, as the painting was being imagined in the mind of the artist, we could see it formed in real time onstage. After all, this was a play about a painter painting a portrait of a woman writing about having her portrait painted. Thus, for the New York production, we framed the whole proscenium with a bright yellow border that recalled that of an Indian miniature. Inset into the upstage walls were deep windows painted cobalt

FIGURE 9 *Brenda Meaney and Firdous Bamji in* Indian Ink, *Roundabout and American Conservatory Theater, 2014. Scenery by Neil Patel, lighting by Robert Wierzel, costumes by Candice Donnelly. Photo courtesy of Kevin Berne.*

blue. It was thus possible to turn the entire stage into the framed image of the painting Das ultimately makes of the naked Flora, which he gives to her at the end of the play. We created the live image in the following way: when Flora has her attack at the end of Act 1 and sends Das off to fetch tea, the stage directions indicate that she takes off her clothes and lies naked beneath a mosquito net. In our production, a white gauze "tent" floated down center stage, and a simple platform bed rose up from beneath the stage floor to meet it. We shaped the stage picture such that Flora lay on the bed beneath the netting (her "Wendy house"), echoing the posture Anish describes in his father's final painting. Surrounding the image of the naked woman on the bed was our golden border, inscribed with details evoking Das' miniature. Painted in the corner of the wall was a tree and a green vine; this wall devolved to a deep shade of blue when Flora got into bed, and cutouts of a moon and birds appeared in the empty window frames. Thus, when we lit Flora's naked body gently through the netting, the audience instantly remembered a line in Flora's letter to Eleanor, first read by the biographer Eldon Pike: "perhaps my soul will stay behind as a smudge of paint on paper, as if I'd always been there, like Radha, the most beautiful of the herdswomen, undressed for love in an empty house."

What is so satisfying about the end of Act 1 as Stoppard has crafted it is that the moment is doubled in time: as Flora lies in her bed behind the netting in 1930, Anish (in present day Shepperton) hands Eleanor a watercolor nude. "Oh heavens!" Mrs. Swan exclaims, "Oh ... yes ... of course. How like Flora." By expanding the image of the miniature to fill the stage, we were able to immediately share the image that Eleanor is looking at, a beautifully painted vision of her naked sister, made fifty years earlier. This is where scenography contributes its own *rasa*, playing with scale and color such that a tiny image becomes a large theatrical gesture, and then magically disappears.

Having recreated Das' miniature as a complete "stage picture" in Act 1, it was easier to understand Flora's outburst of emotion when she was given the nude watercolor in Act 2; she feels she finally understands what *rasa* is. So potentially explosive is this tiny miniature that Anish has hesitated to give it to Eleanor. "She had a romance with my father," says Anish. Eleanor, in her usual pragmatic way, replies: "Quite possibly. Or with Captain Durance. Or His Highness the Rajah of Jummapur. Or someone else entirely. It hardly matters, looking back. Men were not really important to Flora. If they had been, they would have been fewer. She used them like batteries. When things went flat, she'd put in a new one." But in spite of her joking response, it is clear that this piece of art contains enormous significance both for Eleanor and Anish, so much so that that they refuse to hand it over to Eldon Pike. "If you decide to tell Mr. Pike about the watercolour, I'm sure Flora wouldn't mind," Eleanor tells Anish. To which he replies, "No. Thank you. But it's my father I'm thinking of. He really wouldn't want it, not even in a footnote. So we'll say nothing to Mr. Pike." Eleanor is delighted by this decision. "Good for you. I don't tell Mr. Pike everything either." The bond between Eleanor and Anish is movingly completed.

The secret of the erotic watercolor is one of the most delightful parts of the "game" of *Indian Ink*, deftly woven into both past and present plot lines and highlighting the misbegotten quest of the biographer, Eldon Pike, who *nearly* gets it right. Early on in the play, Eleanor has warned Pike, "biography is the worst possible excuse for getting people wrong." Pike correctly surmises that the "smudge of ink on paper" that Flora describes in her final letter to Eleanor is a nude watercolor, and he's determined to find it. First, he hopes Eleanor has it (which she does not, not yet), then he hopes perhaps he will find it in India. But when he visits the descendant of Flora's Rajah and is handed a thank you note Flora wrote the Rajah after having received the *Gita Govinda* print, he is deeply disappointed. In a fatal misjudgment, he assumes the nude referred to in that note is what he had hoped would be a watercolor nude of Flora. Thus, his quest is derailed. "It's like the Aspern Papers," Stoppard happily explained in rehearsal. "Pike is on the hunt for the nude painting and the Rajah's reference throws him off the scent. He mistakenly thinks he's been on a false trail, when in fact his instincts are right all along. But he never finds that out." Nothing pleases Stoppard more than derailing a biographer's quest for certainty by teasing and surprising the audience just when they think they know what is happening. As the

Junior Rajah gives Pike the copy of the *Gita Govinda*, Eleanor hands the "same" piece of paper to Anish; for our 2014 production, Stoppard streamlined the text so that these two events were absolutely back-to-back, and the audience got to witness Pike's confusion and Anish's clarity simultaneously. Anish explains: "From the *Gita Govinda*. Late eighteenth century, I think" and Eleanor avers, "It was in her suitcase." But it is not what Pike was looking for. That truth about the past has been judiciously hidden from his sight.

Indian Ink keeps revealing and concealing secrets as it progresses. As we rehearsed, what was most important to Stoppard was that the internal logic matched the external form. I began this chapter by saying that the impulse to write *In the Native State* came from an idea to write about a painter who was making a portrait of a poet while she was writing a poem about being painted. This may sound like a gimmick, but in discovering *rasa*, Stoppard put a name to something he was already exploring intuitively. The painter is in communion with the poet when she is writing a poem about being painted. Then one day, she shows up to be painted but instead of writing a poem, she writes a letter to her sister. Something is wrong. The sitter has changed. It is as if suddenly, one of the players is cheating at the agreed upon game. Das feels this instinctively—he is a good enough player to know.

In his notes after a run-through one day, Stoppard tried to parse the emotional details of the scene to Art Malik (who played Das in our 1998 production): "Something troubles Anish at the top of the scene but he doesn't know what it is, he just senses it. When he realizes that she's writing a letter, he doesn't know what to make of it—he feels upset without initially being able to articulate why." But we know why. Flora has taken a look at Das' oil painting when he was not looking and is disappointed by what she has seen: to her, the painting feels like Western knock-off, not like the "Indian" painting she had hoped it would be. So, she says nothing. Das guesses that she has looked at the painting. He takes her silence as disapproval and becomes distraught. His emotions confuse him; all he knows is that somehow she has broken the rules—the pact was that she write poetry and he paint her doing so. Stoppard thus reveals in real time what the absence of *rasa* actually *feels like*: when Flora becomes a woman writing a letter rather than a poet creating a poem, there is no *rasa* for Das to paint. This leads to an emotional break between them. "A letter?" he asks, distraught. "I am not the same sitter. How thoughtless of me," Flora quickly replies. They try to engage in conversation to cover over their discomfort, but it fails; they cannot understand each other. He wants an approbation that she withholds. "And all because I said nothing," Flora exclaims. "Are you at the mercy of every breeze that blows? Are you an artist at all?" In his humiliation, Das snatches the pencil sketch he has given Flora at their first meeting (Portrait 1) and tears it up. The argument escalates to a fight over the oil painting, until finally Flora has an attack, cannot continue, and retreats to her bed.

When Das and Flora finally speak about this again, she is lying naked under the netting, a very ill woman recovering from breathlessness.

The scene is extremely complex to play; once again we were wrestling with how to excavate subtext in Stoppard while preserving the external form of the language. In her frustration at trying to explain what she disliked about his painting, Flora says, "You're trying to paint me from my point of view instead of yours—what you *think* is my point of view. You deserve the bloody Empire!" To which Das replies (*sharply*): "May I sit down please?" Why does he say this "sharply"? we asked Stoppard in rehearsal. What is actually happening to the character in this moment? We watch Das sit, smoke, and seem to calm down. The conversation continues. Then Flora, innocently trying to make friends again, says cheerfully: "That's what I love about my little house—you can see out better than you can see in," and Das explodes. As we wrestled with this sequence of events in rehearsal, Stoppard spoke eloquently about his struggle to create a plausible emotional outburst for a character (Das) who is normally so reticent. The right language, he said, kept eluding him. In the 1998 version, Das' retort to Flora was, "But you are looking at such a house." In 2014, that line no longer seemed clear. But was it the line, or our playing of it?

Stoppard sat very patiently in San Francisco as Brenda Meaney (Flora) and Firdous Bamji (Das) tried to figure out how to match the image in the line with the emotional intention beneath it. One thing that became clear was that we were mistakenly looking for an evident dialectic between Flora and Das, an "even argument," if you will. But in this case, despite his love of argument, Stoppard explained that such directness was impossible. This man and woman come from such radically different cultures, they have no idea how to bridge their differences or heal their wounds. "Das doesn't have the confidence to be a peer arguer," Stoppard told us. "He's not someone who argues back. He watches. Thinks. Even when she attacks his authenticity." That was a helpful note and one the actors could play. Then, Stoppard explained, that stance suddenly changes. "She begins pontificating about his authenticity as if he's *chosen* it," Stoppard said. So when she makes the offhand comment about seeing out of her netting better than you can see in, he finally erupts. Stoppard paraphrased for us what Das is thinking: "I didn't choose my inauthenticity; you British came in and destroyed our tradition. The Empire finished off Indian painting! So now I'm a phony Western artist, because that's all I can be!" But all Das actually says is, "But you are looking at such a house!" The line had to carry a lot of freight. Stoppard's generous notes to the actors helped them internalize the minute transitions of the scene, but even then, Stoppard realized that the line was not landing. Sitting in his corner of the studio, devouring sweets and coffee, he rewrote that one line a dozen times over the course of rehearsal until he finally ended up with "You can see but you do not understand!" A simple change which put the burden of the problem back on Flora's own cultural myopia.

What I learned from this encounter was how subtle the interiority of Stoppard's characters can be. "I like Das putting his emotional energy into 'May I sit down,' where you least expect it, instead of an argument being batted across the net," Stoppard told me. He urged us to trust that sometimes a character is enraged without knowing why, or at least, without being able to articulate why. ("Which goes to show that people are surprising," Eleanor tells Anish.) For Stoppard, that feels more authentic, even though (as I noted in Chapter 3), American actors like to understand their characters' motivations and to clarify their behavior. But in Stoppard's universe, human beings are unpredictable and emotion comes where you least expect it, which is why he is loathe to over-explain.

An opposite kind of surprise occurs in the Anish–Eleanor scene in which she shows the young painter Das' oil portrait of Flora. Unlike his reticent father, Anish is worldly, articulate and self-confident; we do not expect him to ambush us with emotion. But as soon as Eleanor unfurls the painting and Anish sees it, he begins to weep. It does not matter that the painting is "garish" or incomplete; it is his father's hand, and he feels the connection instantly. When Eleanor sees Anish's genuine and deeply felt response, she quickly recants: "Yes, book jackets and biscuit tins are all very well, but obviously there's something that stays behind in the painting after all," she realizes. Stoppard loved that moment. "Anish recognizes it immediately as one of his father's works, and thus to him, it has *rasa*," he explained. Art is never objective, it is about how it communicates to a given viewer. The painting's emotional impact on Anish, fifty years later, is one of the most palpable examples of *rasa* in the play.

Because Stoppard trusts his audience to excavate the subtext and emotional undercurrents without their being pointed out, the director and actors have to help focus an audience's attention on little ripples or undercurrents that can be exposed. He was vociferous when rehearsing *Rock 'n' Roll* in London that Rufus Sewell not become "so highly emotional about England that what he was uttering became secondary to the passion."[1] A beautiful example of the relationship of restraint to surprise occurs in Act 2 of *Indian Ink*, when Captain Durance (the young English Resident who has fallen in love with Flora) takes her for a ride. As staged, the actors sit on high stools and imagine they are on horseback in the early morning mists in India. The dialogue is as follows:

Durance   Flora.

Flora   No.

Durance   Would you marry me?

Flora   No.

Durance   Would you think about it?

Flora   No. Thank you.

Durance Love at first sight, you see. Forgive me.

Flora Oh, David.

Durance Knees together.

Flora 'Fraid so.

What makes this exchange so acute is the surprise of the proposal coupled with both the setting in which it happens and the lack of sentiment with which it is made. Durance longs to consummate his feelings for Flora but (a) he is a British official and (b) he is on horseback next to a woman who does not know how to ride. The tension between his desires and the circumstance are what make the scene both moving and comic. There is not a single pause marked in the exchange, and Stoppard felt strongly that the whole terse proposal (and subsequent wry apology) be played straight through with no break. He assured us that the more masked the emotion and brisk the delivery, the more resonant the scene would be. But in our first outing of *Indian Ink* in 1998, our Durance wanted to make *sure* the audience understood the depths of his feelings for Flora and his despair in being rebuffed. Thus, during the first few previews, he freighted each exchange with a pause and a sigh, while Stoppard stood in the back of the theater shaking his head, longing to convince the actor to play the music as it was written. In fact, the only thing that kept Stoppard calm during rehearsals of that particular scene was to light a cigarette at the back of the house; occasionally an usher would appear in the darkness and say, "Sir, you can't smoke in here" to which he would reply "Yes, I know" with infinite charm, and then keep right on smoking.

Just as Pinter urged the actors in *The Birthday Party* not to carry the emotion of the previous scene too literally into a subsequent scene but to allow the next round of the boxing match to start afresh, Stoppard urged the actors in *Indian Ink* to avoid setting up the Flora/Das pairing as a love relationship from the start, but to let each scene between them have its own trajectory and quality. The play tricks the audience into believing that Durance is going to be the source of romance for Flora, and years later, Eleanor still believes that he might have been the one her sister had an affair with. Because Stoppard never wants to telegraph to the audience where he is heading, he insisted that it was neither useful nor interesting to *play* the Flora–Das love story too obviously from the beginning of the production. Keep the audience guessing, he insisted. It took a lot of vigilance not to "signal" too much in the early parts of the play.

As I noted with regards to Pinter's work, actors (particularly American actors) often try to construct a clear "arc of experience" that moves inexorably and clearly toward the climax. But for both Pinter and Stoppard, it is a richer theatrical experience when one beat or mood is not carried over to the next but invites a third thing to happen. Since life, in their view, rarely follows a linear emotional path, why should theater? Or as Stoppard himself put it, in a letter to me regarding a question about *Arcadia*: "It's not *tidy*; it's more like life or incompetent playwriting, which resemble each other, luckily." Resisting tidiness and searching for surprises became important "rules of play" in my encounters with Stoppard's work.

The initial instinct of the actors playing Flora and Das was, as I said, to begin the play by carefully planting the seeds of their future romance, so that the audience would be prepared to look for clues and watch the affair evolve. But this negates the delicious reversal that erupts at the end of the play. Over the course of the story, as Flora writes poetry on her verandah, Das paints her. His first attempt is, in her eyes, a garish imitation of Western painting that disappoints her terribly. (In rehearsal, however, Stoppard was quick to point out that Flora's and Eleanor's evaluation of the painting is not necessarily to be taken at face value. "Eleanor reaches for a comparison that makes sense to her—'a Technicolor cinema poster,'" he explained, "but that doesn't mean it was bad, only that it was westernized and not at all what either sister expected.") Das cannot understand Flora's attitude to the painting—she accuses him of not being "true" to his Indian self, without understanding that the Empire has robbed Indian painters of their own traditions and substituted British values that are not their own. Ultimately, after a tussle that becomes a physical fight and leaves Flora breathless and ill, Das begins to paint her a second time. His completely private feelings for Flora, which are profound, allow him to paint the delicate miniature which becomes such a crucial plot point in the play. But in making this moving representation of Flora, he has no expectation of having what Eldon Pike later calls "a relationship" with her.

In fact, Flora, who up until this point has felt no more than compassion for Das, falls in love with him the instant she sees this second painting.

Flora   It's going to be a drawing, isn't it?

Das (*nervous, bright*)   Yes! A good joke, is it not? A Rajput miniature, by Nirad Das!

Flora (*not heeding him*)   Oh . . . it's the most beautiful thing . . .

Das (*brightly*)   I'm so pleased you like it! A quite witty pastiche.

Flora (*heeding him now*)   Are you going to be Indian? Please don't.

Das (*heeding her*)   I . . . I am Indian.

Flora   An Indian artist.

Das   Yes.

Flora   Yes. This one is for yourself.

Stoppard urged the actors not to get ahead of this moment or to signal in any way that it was coming. "Das has a completely private feeling for Flora which enables him to paint the picture he paints," Stoppard commented in rehearsal. "But he has absolutely no expectations of sleeping with her, it is just a fantasy. Flora falls in love with him the moment she sees the painting and not before—it is then she invites him into her bed. There is nothing leading up to that moment that would suggest this is going to happen, in fact the contrary." Stoppard made it clear that the audience's point of view needed to be aligned with Eleanor's, for whom such an idea was (until she met Anish) inconceivable. It is impossible, and then, in an instant, it becomes possible, in a way that only the theater can truly imagine. Did it really happen, the night of lovemaking between Flora and Das? Or did it not? Was her lover perhaps not Das but Durance? Or even the Rajah? In Stoppard's work, there are wonderful moments when something unthinkable suddenly becomes real.

Indian Ink is a delicate play to pull off, and in New York we had numerous challenges, from temperamental actors to a technical crew that was overstretched to props that failed to do their job. One evening, as we got to the stunning moment in which Eleanor begins to remember the beloved fruit trees from her life in India ("Orchards of apricots—almond—plum—I never cared for the southern fruits, mango, pawpaw and such like. But up in the North West . . . I was quite unprepared for it when I first arrived. It was early summer. There was a wind blowing. And I have never seen such blossom"), disaster struck. The design called for delicate white blossoms to rain down around Eleanor and carry us all the way back in time to her first encounter with India and her meeting with Eric, with whom she fell instantly in love. Instead, huge white objects began to crash down from the flies like snowballs, narrowly missing the head of Rosemarie Harris as she stood center stage delivering her beautiful speech. Evidently, the petals had not been separated properly in the scene shop and had, instead, adhered to the glue. Our blossom bombs attacked the stage like weapons, miraculously sparing Harris as they bounced off the stage floor.

Once we moved past that crisis, all was going well until we got to the middle of Act 2, when Dilip appeared with the jacket he had procured for his friend, biographer Eldon Pike, to gain him entry to the Jummapur Club. Just as with the extreme specificity required of Pinter's props, this garment demanded a precise and poignant visual form, and alas, our store-bought jacket failed the test. The costume needed to function as a conduit to secrets of the past; it belonged to an old man who worked in the cloakroom of the Jummapur Club and who remembered that, as a small boy many years before, he had witnessed a naked English lady (Flora) fall ill under her mosquito netting. The jacket thus had to hold, inside its unprepossessing shape, the promise of a major discovery for Pike and his biography. Indeed, as soon as Pike sees it, he wants to dash into the cloakroom and interview the old man immediately, in case he should die while Dilip and Pike are at dinner. In order to help, Stoppard explained to costume designer Candice Donnelly that the jacket should be "crummy and limp and sad, but ostentatious," a wonderful revelation of the way an article of clothing can provide intricacies of character and a specific moment in history. Donnelly understood. She had very much wanted to build the costume from scratch so as to achieve the necessary effect, but since the jacket was only on stage for a short time, it had not merited the expenditure. Donnelly did everything she could to "distress" our store-bought jacket and give it some character, but it never quite became that symbol of faded prestige and lost formality that Stoppard held in his imagination. As with Pinter, Stoppardian magic only truly works when the magician's tools are precisely attended to.

After many long nights of tech and two weeks of previews in New York, we were able to successfully realize our vision of *Indian Ink*, and by the time the production arrived at A.C.T. we felt satisfied that we had finally achieved the degree of *rasa* we had hoped for. To salute the hilarious and often complicated struggles we went through during those long rehearsals of, and revisions to, the play, on opening night Stoppard gave me a set of Indian prints which looked as if they came from an old collection, perhaps something he had found on Tottenham Court Road while searching through bins of used books. Taken together, they were like a *rasa*-filled comic book version of our rehearsal process for *Indian Ink*. The first image was of a determined woman with her arms raised over her head, holding an unsheathed scimitar in her hands; the inscription read, "Carey—How I see you, with love from Tom." Each subsequent print came accompanied by a Stoppardian witticism or pun: a man leaning over a woman and holding a bloody knife was identified as "Critic," while an exhausted woman collapsed on the sand was labelled "The Board Meets," in remembrance of the difficult days in rehearsal when I had to leave the studio to attend a board meeting and commit to raising yet more money on behalf of the work. A sleeping turbaned man with a genie floating above him had a thought bubble affixed with the words, "Maybe if I Fired Him," perhaps a sly reference to the actor of many pauses. A double image of a woman behind bars and one lying on a bed of tears was called "Box Office" and "Admin," while a woman lying on her stomach with her head in her hands and a frustrated look on her face was called, "Waiting for the Director." Two figures floating against a canopy of deep blue star-studded skies was appropriately described as "A Higher Stage of Development," in honor of Coomaraswami, Stoppard's cheerful existentialist in *Indian Ink*. The last image was my favorite—a woman standing on a swirling bed of sand, stars shining above, her eyes closed, her arms framing her head, looking up and imagining. Stoppard called this one "A Moment of Optimism."

The set of annotated drawings captured everything Stoppard knew and loved about the impossible process of making theater, a process so memorably described in *Shakespeare in Love* by the theater manager Henslowe: "Let me explain about the theatre business. The natural condition is one of insurmountable obstacles on the road to imminent disaster. One must never expect a manuscript at this stage. That is an impediment to look forward to. But it always works out in the end . . . It's a mystery." Stoppard's ongoing wonder at the impossibility of getting a play "right" coupled with his insatiable desire to do so makes him a vigorous and inspiring collaborator. One always has the sense with Stoppard that everyone is "in it" together and that at any moment, someone might come up with the solution that solves the moment that solves the evening. Again, collaboration is all. One must keep hoping for "a moment of optimism" in a landscape of pessimism.

It was during rehearsals for the Roundabout production of *Indian Ink* in 2014 that I lost my brilliant and beloved father Joseph Perloff. He had been ill for some months, and I had spent "days off" from rehearsals in New York flying back to Los Angeles to see him one last time. Rosemarie Harris was aware of my situation and deeply sympathetic, as her own spouse John was going through a similar precipitous decline. I remember sitting with Rosemarie on stage during tech rehearsals of *Indian Ink*, the night of August 19, right after my father had died. "There are nine *rasa*, each one a different color. I should say mood. But each mood has its color," Das was explaining, "white for laughter and fun, red for anger, pale yellow for tranquility." "Oh . . . is there one for grey?" we heard Flora ask Das. Rosemarie reached out and took my hand. "Grey is for sorrow," replied Das.

6

From 9/11 to the Recession:

Pinter's Terror and the Collapse of Certainty in *Celebration*, *The Room*, and *The Homecoming*

If *Indian Ink* in New York coincided with a period of personal loss for me, the American premiere of the one-act double bill of Pinter's *Celebration* and *The Room* at A.C.T. opened at a moment of immense national loss in the United States. Our plan had been to mount this production as a celebration not only of my ten years at A.C.T. but of Harold Pinter's extraordinary life and career in the theater; he was looking forward to joining us in San Francisco with his wife Antonia Fraser for the opening and to participate in an evening of conversation about his work. The first preview of the two one-acts was set for September 13, 2001.

And then came 9/11. By the time those of us in California awakened on that day, the first of the Twin Towers had already collapsed and the south tower was headed for the same destruction. I was horrified to realize that I had been scheduled to be on a plane from Washington D.C. back to San Francisco on September 11, having agreed to sit on a new-play panel at the Kennedy Center on my day off from Pinter rehearsals, which I canceled at the last minute because we had to replace an actor in the show. Grateful that I was safe in San Francisco, I spent the day with the rest of the company calling friends, colleagues, and family in New York, as we tried to wrap our heads around the scale of the disaster. We listened to Mayor Giuliani speak from Ground Zero and to President Bush vow swift retaliation against the perpetrators. Shortly afterwards, Pinter sent me a letter in which he apologized profusely for not being able to join us for the production, but explained,

The atrocities last week were totally appalling and I am aware of the depth of suffering—on the part of many people—which will never go away. But I am very concerned about the gung-ho rhetoric which has ensued at government level. As you know, I've always been highly critical of the US government's policy and actions. My presence in the US—in the present climate—would seem to me to be a very odd presence indeed. I think it would be hypocritical, impossible to sustain.

Pinter's stance was consistent and clear; he could in no way square his antipathy toward President Bush's foreign policy with a visit to America to participate in the production of one of his plays. I admired his fierce lack of hypocrisy and appreciated his ongoing kindness to the company, all the while mourning the loss of an opportunity to explore his work together. Meanwhile, we had to decide what to do about the production: was it appropriate to continue? Would anyone choose to go to the theater in the wake of that tragedy? And if so, how might an audience feel seeing two such unsettling plays? Ultimately, we were too far along with the work and too committed to the project to turn back, so we plowed ahead and held the first preview on September 13 as planned. I gave a brief curtain speech to welcome everyone and to acknowledge the fraught atmosphere in which we were all about to share this piece of theater. I remember standing on the lip of the stage, asking each audience member to look down the row they were sitting in and take a moment to acknowledge the people around them, to recognize that although we were perhaps strangers to each other, we had all gathered because we had evidently decided that being together was better than being apart. And then *The Room* began. Pinter's unquenchable courage, ferocity, humanity, and humor filled the Geary from the first words spoken: "Here you are. This will keep the cold out." Which is exactly what the play did. For those of us who were there, whether in the audience or onstage, that evening was an unforgettable experience, reaffirming our belief that live theater still had the power to *matter* at the most fractured and difficult of times.

I should begin with a brief explanation about the nature of the evening. Pinter had written a new one-act, *Celebration*, in 2000; it is a savage farce about two "masters of the universe" who take their wives to a celebration dinner at a trendy contemporary restaurant, where one of the employees is a literary Waiter fond of making surreal interjections about his family. When Pinter himself staged the premiere for the Almeida Theatre in London in March 2000, he decided to pair it with his first play, *The Room* (1957), which gave audiences a rare opportunity to watch the evolution of Pinter's work and to see how the early themes of isolation, violence, paranoia, and the power of food played out forty-four years later.

My own connection to the work came about over lunch with the playwright the following spring. Approaching the end of my first decade at A.C.T. (which filled me with both pleasure and a certain degree of apprehension, as anniversaries always do), I was in the midst of setting the slate of plays for the 2001/2 season, which also marked A.C.T.'s thirty-fifth year in San Francisco. On a warm London day, Pinter and I met for lunch at

La Caprice. Within five minutes of sitting down, he said, "I have a play for you to read, and it's called *Celebration*." Since I had missed its London debut, Pinter described it to me with great relish, quoting whole swaths of dialogue by heart as we ate and drank our way through a very fine meal. His delight in sharing the scabrous world of the play with me was infectious; it was as if he were describing people he had actually met rather than characters he had recently invented. When I asked what he thought these characters should *sound* like, he quickly replied, "I don't know what you'd call their particular accent, but I do know they all enjoy words and using words, they love it, and that's it." Then he grinned. "One also has to remember, of course, and this is all a question of balance and degree, that they're all very drunk." As I sat listening to him revel in the crudity and beauty of his new characters' speech, I asked him a question about the fantasy-spinning Waiter who interrupts the action in *Celebration* with wild disquisitions about his grandfather's exotic life. "Is he making it all up?" I asked. "I think he is," Pinter replied. "He's a wonderful improviser, isn't he? But I think the crucial point is that the Waiter himself is in love with literature."

That moved me enormously, coming from the mouth of a man for whom literature was a key to salvation. Pinter and I covered a great deal of ground during that lunch, from politics to plays and back, but one thing was viscerally clear: at the age of seventy, Pinter still found words fascinating, surprising, dangerous, elusive. "I once sat next to Ralph Richardson's wife at a dinner," he related with glee. "She had wonderful stories about Vivien Leigh. At one point she lowered her voice and said to me, 'You know that Vivien was very interested in sex.' And I was stopped dead by that use of the word 'interested.' Interested in what way? What did it mean? I used the word just as I'd heard it in *Celebration*." (Sonia, the hostess, says, "Yes, it's funny you should say that. I met a man from Morocco once and he was very interested in sex.") Pinter's visceral love of language and hunger for the creative act was moving to witness, particularly since he was a writer who had often suffered from the paralysis of *not* being able to write. I was reminded of a comment he had made years before to Mel Gussow: "Writing for me is an act of freedom and celebration. Whatever I'm writing about, it's a celebration. What you're celebrating is the ability to write. There's an excitement about it that certainly transcends anything you might have been doing before. It takes you way out into another country."[1]

Sure enough, when I took the script back to my hotel and read it, I was struck by its vitality and appetite; this was the work of a writer filled with the desire to create, to express, to relish the possibilities of theater again. *Celebration* is a study of violence, greed, and sexual predation in the elegant world of global finance; it is also, like *The Room*, about the longing for intimacy and the search for home in a hostile and dangerous world. And it is extremely funny.

I committed without hesitation to opening A.C.T.'s 2001 season with the double bill of *Celebration* and *The Room*, drawn to the idea not only because presenting an early Pinter with a brand-new Pinter felt so congruous with my own tenure at A.C.T., but because this gave me an opportunity to celebrate my newly-formed Core Company of actors. Versatility and transformation have always been the qualities I admire most in an actor; my first experience with Pinter at CSC had also involved creating a "rep company" in which six actors played radically different kinds of roles in two plays, so this felt like a kind of homecoming for me. I remembered how fascinating it was for CSC's audience, so many years before, to witness the silent and frightened Elderly Woman at a political prison (Jean Stapleton) turn into the ebullient and loquacious Meg in *The Birthday Party*, and conversely to experience the aggression and viciousness of David Strathairn's Sergeant morph into the beaten-down despair of Stanley; that "rep" had been a true celebration of the transformative power of theater. One aspect of A.C.T. that most appealed to me was that William Ball had founded it to support a permanent and highly trained acting company, an ensemble that made a great impression upon me when, as an undergraduate at Stanford in the late 1970s, I had witnessed A.C.T.'s work in action. Although by the time I arrived as Artistic Director in 1992, the Loma Prieta earthquake had destroyed not only the Geary Theater but the resources necessary to sustain a company, I continued to believe that audiences develop the deepest appreciation for how the art of acting actually *works* when they get to watch an ensemble of actors transform and perform multiple roles across a season. Sadly, the American theater has all but abandoned this idea; for the most part, actors are (in the words of Arena Stage founder Zelda Fichandler) "piece-workers" jobbed in for a given production and then released back into the world of unemployment.

Nevertheless, by the millennium I had decided it was time to initiate the beginnings of a new company at A.C.T. I thus made a long-term commitment to four transformative actors from diverse backgrounds capable of performing a wide variety of work: they were Marco Barricelli, Rene Augesen, Steven Anthony Jones, and Gregory Wallace. I paid them for fifty-two weeks of the year and gave them as much visibility and creative control as possible. In subsequent years the company expanded, and for a decade my commitment remained steadfast: to give actors a central role in the decision-making of a major theater, advising on repertoire and artistic policy, teaching and directing in the Conservatory as well as playing large and small roles on stage and engaging regularly with our audience. Pinter, being a veteran of rep, was especially enthused about the idea of this ensemble because he knew what it could offer both actors and audience. Indeed, having just directed the rep of *Celebration* and *The Room* himself, he regaled me with stories about his tricks of transformation for that production, such as launching the evening with the beautiful Lindsay Duncan in a shapeless turban for her portrayal of Rose; beneath the turban were curlers that came off at the interval to reveal a glorious head of blonde curls for Prue in *Celebration*. This sleight of hand pleased him; he admired the virtuosity that allowed an actor to fully inhabit a role and then to turn on a dime and play someone completely different. After all, he had done it himself, many times.

Pairing *The Room* and *Celebration* proved to be a thrilling challenge for the actors because the tone and circumstances of the two plays are so different: *The Room* is about poor people barely eking out a living in rented rooms in London, *Celebration* is about rich businesspeople at a fancy restaurant celebrating an anniversary. The tone of *The Room* is desperate, fierce, and quiet, while *Celebration* is outrageous, aggressive, and loud. But ultimately, both plays are about terror, exposure, and the attempt at dominance. And, equally importantly, about love, family, and friendship. It turned out that when placed side by side, the two plays illuminated each other beautifully, just as we had found all those years before when we paired *The Birthday Party* and *Mountain Language*. Because the set requirements of two plays in rep were complex, the focus on precision and spareness which Pinter's world always demanded became even more crucial.

The evening opened with *The Room*, which Pinter had written in 1956 at the request of his best friend, Henry Woolf. At the time, Woolf had been doing a post-graduate year at Bristol University's recently founded Drama Department, and was looking for one-acts for the students to perform. Woolf remembered Pinter telling him he had had an idea for a play, based on a surreal event he could not get out of his mind: while performing in rep in Colchester, Pinter had gone to a party in a large house in Chelsea and was invited upstairs, where he discovered a

> little man with the most extraordinary colour hair, bare feet and extremely fluid clothes. . . . He welcomed us in, gave us a cup of tea . . . And all the while at the table sat an enormous man with a cap on reading a comic. The little chap was dancing about cutting bread and butter, pouring tea and making bacon and eggs for this man who remained quite silent through the whole encounter. . . . We left after about half an hour and I asked the woman what the little chap's name was and she said Quentin Crisp.[2]

In *The Room*, that loquacious man became a woman; Pinter proceeded to write the play in four days in November 1956 (while performing in Terrence Rattigan's *Separate Tables*) and it was staged in May 1957 in Bristol. The budget was four and sixpence. It was subsequently remounted for a student drama festival at which Harold Hobson was in attendance, and his enthusiasm decisively launched Pinter's playwriting career.

This early play is already characteristic Pinter, taking place in a claustrophobic space occupied by a recluse named Rose (Pinter's mother's name) who lives with an uncommunicative man named Bert. Over the course of the play, we gather that Rose is in hiding from her own past; her terror seems located, metaphorically or literally, in the basement of the house where a silent figure lurks. When Rose's husband goes off in his van after having been fed bacon and eggs by his devoted wife, there is a moment of peace before the inevitable "knock on the door." First comes her landlord, Mr. Kidd, followed by a couple, Mr. and Mrs. Sands, who are looking for a room to rent. Rose becomes more and more terrified of being evicted from her cocoon until, at the climax of the play, Mr. Kidd brings in a large blind Black man whom he says has been in the basement waiting to speak to her all weekend. "My name is Riley," the man announces. Quickly Rose contradicts him: "I don't care if its—what? That's not your name. That's not your name."

The anxiety of buried identity discussed in Chapter 1 emerges in full force here. "Your father wants you to come home," Riley insists. There is a pause before Rose says, "Home?" The vulnerability of that question hangs in the air until Riley urges, "Come home, Sal." Initially Rose denies that Sal is her name, but as Riley repeats it, she begins to acknowledge the truth: "The day is a hump. I never go out." Finally, with a kind of deep familial connection, Rose touches Riley's eyes, the back of his head, and his temples. That ritual is tragically violated by Bert, who bursts back into the room, speaking for the first time, describing his experience driving the van through the icy weather as if it has been a particularly violent act of sex ("I drove her down, hard"). Bert sits beside Riley. Then, in a final gesture of wanton aggression, he tips the Black man off the chair and kicks him in the head until he stops moving. The play ends with Rose covering her eyes and moaning, "Can't see. I can't see. I can't see."

There were many tropes in *The Room* which were familiar to me from *The Birthday Party* and deeply resonant to explore. The fundamental acts of standing, sitting, crossing, looking, became dangerous acts in that constricted space. Rose, like Stanley, lives in terror of being "found out" and ejected from the fortress that is her room; she is guilty of a nameless crime that makes her vulnerable and afraid. This time, I knew better than to spend the rehearsal period trying to figure out Rose's literal biography. Instead, we anatomized her concrete behavior: the obsessive caretaking of Bert, the endless chatter to cover up the fear of silence, darkness, and cold that hovered menacingly outside the window. Rose's behavior requires the kind of choreography that will characterize Pinter's subsequent work, as every move of Rose's and every response of Bert's is calculated to raise the stakes of their tense relationship and to expose his power and her extreme need. The timing of the food service needed such precision that we decided to hold daily prop and cooking rehearsals, just as we did for the breakfast scene of *The Birthday Party*, to drill the making, serving, and clearing up of food so that the actions timed out cleanly with the requirements of the text.

What is remarkable about the first section of the play is Pinter's deployment of *silence* and *stillness*. Rose never stops chattering away, while Bert says nothing. She rushes back and forth from the stove to the table, from the window to the door, while he does not move a muscle except to turn the page of his comic and eat his eggs. Rose feeds him, flatters him, pleads with him, warns him, confides in him, flirts with him, and apologizes to him, but gets not a word or a move back. Thus, when Bert suddenly stands up, the event feels seismic, made all the more dramatic in our production by the size of Marco Barricelli, our Bert. We saw him tower above Rose as she fixed his muffler, and then suddenly he was gone. The thing Rose was most terrified about had happened: she was alone.

Pinter's visual imagery in *The Room* is potent and precise; there is no random movement in the play, everything is sculptural and calculated for maximum effect. The one escape route is a door, center stage, which becomes the locus of Rose's terror. When she opens the door to empty her waste bin, she suddenly encounters two figures standing and facing her. Who are they? What are they doing outside her door? When Diane Venora as Rose gasped to see them, that 9/11 audience gasped with her. When she described the terrifying hidden zones of the house (the damp basement, the dark corridors, the mysterious empty rooms), the audience understood that the house was a war zone that required acute vigilance. What had been abstract in 1957 felt completely recognizable by 2001, so much so that a quote from the Polish theater critic Jan Kott came back into my mind: "In Poland, when we want fantasy we do Brecht," he said after the war, "and when we want realism, we do Beckett." After 9/11, *The Room* felt like realism.

During the first outing of the play in 1956, many theories circulated about what it signified and, in particular, how to interpret the character and behavior of Riley. Was he a figure of Christian salvation coming to rescue Rose? Or a primal force that had escaped from the dark confines of the basement to destroy her? When I met with Pinter in New York to discuss the play prior to rehearsals, I asked whether he still believed, as he had said years before, that Riley was Rose's liberator, arriving to release her from her imprisonment with Bert. "I don't want to make any great claims about Riley," he replied. "Riley is Riley. I prefer to keep it on a very concrete level. Riley comes in and says, 'Your father wants you to come home,' and calls her by a name, 'Sal,' that clearly was once hers, that strikes a very profound chord in her that she finds irresistible. I think releasing her from imprisonment is right, but it's an imprisonment *she doesn't know she's enduring.*" As always with Pinter's notes, I found that one extremely useful: we were back to the trope of "forgetting" or "not knowing" that Pinter had stressed with *The Birthday Party* and that encouraged an actor to operate entirely in the present tense. When Riley enters the room, Rose is as shocked and confused as the audience is. Who is this man? Why is he calling her by another name? The less we have been "prepared" for this moment, the more startling it becomes. We did not need to answer literal biographical questions in rehearsal to understand that Riley triggers in Rose a memory of a crucial time in her life that has been buried; when that memory is triggered by the name "Sal," it erupts with full force.

In a similar vein, Pinter believed that the actress playing Rose should commit wholeheartedly to her desire to please Bert without being conscious that her marriage was a form of domestic terrorism. Never anticipate disaster, he urged. Let it simply arrive at the door. He reminded us that the experience of rehearsing the play echoed his own process of writing it: once he had established the primary image, he himself never knew who was going to arrive to upset the equilibrium, so why should the actors know? That sense of palpable surprise is what gives Pinter's work such vitality; when the present tense of the audience and the present tense of the actors is one and the same, the collective experience can be electrifying.

By the time I staged *The Room* in 2001, I had known Pinter for over a decade, and it felt evident that this was a highly personal piece of writing. Despite its elusive setting and often surreal dialogue, at its core the play is about the emotional freight of *family*. It is interesting to note that some six weeks before writing the play, Pinter had married Vivien Merchant, an event which shocked and upset his Jewish parents. Pinter's attachment to his own family was fierce; his parents had already persuaded him not to wed Pauline Flannigan, an Irish-Catholic girlfriend whom he brought home after performing a season of rep together. Now he had done something much more transgressive: on an impulse he had gone to a registry office and married a non-Jewish girl, and, even worse, he had accidentally done it on Yom Kippur. Pinter's guilt at this familial betrayal must have been considerable. His parents were not in attendance at the wedding of their only child. It is possible that Riley's exhortation to "come home" echoed a refrain Pinter heard in his own mind after having married "outside the tribe." The loss of family is a theme that runs throughout Pinter's work; in *Mountain Language*, the elderly mother repeatedly tells her son that "the baby's waiting for you, we're all waiting for you," but it is clear that the father will never see his child, just as in *Moonlight* a mother calls her sons to urge them to come home and see their dying father, but to no avail. The exhortation to "come home" has a profound effect upon Rose at the end of *The Room*; Bert intuits a change in her emotional state as soon as he returns. In fact, one could argue that Bert destroys Riley in order to kill off any possibility of Rose returning to her previous life. No wonder she "can't see" at the end of the play.

On a sociological level, *The Room* makes visible the anxiety, poverty, and racism of post-war Britain in a way that was rare in the drama of the period but that feels extremely resonant today. Rationing was still in effect when the play premiered, and many people did not have enough heat or food. If Jews were victims of widespread aggression during this period, Blacks were even worse off. Post-war England saw a major influx of West Indians, Pakistanis, Indians, and West Africans, many of whom had fought for the British during the war; often, the only form of survival for the poor was to find someone lower on the social rung to put down. The metaphor of seeing and blindness is deeply connected with the myopia of xenophobia prevalent in British post-war culture and the difficulty of "seeing" beyond one's own four walls. Pinter will raise this theme again in *The Caretaker*, in which Davies tries to assert his status as an "Englishman" by doing "foreigners"

FIGURE 10 *Steven Anthony Jones and Marco Barricelli in* The Room, *A.C.T. 2011. Scenery by Loy Arcenas, Lighting by Peter Maradudin, Costumes by Deborah Dryden. Photo courtesy of Kevin Berne.*

out of jobs: "What they want to do, they're trying to do away with these foreigners, you see, in catering," he explains to Aston. "They want an Englishman to pour their tea, that's what they want, that's what they're crying out for." Such is the racism borne out of a fear of being "replaced" or erased. Critics initially considered *The Room* an abstract play, but to many oppressed people living in Britain, it might have felt very true.

The language of this epic one-act is startling. As noted in Chapter 1, Pinter had discovered, with his very first play, something characteristic about natural human speech that most writers rarely address, namely that it is full of *non sequiturs* and digressions. This renders communication not only difficult but often hilarious. "I think my mum was a Jewess. Yes, I wouldn't be surprised to learn that she was a Jewess. She didn't have many babies," says Mr. Kidd. He claims his sister had a resemblance to his old mum. "When did she die then, your sister?" Rose asks. "Yes, that's right, it was after she died that I stopped counting," Kidd responds irrelevantly. The more Rose asks her landlord specific questions, like "How many floors you got in this house?", the more peculiar his replies become. "Floors" (*he laughs*). "Ah, we had a good few of them in the old days." Mr. Kidd unleashes memories which are contradictory and bizarre to Rose ("She had a lovely boudoir"), and the results are unsettlingly funny. The arrival of two strangers aptly named Mr. and Mrs. Sands, like the arrival of Goldberg and McCann in *The Birthday Party*, unnerves Rose completely—they engage in status games of sitting and standing that will re-emerge with full comic force in later Pinter (MRS. SANDS: "You're sitting down!" MR. SANDS (*jumping up*): "Who is?" MRS. SANDS: "You were." MR. SANDS: Don't be silly, I perched.") as they warn Rose that the landlord indicated a vacancy in room number seven, Rose's room. The precise and forensic use of the *pause* is already in evidence here as well: when Rose hears "number seven" there is a crucial pause as she takes in this enormous threat. Only then does she manage to utter, "That's this room." The play ends with an act of gratuitous violence that makes manifest what is suggested in *The Birthday Party* with the snapping of Stanley's glasses and the breaking of his mind. For all of these reasons, it was a revelation to work on *The Room* in light of what I had learned from working on Pinter's later work. Every seed was there.

Even from a distance, Pinter was very engaged with our pre-production work on *Celebration* and *The Room* at A.C.T. He worked closely with me to determine how the evening should be cast; Pinter was always interested in providing actors the chance to move quickly from dominance to submission and back, a transformative requirement for any Pinter play but particularly necessary when performing in rep. Selecting actors for *Celebration* and *The Room* reminded me again that casting Pinter's work is like putting together a sports team: one must find players of equal talent but distinctive voices, capable of sustaining a ferocious and often highly contained energy with precision, panache, and complete concentration. The doubling of roles was handled somewhat differently in our production than in his. While the actresses playing Rose and Prue (Diane Venora) and Mrs. Sands and Suki (Rene Augesen) doubled exactly as had Lindsay Duncan and Lia Williams in Pinter's production, we decided to assign the male roles in different combinations. Thus, the large powerful Marco Barricelli (who would go on to play a terrifying McCann in *The Birthday Party* in 2018) played the hulking Bert and then the nasty sidekick Matt, while Peter Riegert (of Goldberg fame) carried Mr. Kidd (a role full of Jewish locutions, given to Pinter's childhood friend Henry Woolf in London) as well as Lambert, obnoxious host of the dinner in *Celebration*. Pinter liked the "scale" of the actors: Marco's size made for a formidable Bert, and then there was something comic about him playing the "second banana" to Peter Riegert's vicious but much physically smaller Lambert. Anthony Fusco, a future company member, had the opportunity to play both the hen-pecked Mr. Sands and the supremely suave restaurant owner Richard, an interesting study in contrasts.

But the most important piece of casting for the A.C.T. production was Gregory Wallace as the Waiter. Gregory had been part of A.C.T.'s creative

FIGURE 11 *Gregory Wallace in rehearsal for* Celebration *(above) and* Waiting for Godot *(below), A.C.T. 2011 and 2003. Photos courtesy of Kevin Berne.*

life since his starring role as Belize in *Angels in America* in 1994; a Black actor of consummate linguistic skills and with a great love for physical comedy (he subsequently played a memorable Estragon in *Waiting for Godot* at A.C.T.), Gregory turned the Waiter into the beating heart of *Celebration*. His presence in that play meant that each of the two one-acts was anchored by an African-American: Gregory in *Celebration*, and Steven Anthony Jones, who had led A.C.T.'s work for decades before I had even arrived at A.C.T., as Riley in *The Room*. (It was that performance that inspired me years later to cast him as Charon the Ferryman at the River Styx in Stoppard's *The Invention of Love*.) This helped ground the work in our own immediate universe.

After the terrifying final moments of *The Room* on that night of September 13, 2001 came a much-needed intermission, and when the audience returned, they were welcomed into the spare but supremely elegant dining room of

Celebration, where we saw two banquettes side by side, one occupied by four people and one by a couple. Although the setting is upscale, Pinter had created a scenography of imprisonment parallel to that of *The Room*. In *Celebration*, the characters are trapped in their restaurant banquettes like Beckett characters in an urn, forced to confront each other in close quarters and to mitigate the extreme tension of their entrapment by the use of violent language and excessive alcohol consumption. Like *The Room*, *Celebration* begins with food, but instead of the bacon, fried eggs, and toast which Rose offers Bert, the cuisine has become decidedly *haute*: "Who's having the duck?" asks the Waiter. "The duck's for me," asserts Lambert, instantly claiming control of the table ("Table One") in spite of the fact that the duck is not actually for him.

With this first line, I was reminded of a disquisition Pinter had given the cast after the first read-through of *Mountain Language* in New York, explaining with great relish that the word "fuck" is one of the most valuable in the English language, demanding of the actor a wide-open mouth for the vowel and then a satisfying plosive "k" which rendered the word both violent and sonically pleasing. Pinter deployed the word "fuck" in increasingly violent ways in later plays such as *One for the Road*: the torturer Nicolas asks his victim, Victor, "Does she . . . fuck? Or does she . . .? Or does she . . . like . . . you know . . . what? What does she like? I'm talking about your wife. Your *wife*. (*pause*) You know the old joke? Does she fuck? (*heavily, in another voice*): Does she fuck!" The word becomes more terrifying with each repetition.

But *Celebration* is a comedy, so it begins not with "fuck" but with the equally suggestive but initially more palatable "duck." When Lambert asserts that "the duck's for me," his wife Julie contradicts him ("No it isn't") and the power games begin. Scene 1 is an obscene riff on food as weapon: LAMBERT: "Well I knew Osso was Italian but I know bugger all about Bucco." MATT: "I didn't know arsehole was Italian." LAMBERT: "Yes, but on the other hand what's the Italian for arsehole?" Within the first moments of *Celebration*, it becomes clear that food is no longer the source of sustenance and human connection that it is for Meg with her cornflakes or Rose with her bacon. It has become a way to demonstrate the power and superiority of those who can pay. For these characters, money is the sole determinant of human value: as Suki (the plump ex-secretary at the next table) says, "I mean, listen, I want you to be rich, believe me, I want you to be rich so that you can buy me houses and panties and I'll know you really love me." Her husband Russell (at "Table Two"), desperate for approbation, sinks further and further into anxiety as Suki, while professing to love him, uses a language of blatant sexuality to negate any real emotional connection between them. "I would never do all those things now I'm a grown-up woman and not a silly young thing, a silly and dizzy young girl, such a naughty, saucy, flirty, giggly young thing, sometimes I could hardly walk from one filing cabinet to another I was so excited."

As in *Old Times* and *The Homecoming*, the language of seduction becomes the language of power, particularly potent in the hands of a woman who must deploy all the verbal tools she can muster since she is trapped physically inside a banquette. (Rene Augesen's luscious and charismatic Suki was in some ways a practice run for her Ruth in *The Homecoming* in 2008.) The notion of "intimacy" in *Celebration* disappears inside a lexicon of cliché: "You can ask me absolutely anything you like," says the *maitresse d'hotel*, while revealing absolutely nothing. "You really want me to tell you? You're not being insincere?" Russell asks his wife, in reference to his mother's cooking. "Darling. Give me your hand. There. I have your hand. I'm holding your hand. Now please tell me. Please tell me about your mother's bread-and-butter pudding. What was it like?" Suki cares not an iota about Russell's mother or her cuisine. In the universe of *Celebration*, each performative verbal gesture masks an emotional desert.

At least Meg in *The Birthday Party* is capable of love, Petey is capable of decency, and Lulu is capable of honesty. In *Celebration*, we discover the emptiness that occurs when greed has replaced personality: "I think you could have quite a nice character but the trouble is that when you come down to it you haven't actually got any character to begin with—I mean as such, that's the thing." The patrons of the restaurant are for the most part rootless and alone, power brokers in the anodyne world of high finance and chic cuisine. In *Celebration*, Pinter's long-standing obsession with community and with the pleasures of friendship butts up against the anonymity of contemporary urban life in ways that are both funny and deeply sad. In this loveless universe, we return to the theme of the son who has betrayed his family: "His mother always hated me," asserts Prue about Lambert. "The first time she saw me she hated me," to which Julie replies, "All mothers-in-law are like that. They love their sons. They love their boys." And then that favorite violent word: "They don't want their sons to be fucked by other girls. Isn't that right?" "Absolutely," replies Prue. "All mothers want their sons to be fucked by themselves." Love is possession, and fucking is its most visible expression. At this wedding anniversary, a husband and wife who despise each other celebrate with their friends by talking about fucking their own sons. Family provides little solace in this universe of predators. "They have no memory," Matt says about children, or at least his children. "They remember nothing. They don't remember who their father was or who their mother was. It's all a hole in the wall for them. They don't remember their own life." In a faceless world of money and manipulation, corrupt behavior is masked by the blandishments of euphemism. "Well, we're consultants, Matt and me. Strategy consultants," Lambert explains. "Strategy consultants," Matt concurs. "It means we don't carry guns," Lambert laughs. "We're peaceful strategy consultants," Matt says. "Worldwide. Keeping the peace." These men are engaged in activities of destruction and deception all the more horrifying for being described in recognizable "corporate speak."

By the time we arrive at *Celebration*, the graphic violence of Pinter's early work has become global, invisible, financial, and untraceable. Pinter's appetite for linguistic aggression goes back to his very first plays, which skewered the phony humanism characteristic of much contemporary drama, and indeed, of much contemporary life, revealing how we employ a false lexicon of "caring" to disguise our destructive desires. I found it to be a rule of thumb that as soon as one of Pinter's characters assumes a "humanistic stance," the rest of the room must go on immediate alert. We see this with Goldberg's birthday toast in *The Birthday Party*, and with Max's prostitution negotiations in *The Homecoming*: "Lenny, do you mind if I make a little comment?" his father asks with false sweetness. "It's not meant to be critical. But I think you're concentrating too much on the economic considerations. There are other considerations. There are the human considerations. You understand what I mean? There are the human considerations. Don't forget them." In *Celebration*, "human considerations" are what you pay for to keep "undesirables" at bay, but they offer no warmth or comfort. The hostility to "foreigners" and the fear of the known world being overtaken by the "other" that emerges so clearly in *The Room* (Rose: "You're all deaf and dumb and blind, the lot of you. A bunch of cripples. . . . My luck. I get these creeps come in, smelling up my room. What do you want?") emerges with equal force in *Celebration*, in which the seemingly elegant *maitresse d'hotel* asserts, "I had a sister. But she married a foreigner and I haven't seen her since."

There is one notable exception to the club of venality in *Celebration*. What makes the play more than a topical farce about the corrosive impact of money on human relations is the extraordinary Waiter at the center of the play. In the midst of a despairing conversation between Russell and Suki (RUSSELL: "I wanted to be a poet once. But I got no encouragement from my dad. He thought I was an arsehole") this Waiter arrives with great energy and, as he pours the wine, dives right in. "Do you mind if I interject?" Russell is startled to hear the Waiter speak. "Eh?" The Waiter repeats: "I say, do you mind if I make an interjection?" He then proceeds to talk: "It's just that I heard you talking about T.S. Eliot a little bit earlier this evening. . . . And I thought you might be interested to know that my grandfather knew T.S. Eliot quite well. . . . I'm not claiming that he was a close friend of his. But he was a damn sight more than a nodding acquaintance." This loquacious character goes on to concoct an ever-widening tissue of connections that supposedly existed between his grandfather and all the literary greats of the 1920s and 1930s, culminating with, "He was James Joyce's godmother."

When I asked Pinter at lunch to tell me more about the genesis of the Waiter in *Celebration*, he asked me if I had ever held that particular job; I promptly told him about my adventures as a waitress in Palo Alto during my Stanford undergraduate career and the day I got released from my shift with full pay owing to a 4.6 earthquake that had left liquor bottles scattered across the restaurant. He laughingly replied, "I'll bet you were a damned fine waitress," and then told me about his own table-waiting experience. "I was a waiter—this has been a long career, you know," he began.

I was out of work as an actor, so I did a bit of waiting at the National Liberal Club—it's a fitness club in London. This was the early 50s. I actually heard two men having lunch and talking about Kafka and the publication date of *The Trial* and *The Castle*. I stopped at the table and said, "No, no, *The Trial* was published in 1922" or whatever the date was, and they said, "Really? Was it? We thought it was later than that!" I said, "No, you'll find that I am right" and I went back into the kitchen and was fired on the spot for talking to the customers. That was my experience as a Waiter. So in a sense, I think the Waiter in *Celebration* may have come from that.

He recounted this event with the same detached fascination that he might bring to events that overtake his characters, which reminded me once again that in many ways, Pinter himself was his own most interesting character; he was capable of observing events that happened to him with such acuity and objectivity that they retained their mystery while becoming instantly concrete and "usable" from a dramatic point of view. The Waiter is the pulse of *Celebration* because he is the character who possesses *imagination*. Belonging nowhere, he longs for human connection, and when he cannot find it in the flesh, he conjures it in capacious fantasies that link him to great minds and great moments from the past. Like Rose in *The Room* and Stanley in *The Birthday Party*, the Waiter lives in terror of being ejected from the one place where he is left in peace. When Russell nastily asks him, about the restaurant, "You going to stay until it changes hands?" the Waiter panics. "Are you suggesting that I'm about to get the boot?" he asks. "To be brutally honest, I don't think I'd recover if they did a thing like that. This place is like a womb to me. I prefer to stay in my womb. I strongly prefer it to being born." When Russell tartly replies, "I don't blame you. Listen, next time we're talking about T.S. Eliot, I'll drop you a card," the Waiter is thrilled. "You would make me a very happy man. Thank you. Thank you. You are incredibly gracious people."

Fantasy is salvation. As Pinter discovered in writing his Proust screenplay, the only thing that redeems the despair of lost time is the creation of art, and that creation is connected to the tangible transformation of memory. The Waiter in *Celebration* appropriates the lives of every artist he can name so as to conjure a magical past that will give his aimless present some sense of destiny and meaning. The actor's task is to keep his imagination actively deployed at all times. Just as Meg survives in *The Birthday Party* by concocting a fantasy past that involves a little pink bedroom and "little sisters and brothers in other rooms, all different colors," the Waiter's existence in *Celebration* revolves around an invented past of infinite longing and aesthetic delight. A desire to transcend language and to find a momentary union with another person has always anchored Pinter's work, and the Waiter in *Celebration* is one of the finest exponents of that desire. A consummate outsider, the Waiter creates a parallel universe in which the personal, the historical and the aesthetic can safely merge, putting us all in a magical continuum with the writers who had been Pinter's beacons as a young man: "He was a bit of a drinking companion of D.H. Lawrence, Joseph Conrad, Ford Maddox Ford, W.B. Yeats, Aldous Huxley, Virginia Woolf, and Thomas Hardy in his dotage," he exclaims.

But the Waiter also acknowledges the loneliness of existence and the constant threat of diminishment and loss: "He had a really strange life," he says of his grandfather. "He was in love, he told me, once, with the woman who turned out to be my grandmother, but he lost her somewhere. She disappeared, I think, in a sandstorm." Occasionally, in describing his grandfather's "boon companions," we arrive back at the violence and terror of war time: "He knew these people where they were isolated, where they were alone, where they fought against savage and pitiless odds, where they suffered vast wounds to their bodies, their bellies, their legs, their trunks, their eyes, their throats, their breasts, their balls"—the language of the Holocaust exploding into our contemporary consciousness. The fact that Gregory Wallace was the only Black person onstage gave these speeches extraordinary force, reminding us of the vast inequality and brutality of contemporary life which we mask with illusions of civilized behavior.

It is difficult to describe what it was like to put those two plays onstage at the Geary two nights after the events of 9/11. After watching endless loops of buildings falling and massive urban destruction, the deaths of 3,000 people loomed very large on September 13 as the curtain rose to reveal an anxious little woman in a bedsit, bustling around and desperately wishing that her husband would not leave for work. If *The Room* on its first outing in 1957 provoked a certain degree of confusion, it was clear by 9/11 that this room was Rose's only safe harbor, and that outside lurked a danger and violence that was more frightening for being faceless. The audience understood in a visceral way why Rose was cocooned inside, terrified to go out. The night of our first preview at the Geary, the price of racism also felt loud and clear, as well as the price of misogyny. The moment of spiritual connection between Riley and Rose was a momentary balm, a balm subsequently destroyed by Bert's violence.

The audience was strangely quiet for the entirety of *The Room* that night; they seemed frightened and fascinated, in equal measure. At intermission, I still could not tell if this whole evening had been a good idea or a misguided one. And then came *Celebration*. The sound that erupted within the first few lines was unlike anything I can remember in the theater. As Riegert later commented, "They made a noise of laughter as if they were breathing for the first time." Clearly, the audience needed a release, something guttural and explosive. Remember that we were in San Francisco, where the lies and clichés of President George W. Bush felt like a particular assault; suddenly the country was full of jingoism and calls for revenge, a "force majeure," exactly as Pinter had described it. With Lambert and Matt in charge, *Celebration* seemed to say, it was no wonder the world had no moral compass. The audience laughed in horror at the barbarians occupying the fanciest booth at the fanciest restaurant in town; they recognized them immediately.

But it was the Waiter who provided them with a point of view. The more fanciful and absurd his stories became, the more drawn they were to him, responding with pleasure when he confided that his grandfather was "one of the very few native-born Englishmen to have had it off with Hedy Lamar." They intuited that the Waiter was Everyman, looking through a keyhole at a mysterious world on the other side. His confusion was our own. And so was his desire to connect, to speak directly to us. Pinter ends the play with the Waiter urgently addressing the audience. In our production, as Wallace stepped downstage, we lit the walls from behind, revealing them to be opaque; slowly, the whole frame of the set seemed to disappear, leaving the Waiter marooned alone in a vast and empty space. "My grandfather introduced me to the mystery of life and I'm still in the middle of it," he told us. "I can't find the door to get out. My grandfather got out of it. He got right out of it. He left it behind him and he didn't look back. He got that absolutely right. And I'd like to make one further interjection." And then the actor stood in silence, as suspended as his character, while the lights faded.

The existential questions posed by *The Room* and *Celebration* lingered long after the evening concluded: how do I get out? How do I find purpose? How do I unlock the strangeness of life? How do I make a connection, even for an instant, with another human being? "And I'd like to make one further interjection," the Waiter pleads. But the play ends before he can say another word. The day Pinter gave me the script in London, he had told me he believed *Celebration* would be his last play. "I've written 29 plays, for God's sake. I think it's enough." But I knew that, like the Waiter, Pinter would always attempt to make "one further interjection," because to write was to live. To imagine was to feel human. Even in the darkest of circumstances.

The double bill of *Celebration* and *The Room* had an enormous impact upon A.C.T.'s audiences, providing a palpable correlative to the anxiety they were experiencing, as well as offering a welcome collective release. The experience made me more aware of the mythic dimensions of Pinter's work; embedded in his uncompromising poetic realism is a metaphoric landscape that makes his plays perfect touchstones for a range of charged historical moments. Surprisingly, the experience of seeing two such radically different views of imprisonment and entrapment made each play feel more universal. By this time, A.C.T. audiences were beginning to find the strange world of "Pinterland" more familiar and rewarding, having enjoyed *Old Times* (starring Pamela Reed and Graham Beckel) in 1998. Our only sorrow was that we had not been able to share the experience with the playwright himself.

One happy result of *Celebration* was that Marco Barricelli, a favorite collaborator of Stoppard's who played Matt in Pinter's one-act, got to spend an afternoon with the two great men in London not long after the run. Stoppard graciously offered to introduce Barricelli to Pinter over lunch at the Ivy; when Barricelli arrived and saw Pinter and Stoppard sitting companionably together at the table, he was so nervous he desperately had to pee. But finding himself squeezed into an elegant banquette between two lions of the British theater, he did not dare slip off to the men's room. The result was that he remained in agony during the entire lunch. When Pinter asked him what role he had played in *Celebration* (Matt), Barricelli could not for the life of him remember the character's name, throwing out options that were not even in the play. I am sure Pinter did not mind; Barricelli is a true man of the theater with deep Shakespeare background and a love of language that rivals that of both his favorite playwrights, and Stoppard assured me that the three of them had a wonderful lunch. But all Barricelli could remember of that day was the pain of sitting entrapped between his heroes, and the immense relief he felt when the lunch concluded. Like AEH in *The Invention of Love*, he must have wished he could say to them both, "and now I really do have to go."

My own reunion with Pinter was never to happen, although we stayed in close touch over the years, because on December 24, 2008, Harold Pinter died of esophageal cancer. I could not believe that the writer who had done so much to re-animate theatrical language died of a disease that meant he could not speak. I thought about our collaboration on *Mountain Language*, and how moved he was by characters who had been forbidden to speak; for Pinter, to speak was to live. We were heartbroken at the loss of his voice in our universe. His death came at a bleak time in the world and a particularly bleak time in the theater, a time of global financial collapse when those of us in the profession wondered whether and how we would emerge from wreckage. In an obituary of Pinter for the *San Francisco Chronicle* on December 20, 2008, I wrote,

> Pinter died just as all of us in the American theater are wrestling with the role we ought to play in this enormous and difficult new moment in American political history. Having capitulated for years to the crass forces of "relevance" and television commercialism in our quest for attention in an increasingly noisy world, the American theater has run out of resources and audiences just at the moment when what we do ought to matter more than ever. It is up to us to assert that the potency of two people in real time in a live encounter onstage can engage us more deeply and fully than all the blogs and special effects in the world.
>
> So perhaps the passing of this astonishing writer is the wake-up call we need, to dare again to do work that is fierce and nuanced, that demands imagination and play, that questions the tyranny of political double speak, that revels in the virtuosity of great acting, that refuses easy

answers and earnest palliatives but demands that we examine ourselves in all our complexity and mystery. Pinter's is a theater with no agenda other than itself—pure theater, pure experience, caught in the moment of creation.

It was cathartic to write about Pinter's bracing theatricality during such uncertain times, and I began to find myself carrying the script of his masterpiece *The Homecoming* around with me as a kind of talisman. Its pungent language and uncompromising insistence on being exactly what it wanted to be was a useful reminder of why I had gotten involved in the theater to begin with. My husband and I honored Harold's death by reading aloud our favorite sections of the play, reveling in Lenny's deranged speech about the clock ("I've been having a bit of a rough time with this clock. The tick's been keeping me up. The trouble is, I'm not at all convinced it was the clock") and Max's hilarious and horrible comments about his dead wife Jessie ("I've never had a whore under this roof before. Ever since your mother died. My word of honor"). Despite having to make significant cutbacks in staff and operations because of the 2008 recession, I had fought hard to keep A.C.T.'s Core Company intact, which seemed like an important goal. *The Homecoming* began to feel like the right play for them to do at that moment in history, just as Pinter's one-acts had inaugurated the Company right after the millennium. Thus, for the 2010/11 season, I decided to produce the play to celebrate Rene Augesen's tenth anniversary as our leading lady (Ruth had always been on the top of her wish list of roles to play), and most importantly, as a homage to the writer we had lost.

If cornflakes and newspapers define the landscape of *The Birthday Party*, *The Homecoming* is built around the erotics of a glass of water, the territorial importance of a cheese roll, and the dangers of climbing a staircase. At its core, it is a play that tries to parse the many meanings of the word "home," and to ask who inherits that territory when the patriarch fails. We were about to discover that the mapping out of territory on which this primal battle takes place is even more critical and specific than it was in, say, *The Birthday Party*. In *The Homecoming*, every corner of the room is terrain to be won or lost. There is emasculation in a sip of water, and victory in occupying an armchair. *The Homecoming* has been interpreted as, among other things, an Oedipal drama, a Jungian battle of the sexes, a post-war political reckoning, an enactment of a Golden Bough-inspired fertility ritual, and a feminist tract. It centers around the return of Teddy, a professor who now teaches in America, to his childhood home in London. Anyone who has seen the film *Accident* (for which Pinter wrote the screenplay at roughly the same time as he was working on *The Homecoming*) will recognize Pinter's deft characterization of the academic philosopher, who strives to disconnect from responsibility for basic human interactions by living in the rarified zone of dialectical thought.

In the home to which Teddy returns, his two grown brothers, Lenny (a con artist) and Joey (an amateur boxer) still live with their father, Max (appropriately, a butcher). Their mother Jessie is dead, but her legend hangs over the house like moss. The other denizen of this house is Sam, Max's brother, a chauffeur. The inspiration for the play's plot was most likely the story of Pinter's childhood friend Morris Wernick, who married a Gentile in the mid-1950s and was so anxious about his family's reaction that he moved to Canada and did not tell his family for ten years. Such was the anxiety of a Jewish son marrying outside the tribe. Finally, in 1964 (the year *The Homecoming* was written), Wernick made the trip home to London with his wife and children to introduce them to his family. The seeds of his friend's story obviously lodged in Pinter's imagination, even though the actual response of Wernick's family to his "betrayal" was nowhere near as violent as the family reaction in Pinter's play. By the time I began preparing to direct the play, my understanding of how Pinter's Jewish background impacted his dramaturgy was more deeply developed.

Interestingly, early drafts of the play reveal[3] a more literally Jewish context than the final version employs ("I used to knock about with a man called Berkowitz. I called him Berki" became "I used to knock about with a man called MacGregor. I called him Mac") but the play is clearly set in the Jewish London of Pinter's childhood. As he told Michael Billington, "The image of the old man—who was Moishe Wernick's father—may have been a kind of source. I didn't know him well. We didn't discuss our parents in those days. But the image of Moishe's father in cap and plimsolls was one I carried with me. I knew him to be a pretty authoritarian figure. A really tough old bugger."[4] In fact, the only person tougher than Max in his self-enclosed world was obviously MacGregor, the butcher friend who, as we intuit early on, screwed Max's wife Jessie in the back seat of Sam's cab. The extreme specificity of the play only adds to its universality, and as I mentioned in Chapter 1, despite the fact that the men in this family are vile and aggressive toward each other, there is an undercurrent of love and longing that gives the play incredible poignancy. These are men without a woman, sons without a mother, a father without a wife. "Even though it made me sick just to look at her rotten stinking face, she wasn't such a bad bitch," says Max about Jessie. The naked desire for control exercised by the men is met, however, by the one woman in the play: Ruth. Married to Teddy and living in America with her three sons, Ruth arrives in this household as the stranger, and proceeds to take it over. Her psychological behavior is mirrored by her physical behavior: from the moment she walks across the threshold, every move she makes is about status and control. Ultimately, as is often the case with Pinter's work, the play is about Ruth's growing freedom to exercise her will and live her life as she sees fit. It is about a woman's conquest of male territory. The play is Ruth's homecoming.

In attempting to stage this richly imagined play, it helps to begin quite concretely with what that territory might look like. The subtle balance of realism and metaphor which pertained to the design of *The Birthday Party* is even more complex with *The Homecoming*. We are looking at Max's kingdom, a kingdom which, like Lear's, is about to slip from the grasp of the patriarch. But we are also looking at a real room in a real house in post-war London. "This is my house as well, you know," Sam reminds Max. "This was our mother's house." And also, he remembers, "Our father's house." The giant half-empty room holds the entire history of the family. As I began working on the production with set designer Daniel Ostling and lighting designer Alexander V. Nichols, we took a close look at how each character describes the house, and at what the choreography of their struggle demands of the space. Pinter describes the landscape as follows: "*An old house in North London. A large room, extending the width of the stage. The back wall, which contained the door, has been removed. A square arch shape remains. Beyond it, the hall. In the hall, a staircase ascending U.L., well in view. The front door U.R.*" There is something strange about this room: it is like a giant waiting room rather than a recognizable living room. For what purpose had the back wall been removed? What was being exposed? When did it happen? How evident should this be? The night of their arrival, Teddy gives Ruth the room's history: "Big isn't it? It's a big house. I mean, it's a fine room, don't you think? Actually, there was a wall, across there . . . with a door. We knocked it down . . . years ago . . . to make an open living area. The structure wasn't affected, you see. My mother was dead." It's a chilling description of a space devoid of all feminine comforts or intimacy, and designing it is one of many challenges in bringing *The Homecoming* to the stage.

Equally interesting is that the *staircase*, which had been "offstage" in the original set description in *The Birthday Party* but had become such a feature of our CSC production, had made its way to a position of absolute centrality ("*well in view*") in *The Homecoming,* a giant phallic object bisecting the space. Because this staircase, conduit to the bedrooms upstairs where Ruth exerts her sexual power, is "well in view," we get to watch the visible and visceral journey toward danger which will be shaped by the ascent up the stairs. Pinter also describes the room's furnishings: there are two large armchairs, a large sofa, and a sideboard against the right wall. These pieces of furniture will become islands to be conquered. The central armchair is Max's "throne," a fact that Teddy quickly asserts all these years later; as soon as Ruth eyes it, he says, "That's my father's chair." "That one?" she asks, clocking it. By the end of the play, she will have victoriously occupied the patriarchal chair, leaving Max to grovel on the floor.

In creating a visual world for *The Homecoming* at A.C.T., we had to take into account that the Geary was an extremely large stage, so the design would need to help focus the action to achieve Pinter's laser-like specificity of movement and gesture. Two decisions were made: first, that the walls would be huge and canted, leaning slightly inward in false perspective to focus the gaze. The surface of the walls, in a nod to Max's profession, would resemble those of a butcher's abattoir, blood-stained but clean (Richard Serra's rusted steel slabs were a notable inspiration). This was Max's domain. It may be that Max has made his money in blood and bones, but he is

meticulous. "It's my father. He's obsessed with order and clarity," Lenny tells
Ruth. Everything in the space is scrubbed. That is part of what is surreal
about this house—it is not untidy, it is not a slum dwelling, it is Max's
universe. The second decision we made had to do with lighting. We noticed
immediately how precisely Pinter describes light and darkness at each
moment of *The Homecoming*, setting up the convention that the person
who controlled the light switch controlled the universe. We therefore made
the decision early on to divide the stage into zones of light which could be
carefully controlled by the characters as part of the action of the play. Only
when a practical light was called for in the script did we illuminate that area
of the space.

Thus, for example, there was a central chandelier (which could create a
pool of light for the moment when Lenny and Ruth dance and kiss center
stage in Act 2), a standing lamp by the sofa to illuminate Ruth being pulled
on top of Joey ("*He leans her back until she lies beneath him*"), a table light
placed precisely where it could light the infamous glass of water, and two
small lamps on the sideboard which would help focus the crisis of the
"cheese roll" in Act 1. Finally, there was a light at the top of the stairs,
activated by a switch by the door; whoever controlled this switch controlled
the fraught journey up the stairs toward the bedrooms. Outside the window,
and through the glass above the front door, light could bleed through as if
from a streetlamp just outside, crucial for those moments when Ruth stared
out the window as if re-acquainting herself with the mean streets of her
youth.

By the time I directed this particular Pinter, I had his "rules of play" firmly
etched in my mind. Knowing that the choreography was going to be
extremely precise and that the lighting was going to contain each territorial
zone, I decided to conduct rehearsals in an unorthodox way: I asked the
stage manager to board up the windows in the rehearsal studio such that no
daylight could enter. The only illumination would be the practical lights on
the set. This had the unintended consequence of forcing the actors to learn
the text very quickly, as they could not see their scripts in the darkness.
Rehearsals were very focused and without distraction. It also meant that the
action of each moment, the subtle shifts in dominance and retreat, could be
calibrated by light. In the rehearsal studio, we set up the "practicals" exactly
as they would be on stage and marked out the anticipated "light zones" on
the floor with tape so that the actors knew where and when they would land
in the "hot spot." It was a bit like staging a "film noir," which seemed
appropriate since Pinter himself had relished the language of thrillers since
his days as an actor in rep. In the darkness, the stakes became exceptionally
high.

One of the most dramatic light shifts indicated in the play occurs after the
first long scene between Max, Lenny, Sam, and Joey, a scene that establishes
the status of each of the four men in relation to the others. The subtext
throughout has been violent and sexual. Suddenly, in the middle of the act,

there is a blackout. And when the lights come up, the stage has been wiped clean. Where has the family gone? And now who is in charge? As soon as the lights are restored, we meet a new set of characters standing at the threshold: Teddy and Ruth. The intruders. It is a startling entrance that echoes the arrival of Mr. and Mrs. Sands in *The Room*, an echo particularly resonant for A.C.T.'s audience because Ruth and Teddy were played by the same actors, Rene Augesen and Anthony Fusco, that had played Mr. and Mrs. Sands. In our staging, after the lights blacked out, we heard a key turning in the lock, that frightening sound in the darkness that Pinter loved. When the lights came up, the door was open, and a shaft of light as if from an exterior streetlamp lit two figures in silhouette on the threshold. "Well, the key worked," says Teddy. "They haven't changed the lock." After a few lines of dialogue, I asked Anthony Fusco (Teddy), to shut the outside door and turn on the chandelier. Now the center of the room was exposed, and with it, Max's "throne." When Teddy tells Ruth to sit down, she looks right at the central chair, and Teddy quickly explains, "That's my father's chair." Within seconds, the territorial imperatives are laid out. Ruth *"does not move"*—as we discovered with *The Birthday Party*, sitting is usually a sign of capitulation in Pinter, and Ruth is certainly not ready to capitulate. So Teddy makes the long journey up the stairs to see if the family is there.

The staircase Daniel Ostling designed was a truly epic flight— I believe there were twenty-two steps—and climbing it was a commitment and an effort. Ruth stood at the bottom and watched her husband *"stealthily"* make the climb, lit only by a light from the top of the landing. Once he had disappeared at the top and she was alone, she was free to stake out the illuminated territory down below. When Teddy comes back down the stairs, he asks, "What do you think of the room?" and proceeds to explain the destruction of the wall in the same breath as the death of his mother, allowing us to see the space as a kind of gladiatorial arena devoid of female intervention.

We gather quite quickly that Ruth and Teddy's marriage is in trouble. She announces that she is going out for "a breath of air" and he is instantly alarmed: the single light glowing in the center of the room makes the outside world more threatening, menacing, and remote. Ruth walks off into the dark night with supreme confidence; we begin to suspect that the neighborhood outside the house is one that she knew well at an earlier time in her life. That fact is clearly threatening to Teddy, who is terrified at being left alone in his own family house. In a Pinter play, the actions a character undertakes when left alone are always extremely revealing. The stage directions indicate *"Teddy goes to the window, peers out after her, half turns from the window, stands, suddenly chews his knuckles."* And who should be watching Teddy panic but his brother Lenny, who silently appears from the opposite side of the stage.

The scene between Lenny and Teddy highlights the way Pinter uses sound as much as light and physical behavior to ratchet up the tension. We begin

FIGURE 12 *Andrew Polk and Anthony Fusco in* The Homecoming, *A.C.T. 2011. Scenery by Daniel Ostling, lighting by Alexander V. Nichols, Costumes by Alex Jaeger. Photo courtesy of Kevin Berne.*

with the sound of the "k," Pinter's favorite, exploding out of Lenny's mouth. Lenny says he has been awakened by some kind of "tick," a sound whose source he cannot locate. The repeated use of the onomatopoetic word "tick" echoes the "duck" of *Celebration* and the "fuck" of *Mountain Language.* "Have you got a clock in your room?" asks Teddy. Lenny's response increases the threat hanging in the air, "Well, if it's the clock I'd better do something about it. Stifle it in some way, or something." (Andrew Polk's eyes gleamed with pleasure on the word "stifle.") The stand-off between the two estranged brothers ends in a game of chicken to see who is going to drive the other out of the room. Finally, Teddy picks up the suitcases and heads for the stairs. Lenny has won that gambit. What does he do next? As Pinter describes with meticulous stage directions, "*Lenny turns out the light in the room. The light in the hall remains on.*" For a moment, Lenny has trapped himself and his brother in a narrow pool of light together. Then Lenny turns out the hall light and "*turns on the first landing light,*" effectively driving Teddy out of the hallway and up the stairs. Lenny stands at the bottom and watches Teddy slog his way up. Lenny feels victorious. He heads for his own ground floor bedroom, and the stage for a moment is empty.

In that emptiness, the light on the landing goes out, indicating that Teddy has gone into his old bedroom. "*Slight night light in the hall and room.*" There is a moment of suspense and anticipation: who will appear next in this dangerous space? When Lenny returns, he crosses to the window, as if he senses someone is out there. It is an instinct of his; he is a pimp, after all. At that moment, we lit Lenny's face as if from an exterior streetlamp, an image that we repeated later with Ruth, as she looks out and examines her old haunts. Time stopped while we examined his face in the shaft of light from outside. The next light shift is crucial. Lenny leaves the window, crosses to the table, and turns on the table lamp. That becomes the only illumination on stage. He sits by the table and places the clock on it.

Pinter has thus engineered an entirely new lighting state for Ruth's entrance and the subsequent sexual battle, a game revolving around a glass of water. After having given a whole aria about the "tick" and its possible sources, Lenny rises and pours water for Ruth as if it were a fine whisky: "Here you are. I bet you could do with this." "What is it?" Ruth asks. "Water." Ruth sips, and places the glass on the small table center stage, lit by the lamp Lenny has turned on. In our production, we discovered that if that lamp was angled exactly right, the glass would glow in the dark like a beacon of sexual promise. It took hours of technical rehearsals to get the effect of that hyper-intentionality exactly right. When it worked, the beam of the light and the glass half-filled with water created a kind of epiphanic image for the audience, like the effects in a David Lynch movie. We were ready for a magic trick. For a moment, the glass existed outside time. Both Lenny and Ruth were drawn to it like moths.

Thus, when Lenny ultimately tries to remove Ruth's glass, she resists. In this section, the choreography of her hand is as precise as anything Pinter ever wrote. It moves from darkness into the light of the table lamp to grasp the glass. Lenny is annoyed at being flouted. "Just give me the glass," he insists. But Ruth holds the power. "No," she says. "I'll take it then," counters Lenny. "If you take the glass, I'll take you" she replies. This simple prop, glowing under the table lamp, becomes a talisman, a prize only one of these sexual predators will win. Ruth taunts him: "Have a sip. Go on. Have a sip from my glass," and when he will not, she goes further: "Sit on my lap. Take a long cool sip." The stakes continue to rise as Lenny refuses the glass. Then, in a masterful piece of dramatic choreography, Ruth *stands, moves to him with the glass,* dares him to lie on the floor and let her pour the water down his throat, and finally, in one quick move, *"laughs shortly, drains the glass."*

Ruth's draining of the glass is the beginning of Lenny's emasculation at her hands. The right prop filled with the right amount of water lit by the right light will defamiliarize that prop and make it an agent of exquisite danger. Just as suddenly, when Ruth empties the glass and puts it down on the sideboard (out of the light), it reverts to being an ordinary prop again. The magic trick is over. No longer illuminated, it is simply a glass. Lenny cannot figure out what has just happened. "What was that supposed to be? Some kind of proposal?" he yells, as Ruth heads up the long flight of stairs to bed. The epiphanic glass has exposed Lenny as an impotent fraud. Ruth has unmasked him in one deft stroke. This game of wits surrounding the glass of water is a vivid demonstration of Ruth's independence, fearlessness, and wit.

While much has been written about Ruth's status in *The Homecoming* and indeed about whether she is to be judged as a hyper-sexualized male fantasy or as an independent being, we found that exploring her concrete moment-to-moment physical behavior (she is a woman of few words) was more revealing than trying to make any generalizations about her history. Pinter certainly made clear his own feelings about Ruth when he told Mel Gussow, "No one can tell her what to do. She is the nearest to a free woman that I've ever written—a free and independent mind."[5] Obviously this is the playwright's point of view; but there are many possible interpretations of Ruth to be explored. Vivien Merchant was the first to play the role, about which Pinter said, in the same interview, "there's never quite been a Ruth like Vivien. Vivien was a hell of an actress and a woman of undoubted independence of mind." Perhaps because the image of Vivien was in his mind as he wrote Ruth, he has given the character a dark edge and the power of a dancer in a tightly choreographed ballet, knowing that for Vivien, the act of reaching for a glass or crossing a leg would become an erotic demonstration of dominance. It is also possible that with a less potent actress, the role could become a dispiriting display of female subjugation.

To return to the lighting, it is notable that as each act of *The Homecoming* builds to a point of extreme tension, there is suddenly a blackout, right in the middle of the action. In a more conventional dramaturgy, this would signal the end of the act, but in *The Homecoming*, the lights go out mid-act and then instantly come up again on a different set of characters within the same time frame. It is as if a bell had been rung during a boxing match to clear the ring, and the next bout was about to begin. (Pinter had already employed this technique in *The Caretaker,* in which the lights black out suddenly in the midst of all three acts.) In Act 2 of *The Homecoming*, the mid-act blackout occurs just after Teddy's disquisition on "intellectual equilibrium." "You're just objects," he tells his family. "You just . . . move about. I can observe it. I can see what you do. It's the same as I do. But you're lost in it. You won't get me being . . . I won't be lost in it." BLACKOUT. The lights do exactly what Teddy claims he will not do, which is to get lost in darkness. It is a brilliant theatrical coup. Teddy gets "lost," the lights shift, and the subsequent scene begins with vivid momentum, letting Sam take the offensive with a dangerous question: "Do you remember MacGregor, Teddy?" Assuming (as we do by this point in the play) that MacGregor had had a sexual relationship with the boys' mother Jessie (and that it is possible that Joey is actually Mac's son), this is an audacious question for Sam to ask the returning Teddy. And because the line comes right after a blackout, it can be released with full force, a direct punch to the gut.

The extreme light shifts indicated in *The Homecoming* helped remind us of the *attack* necessary to sustain the play, and of Pinter's insistence that the emotions of one scene not be carried over to the next. It takes enormous energy to restart an act right in the middle, with no break other than a light shift. To keep the muscle of the act intact, the actors had to launch each new scene like a fresh group of players up to bat in a competitive and dangerous game. I recalled something Pinter had described to Mel Gussow:

> In the East End of London, where I grew up, it was a very very lively, active kind of world; a lot of people who talked a lot. They talked very fast. It was during and after the war and there was a sense of release. People were just talking very fast. You know this country has changed a great deal. It has now become, for a clear set of reasons, I think, progressively more sullen, more bewildered, more secret. . . . There was a kind of vitality in the world I grew up in.[6]

It is this vitality which gives *The Homecoming* its tremendous impact: the characters are fighting for their lives, while relishing every moment of the struggle.

The second act of *The Homecoming* has divided audiences and critics for years; in fact, when the production was in "try outs" in Boston in 1966, the critic Elliot Norton declared Act 2 to be problematic, and the producers asked Pinter what he was going to do about it. Characteristically, Pinter did not change a word, insisting that he had written exactly what he wanted to write. What we witness is the surreal evolution of an idea that Ruth should stay in London when Teddy goes back to America; not only that, but that she should service all the men in Max's household. How will she earn her keep? By becoming a prostitute in Greek Street, where Lenny plies his trade as a pimp. This was hard for an audience to stomach when it was first performed, and *The Homecoming* still has the power to shock. But if the actors and director have clearly orchestrated the power dynamics of the first act (through the precise deployment of sound, light, choreography, and text), the second act should seem inevitable. In the battle for territorial control of Max's house, someone is going to have to win.

What slowly becomes clear, as Peter Hall discovered during the first production, is that the villain of the play is Teddy. Far from being the weak and pathetic man we initially suppose him to be, Teddy is a cold and calculating adventurer who cuts off his family in order to succeed on his own terms. The warning bells begin to go off early on in Act 2, when Teddy admits to having stolen Lenny's cheese roll. The theft of the cheese role is a shocking transgression, even for a criminal like Lenny; it indicates a complete breakdown of family values. "I'm waiting for you to apologize," Lenny demands. "But I took it deliberately, Lenny," Teddy replies coldly. The cheese roll is a proxy for filial piety; in stealing it, Teddy has deliberately violated the family's moral code.

The next round of the battle comes as Joey descends the stairs from having been with Ruth. The excessive number of steps in Ostling's staircase gave our audience time to watch the complete deflation and humiliation of

Max's youngest son, as he descended onto the deck and admitted that no sex has occurred. Even Max is outraged that Ruth is holding out on them. As a kind of revenge, Max gets an idea. "Who knows? Maybe we should keep her," he decides. "Maybe we'll ask her if she wants to stay." A remarkable negotiation thus begins, in which Joey (a tall, bewildered, and brilliant Adam O'Byrne) offers to "put in a certain amount out of my wages" to keep Ruth, and Lenny (a slickly charming Andrew Polk), who has either known Ruth or someone awfully like Ruth in his own murky past, reminds the men how expensive it can be to provide for such a woman. Only Teddy refuses to "put anything in the kitty"—since clearly, he is not "putting anything in the kitty" with Ruth sexually. The men begin to unleash their imaginations as they invent a solution to the "problem of Ruth."

The last section of *The Homecoming* feels like a precursor to the wild imaginings of the Waiter in *Celebration*. We see a group of impotent men fantasizing about what it would be like to have a woman in the house again. Memories of their mother/wife Jessie collide with images of free sex and feminine warmth as even Sam gets in on the game, conjuring upper-class English names that exist in a world far from this East End Jewish family. "We could call her something nice . . . like Cynthia . . . or Gillian," Lenny imagines. Ruth of the Biblical name understands what she has triggered in these men. She is the "kin" they have lost. She will return the missing feminine principal to their lives. Now all she has to do is negotiate the best deal possible in exchange for her services. Ruth is a realist. She hates America. "It's all rock. And sand. It stretches . . . so far . . . everywhere you look. And there's lots of insects there."

One of those insects is her desiccated husband Teddy. Ruth wants more. She wants the house by the lake that lives in her memory (a lake that anticipates the mysterious lake of death Hirst dreams about in *No Man's Land*). Ruth longs to return to the body she had before "all her children." She wants beautiful shoes. She wants control. And perhaps, depending upon how you interpret the end of the play, she gets it. In the final tableau, Teddy has walked out the door, Ruth is sitting on Max's throne, Joey is kneeling beside her chair with his head in her lap, and Sam is lying prone on the rug, where he has passed out after his big revelation about MacGregor and Jessie. Max begins to panic. "Lenny, do you think she understands?" he asks. Because he knows he has lost. They have all lost. "*He falls to his knees, whimpers, begins to moan and sob. He stops sobbing, crawls past Sam's body round her chair, to the other side of her.*" Lenny stands to one side, watching. Ruth holds court center stage in the sacred patriarchal chair. And before the lights go out, Max begs her, "Kiss me."

Pinter had a unique ability to populate his plays with characters from multiple generations, and to grant each of them a clear claim on the past, the present, and the future. Who will inherit? Who will survive? On what terms? He will pose these questions again in *Moonlight*. In *The Homecoming*, there is no judgment, only a laser-like attention to competing behavior. And Ruth?

The question of Ruth will hang over *The Homecoming* as long as there are academics, audiences, and actors ready to argue about the play. I can only say that for me, as a woman director in a room full of men, I never felt that the play was misogynistic or that Ruth was actually in danger of being controlled by the men in the family. The disposition of characters in space by the end of the play tells a different story. Rene Augesen and I felt that in the final moments, Ruth was becoming something new. Or, as Paul Rogers parsed it in his interview with John Lahr, "She's come home. She knows this area, these people, this behavior ... it isn't a strange dramatic form that Pinter elected to use, it is firmly based in reality."[7] Neither mother nor whore, Ruth has become the negotiator of her own destiny in a collapsing world.

Perhaps this was the reading of a female artistic director desperately trying to keep her organization afloat in an era of financial collapse. After all, the one thing I knew from a career of trying to resuscitate bankrupt theaters is that when things are falling apart, women are often the ones called upon to pick up the pieces. At some point, I learned that the practice even has a name: the "glass cliff," that phenomenon whereby women are empowered when they are most likely to fail, having inherited a mess made by men. As I watched the end of *The Homecoming*, I felt strangely energized by the image of Ruth sitting directly beneath the chandelier in the center of her new kingdom. And I also felt as if, in producing *The Homecoming* at that particular moment, I had returned to my roots, to the theater that actually mattered to me, which is perhaps all one can do when the bottom drops out. In the final moments of the play, Rene Augesen's blonde hair glowed in the light, like a torch. The rest of the room lay in shadows. It seemed clear that the character most devoid of empathy, Teddy, had finally been exiled, a fact which gave Ruth much pleasure. Augesen held center stage with a smile lingering around the corners of her mouth as the lights dimmed on Max's pitiful display of need. It felt extremely satisfying to celebrate Pinter in his own terms. In spite of its bleakness, the end of *The Homecoming* fortified me and gave me renewed confidence in a very complicated time.

7

Anatomizing Guilt:

Stoppard's *Rock 'n' Roll,*
The Hard Problem, and
The Invention of Love

If *The Homecoming* helped mark the end of the financial crisis, Stoppard's *Rock 'n' Roll* marked the beginning. Ironically, we entered into that production (in September 2008) with incredible optimism, hoping that in a post-Bush era, new ideas and new energy would begin to reappear in American arts and culture. Our production of *Rock 'n' Roll*, a play about political turmoil and regime change in Czechoslovakia, coincided exactly with the election of Barack Obama. A few years later, its politics might have felt very different, but in the fall of 2008, while Obama's Chief of Staff Rahm Emmanuel was telling us that "a crisis was a terrible thing to waste" and we were being exhorted to meet the moment with energy and appetite, a new Stoppard play with a vivid and seductive soundtrack fit the bill perfectly. With several key members of my Core Company leading the charge, we dived in, opening A.C.T.'s 2008/9 season with *Rock 'n' Roll*.

Many of my most vivid memories of collaborating with Stoppard have happened while standing over a fax machine (and then, later, a printer) watching handwritten clarifications of complex theatrical moments spew out across time and space from London, and so it was with *Rock 'n' Roll*. Notes responding to our queries about the script had been arriving via fax for several weeks during early rehearsals of the play, but there was a thorny scene late in Act 2 that continued to puzzle the company. I remember that I had run to Macy's during the lunch break to attempt to find a present for my husband, whose birthday it was about to be, when my phone rang. It was Stoppard, patiently prepared to talk me through that troublesome scene one more time. I sat on the floor in a corner behind a pile of dress shirts for over an hour, madly writing his commentary on the back of whatever scraps of paper I could find as the playwright moved from beat to beat, explaining the scene. Naturally, this lengthy exegesis meant that I was late getting back to rehearsal and failed to buy the necessary birthday present, which triggered *another* fax from Stoppard specifically directed to Anthony, apologizing for having disrupted his birthday celebration.

When I recently unearthed those notes (which I could barely make out all these years later) and the series of faxes Stoppard had showered me with about the same set of issues, I was moved both by how willing he was to entertain our confusion and by how frustrating it often is for him to have to explain the emotional trajectory of his writing. While he occasionally resorts to rewriting in order to clarify a moment for an actor (or for a persistent director who keeps pushing to get to the bottom of a moment or a scene), he still holds on to an optimistic belief that his work will find that unique public able to understand his intent. In recent years, that belief has been shaken by the diminution of common knowledge one can expect of any given contemporary audience; indeed, Stoppard was castigated in the press after a National Theatre Platform Talk on *The Hard Problem* for saying that at the first outing of *Travesties* in 1974, everyone in the audience recognized a reference to "Goneril," but by its 1994 revival, few seemed to know that the reference referred to a character in *King Lear*.

While this was undoubtedly true, the press used it as an example of his intellectual arrogance, which I found unfair. It makes sense that Stoppard would long for the kind of literate audience that existed when most general readers accepted the same broad canon of literature; shared perspective helps a playwright's references land. Obviously, this has become a loaded issue in contemporary drama, as the field attempts to broaden its base and engage with audiences who are not necessarily party to or interested in the history of Western culture. But I never found Stoppard abstruse out of disdain for the audience, only occasionally out of love for his subject matter. In a toast he made on the occasion of my twentieth anniversary at A.C.T., he jokingly explained his process:

> Playwrights are often asked whom they write for, and there are two answers which are generally intelligible: to write entirely for oneself; or to write for an ideal audience, eager, generous and bright in just the right way. I understand both ideas but invariably find myself with a third idea, which is to imagine someone I know and trust looking at the page I have just written. The Carey test is a tough test and saves me from glibness, triteness and CMPT—an acronym I picked up from a book recently, standing for Colonic Material of a Taurine Provenance. Of course I wouldn't put that acronym into a play; Carey's hovering spirit would expunge it for pomposity.

Regardless, whenever I have experienced moments of frustration or confusion in the room, when the secrets of a given Stoppard play have refused to yield themselves up, I have gone directly to the source for clarification. Maybe this is laziness on my part; if I were an academic, I would either solve the question analytically or point out perceived flaws in the text. But a director's job is to make the play *work*. I knew that if we built *Rock 'n' Roll* to its climax and then failed to deliver an emotionally coherent conclusion, the let-down would be considerable. I wondered if he could help. Stoppard is unfailingly gracious when these queries arrive. He is anxious to ensure that what he writes is *clear* both to the performers and to the audience (much more so than Pinter, who never felt that it was his problem if the audience found the work oblique), but deeply resistant (as we discovered with *Indian Ink*) to anything that feels too bald and "on the nose." He has also, by the time he commits a story to paper, done more research on the material than anyone reading or experiencing it could possibly have done, with the result that he occasionally assumes knowledge of the given subject that the rest of us could not possibly have, and thus he forgets to fill in the blanks. Throughout Hermione Lee's biography there are references to pleas by directors (particularly Peter Wood but all the way through to Nick Hytner) to clarify an oblique point or to simplify a reference that the audience is bound to miss. I found it wonderful that when Stoppard was working with director Steven Spielberg on the screenplay of *Empire of the Sun*, they had major disagreements about the ending, which, as Hermione Lee recounts it, Spielberg wanted to make more obvious than Stoppard was willing to countenance. "Why don't we give Jim a little dog at the beginning, and then the dog could show up too?" Stoppard wrote his director in frustration.[1]

However, by the time we produced *Rock 'n' Roll*, A.C.T.'s audience had become so accustomed to the experience of watching a Stoppard play that, for the most part, they accepted the challenge with alacrity. It helped that for every production at A.C.T., we published a booklet called "Words on Plays" containing insights about the work at hand; one of my favorite sights, before everything went digital, was to spot A.C.T. audience members at dinner before the show, having torn their copy of Words on Plays in half so that each could read a part of it before curtain time. In all my years of producing Stoppard at A.C.T., I rarely had to eliminate "difficult" sections or apologize for the extreme wordiness of the plays; that was part of their appeal, and the appetite of our particular audience was part of the reason Stoppard worked with us so often.

With *Rock 'n' Roll*, there were two challenges to address: the first was that few Americans have more than a passing familiarity with the history of post-war Czech politics. The second was that one of the lead characters, Max, is quite opaque emotionally, which can make it difficult to bring his scenes to life. To contextualize: *Rock 'n' Roll*, written in 2008 after Stoppard's epic three-part *The Coast of Utopia*, is a time-travel play about art and politics, set in the late 1960s through the late 1980s and chronicling, in part, the Prague Spring and the collapse of "Reform Communism" in Czechoslovakia. It shuttles back and forth between a garden in Cambridge (home to Marxist academic Max, his cancer-stricken classicist wife Eleanor, and their flower-child daughter Esme) and Prague, where a young intellectual named Jan has returned after studying under Max from 1966 to 1968 at Cambridge. The play marks an important step in Stoppard's reckoning with his own past, including his Judaism: Jan, the protagonist (who is forced by the Czech secret police to acknowledge that he is Jewish and who was named Tomas in the first draft), is like a proxy for Stoppard but with the opposite life path. Unlike Stoppard's family (who went to India), Jan's family fled directly to England during the war; like Stoppard, this engendered in Jan a deep and abiding love for all things English, particularly for the English commitment to a free parliament and a free press. Unlike Stoppard, Jan has gone back to Czechoslovakia after the war, returning briefly to England to do graduate work in the late 1960s but ending up in Prague right after the Soviet tanks roll in to quash the Dubcek reforms. Initially optimistic and fairly apolitical, even when faced with Soviet aggression, Jan tries to navigate the system and survive under Communism, but eventually he signs Charter 77, is imprisoned, gets released, and spends a decade doing menial labor (like Stoppard's friend Vaclav Havel) as a baker.

Jan's growing politicization mirrors Stoppard's own growing involvement in the 1990s with human rights issues in Eastern Europe, just as the dialectic of the play mirrors the long-standing arguments between Milan Kundera (a Czech exile living in Paris) and Havel about whether signing petitions and agitating on behalf of political prisoners is "moral exhibitionism" or useful pressure. This aspect of the play intrigued me because Stoppard has often been accused of resisting engagement with political causes, particularly when compared to Pinter. When he and his director Trevor Nunn approached the Royal Court to produce the premiere of *Rock 'n' Roll* in London, there was backlash from director Bill Gaskill (who ran the Court from 1965 to 1972) and a number of the "house playwrights" who felt that Stoppard was too conservative to find a home at the notoriously left-wing Royal Court.

But in the years leading up to *Rock 'n' Roll*, Stoppard had become increasingly involved with issues of free speech under Communism, lending his support to the Belarus Free Theater and to a variety of important and frequently censored writers in Russia and Eastern Europe. He had fought hard to free Russian dissidents imprisoned in Soviet mental hospitals, and had become passionate about the work of Havel, whose absurdism and mordant wit felt congenial to Stoppard; when Havel was arrested in 1977, Stoppard wrote in his journal:

Vaclav Havel, a playwright whose mother didn't marry into British democracy, has been charged with high treason. The minimum sentence is fifteen years . . . His Czechness and my qualified Havel-like predilections as a writer single him out from the battalion of persecuted writers on my conscience. I sit here in this beautiful room surrounded by the commonplace luxuries of a successful writer, and can hardly bring my mind to bear on Havel's present surroundings and on his prospects, his mental state.

That deeply felt personal identification provided fodder for *Rock 'n' Roll*, a complex work about the individual voice in a totalitarian society; Havel's writings from prison (in particular, his *Letters to Olga*) had a major influence on the content of *Rock 'n' Roll*, and Stoppard dedicated the play to him.

The happy accident of learning about the concept of *rasa* during the writing of *Indian Ink* was mirrored in the writing process of *Rock 'n' Roll* by the discovery (via Havel) of a rock band, the Plastic People of the Universe, who became Stoppard's touchstone for artistic defiance and independence of spirit in the play. It is when these "druggy drop-out weirdo friends with their hair down to here" get arrested that Jan's awareness starts to open up and his appetite for political engagement is ignited, impelled, as is so often the case with Stoppard, by the anarchic and surprising power of art: "The Plastics don't care at all. They're unbribable. They're coming from somewhere else, from where the Muses come from. They're not heretics. They're pagans." The liberating passion of paganism is connected to the heartbreak of growing old: while thinking about the play, Stoppard came across a photograph of a bald middle-aged man on a bicycle and realized it was the legendary Pink Floyd lead singer Syd Barrett, whom Stoppard remembered as young and, like "Pan," an emblem of freedom and beauty. The photograph triggered thoughts about change, mortality, and being forgotten, central themes in a play that explores death, survival, and the power of art. It also allowed him to fill the play with something that had meant a great deal to him all his life: the songs of rock 'n' roll.

As Hermione Lee points out, Stoppard was writing *Rock 'n' Roll* exactly ten years after his mother's death. In an interview that year, he speculated, "I wonder whether her death somehow gave me permission to be Czech again . . . I probably began to feel more Czech since then . . . Somewhere working within me quite deep was the sense that I am Czech, I was Czech, I'm English now but I haven't stopped being Czech, and that's that."[2] This represents a real shift in thinking, one that seems to have opened Stoppard's heart to what his Czech compatriots had suffered both during and after the war, and to what responsibility he might bear for having escaped their fate. Perhaps because of that personal connection, I found the Czech sections of *Rock 'n' Roll* the most compelling and emotionally involving, particularly because the lead characters of that section were so young; it felt as if Stoppard were channeling these twenty-somethings while imagining himself in their place.

The plot lines of *Rock 'n' Roll* are complex and sometimes difficult to tease out. We come to learn, by Act 2, that Jan's student days in Cambridge in the summer of 1968 were actually a "spy" effort paid for by the Czech government; we discover subsequently that Max too has had some dealings with the secret police, in this case on Jan's behalf. Things get worse for Jan in Prague as they get worse in Cambridge for Eleanor, who is dying of cancer but still devoted to translating Greek, teaching Sappho, and arguing for the centrality of consciousness. Ultimately the play has three emotional centers: the father/son relationship of Max and Jan, the marriage of Max and Eleanor, and the love between Esme (Max and Eleanor's daughter) and Jan which survives twenty years and ultimately ends the play.

Rock 'n' Roll represented my seventh collaboration with Stoppard; by then, we had developed a kind of shorthand for working together. Even so, during the rehearsal process, I learned surprising things about the dialectical nature of Stoppard's work. Although he repeatedly claims that he begins a play with an argument or a set of ideas to explore and then sets about finding characters to embody those ideas, I have found more and more (particularly with his later plays) that his characters, as in Pinter, often take on a life of their own that does not permit as neat a resolution of argument as the playwright might have wished. The only solution to this interesting "messiness" is to try to move past the surface dialectic and dig into the emotional logic that lies beneath. The most complex section of *Rock 'n' Roll* occurs late in Act 2 between Max and Jan; our queries eventually resulted in that long phone call at Macy's and the accompanying ten-page fax from Stoppard which attempted to anatomize what he was having trouble explaining.

The scene in question was not the first fight between Max and Jan; indeed, all of the scenes between these two characters are contentious, from the first scene when Max accuses Jan of being a weak Communist for rushing back to Prague after the 1967 Soviet invasion. It is clear that beneath the debate lies the emotional neediness of a man whose wife has cancer, whose daughter is a drop out, and who longs for the approval and sustenance of the surrogate son that Jan has become to him. "I picked you out. I put my thumbprint on your forehead. I said, '*You*. I'll take *you*,' because you were serious and you knew your Marx . . . and at the first flutter of a Czech flag you cut and run like an old woman still in love with Masaryk," Max fulminates. When Max and Jan next meet, in Prague several years later, Jan has lost his job as a journalist, Eleanor's cancer has come back, and Esme is nineteen and pregnant. This meeting also ends in a fight; Max is furious that Jan is not grateful enough to the Soviets for having saved Czechoslovakia from Nazism: "You bedwetter!" he sputters. "If it wasn't for eleven million Soviet military dead, your little country'd be a German province now—and you wouldn't be bellyaching about your socialist right to piss everywhere except in the toilet, you'd be smoke up the chimney." Here is Stoppard wrestling with the Jewish "what if"—clearly, if he had not got out of Zlin in 1938, he would have been "smoke up the chimney," just like his grandparents and most of his relatives. The liminal status of Jan's identity is central to his character: neither fully Czech nor fully English, he longs for personal happiness, which Max disdains but Stoppard clearly sympathizes with. "A thousand years of knowing who you are gives a people confidence in its judgment," Jan insists, echoing a sentiment Stoppard himself has expressed many times. "Words mean what they have always meant. With us, words change meaning to make the theory fit the practice." By the time we arrive at Act 2, it is ten years later (the summer of 1987), Eleanor is dead, Esme's daughter Alice (played by the actress who played Esme in Act 1) is 16, and Jan has been in prison for signing Charter 77.

Finally, in the scene which kept tripping us up in rehearsal, Max gets a phone call from Jan out of the blue, on the very day his granddaughter Alice is to meet Candida, her father Nigel's new wife. Max invites Jan for lunch, forgetting the family obligations. As soon as Jan arrives, he encounters Esme, who is overwhelmed and flustered to see him again. "So what's happened?" she asks, mystified. "You phone, you get on a plane, you rent a car, you drive to Cambridge, just to see Max, and you drive back to the airport." Something is up, but Jan does not say what it is. This builds to the big scene with Max, who is clearly nervous about this visit: "You need half an hour?" he asks Jan. "What's the trouble?" "There's no trouble," Jan assures him. Jan produces the file from his briefcase; he tells Max it is his secret police file. Evidently, with the fall of communism, spy archives are being opened and "a lot of stuff is coming out of the woodwork." Jan assures Max that there is not much in it: there is an account of a warning Max had heard at a College dinner in 1968 that "the Sovs were going to bring the hammer down on Dubcek," and a 1977 "briefing paper on the British left." Jan then explains that the 1977 document makes it clear that Max gave the information in exchange for Jan being freed from prison. Jan thus extends the file as a present to Max, to do with it what he will.

It was here that the scene became bewildering to all of us working on it. Instead of thanking Jan for bringing it to him, Max angrily says, "I'll tell you what, Jan. Why don't you take this file and fuck off back to Prague . . . I don't need saving . . . I've done nothing I'm not prepared to defend. So don't expect me to thank you for telling me different. Have we done?" Jack Willis, who was playing Max, could not understand what triggered such anger in Max—surely, he would be grateful to have been spared public humiliation about that file, and pleased that Jan had taken so much trouble to deliver it? But now Jan has another confession to make, namely that he got to study in Cambridge in the late 1960s in exchange for delivering information: "At Cambridge, being your pupil, invited to the Marxist Philosophers meetings, it was a joy for me . . . this house, your family. Pretending to be a good Communist was ridiculous, but what did I care? . . . And all they wanted in return from me was . . . a character study, yes, of Max Morrow." Max has always suspected that Jan had ulterior motives; certainly, he was never a very good Communist. So what does he feel when he discovers that, like him, Jan has also compromised himself with the secret police? Is there relief? Complicity? Derision? Jan asks Max's forgiveness, but "*Max doesn't unbend. It's unsatisfactory,*" the stage directions tell us. Max unkindly says he does not care what Jan does with his file, and when he discovers that Jan's own secret police file has been burnt, he mocks Jan for his confession: "Well

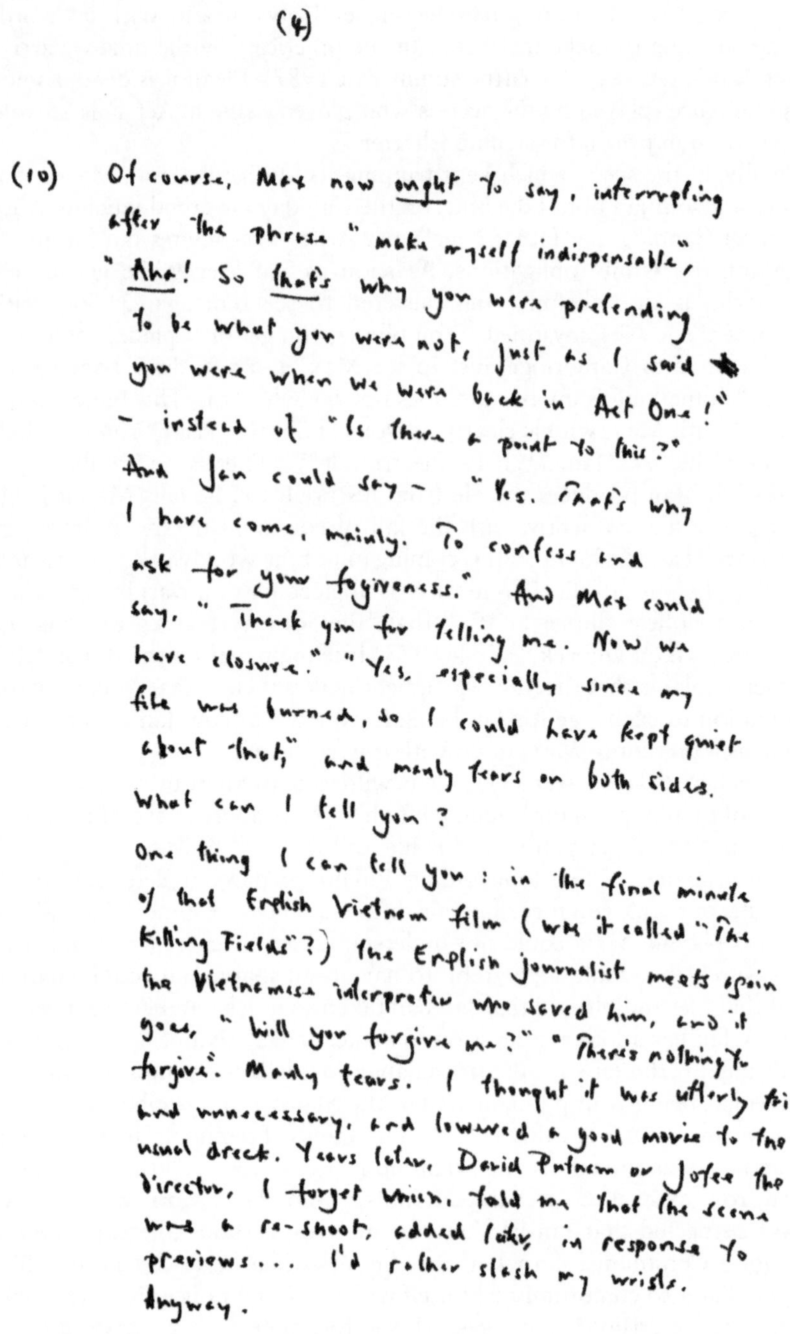

(4)

(10) Of course, Max now ought to say, interrupting
after the phrase "make myself indispensable",
"Aha! So that's why you were pretending
to be what you were not, just as I said
you were when we were back in Act One!"
— instead of "Is there a point to this?"
And Jan could say — "Yes. That's why
I have come, mainly. To confess and
ask for your forgiveness." And Max could
say, "Thank you for telling me. Now we
have closure." "Yes, especially since my
file was burned, so I could have kept quiet
about that," and manly tears on both sides.
What can I tell you?

One thing I can tell you : in the final minute
of that English Vietnam film (was it called "The
Killing Fields"?) the English journalist meets again
the Vietnamese interpreter who saved him, and it
goes, "Will you forgive me?" "There's nothing to
forgive." Manly tears. I thought it was utterly trite
and unnecessary, and lowered a good movie to the
usual dreck. Years later, David Putnam or Joffe the
Director, I forget which, told me that the scene
was a re-shoot, added later, in response to
previews... I'd rather slash my wrists.
Anyway.

FIGURE 13 *Faxes from Tom Stoppard to Carey Perloff about the file scene in*
Rock 'n' Roll, *A.C.T. and the Huntington Theatre, 2008. Content courtesy of Tom
Stoppard, photographed by Carey Perloff.*

(6)

(14) I do find it difficult to ~~explain~~
"explain" Max, but not difficult to
write him. Why is he still being
cynical ("unkind") on " What did
you do with yours?" Max is not "nice".
In fact he's damaged, in some way, out of any
niceness — " (uncharmed) Sweet sixteen" ⟵
from childhood, I guess — from the
beginnings and " the ~~God that~~ failed" has
somehow left him ~~knotted~~ knotted up.
I suppose. I hate ~~them~~ trying to analyse
these things.

FIGURE 13 *Continued*

then, you didn't have to tell me, did you?" It is only when Jan appears visibly upset that he *"unbends enough to oblige Jan with an awkward hug."*

We could not tease out the emotional threads of the scene. Jan seemed to want something from Max that Max refused to give; furthermore, the bombshells he drops about the files did not seem to change the dynamic or to open Max to further understanding; indeed, the scene felt like it ended the way it had begun. Was not something supposed to change? This was obviously a cathartic and important event for both characters, and we felt we were not getting it right. To my relief, Stoppard assured me that Trevor Nunn had had the same struggles and that he (Stoppard) had already been through agony explaining that scene to the London company. At that point, he could have simply done what Pinter would have done and invited us to figure it out for ourselves, but Stoppard being Stoppard, he tried valiantly to help us understand his thinking. Hence the ten-page hand-written fax that arrived to accompany the phone call I took at Macy's amongst the dress shirts.

The cover sheet read: "*Carey—I doubt I'm telling you anything you don't already know, so this probably doesn't help you at all . . .! xx, T.*" The document lays out fourteen points, neatly organized and numbered. He begins by saying, "*I'll break it down, which no doubt will make it (me) look wobbly, but here goes.*" Points 1 through 5 are clear: he explains that during the Cold War in Czechoslovakia, many people over the years had given small bits of information to the secret police in exchange for favors of one kind or another, never assuming that Communism would fall and that they would then be exposed as quislings. Stoppard explains that for it to be revealed that Max was aiding an enemy government would not have gone down well at Cambridge (which is not entirely clear when you read the play); he explains that Jan "*naturally assumes that Max would very much have preferred that his file would never come to light.*" So far so good. Point 6 says: "*Here is where I think I'm confusing you . . . Max knows that Jan is coming with a purpose . . . 'Well, I don't read Czech, so you'll have to tell me—tell me the worst, tell me just how much shit I'm in, if this file ever becomes public.' That's what the scene is about so far.*" He goes on to point 7: "*Now, I suspect you would have no problem if it went, 'Yes, it's a present.' 'Thank you! What a load off my mind! I'm enormously grateful!' So why doesn't he? Why does he say 'fuck off, I don't need saving'?*" Point (7A) sadly acknowledges: "*I can't help you the way you want me to help you. He says, 'Fuck you and your present' because that's what Max would say. I suppose he doesn't want to be beholden to that 'snivelling idealist'. I suppose he resents the logic of Jan's present, that he in some sense betrayed his country, however trivially . . . it makes Max angry that Jan should see him as someone who needs saving.*"

Because the events being talked about happened some time before, Max's hostility so long after the fact seemed extreme and unearned to me—but perhaps that was because I found the character's reflexive defensiveness wearying after a while, and wondered why Max was not in some way more curious about what had happened to Jan and what had triggered this gift-giving. At any rate, Stoppard kept going. Point 8: "*So. Like you, Jan is surprised and baffled,*" Stoppard writes. "*The scene seems—unsatisfactorily—over. 'Have we done?' 'No.'*" Point 9 explains that there is something Jan must get off his chest, namely that in 1968, Max's acts of friendship and patronage to Jan had been solicited and received under false pretenses. And then, in Point 10: "*Of course, Max now ought to say 'Aha! So that's why you were pretending to be what you were not, just as I said you were back in Act One!' instead of 'Is there a point to this?' And Jan could say, 'Yes, that's why I've come, mainly. To confess and ask for your forgiveness.' And Max could say, 'Thank you for telling me. Now we have closure . . .' and manly tears on both sides.*"

"*What can I tell you?*" Stoppard asks me in clear frustration. "*One thing I can tell you: in the final minutes of that English Vietnam film (was it called 'The Killing Fields'?) the English journalist meets again the Vietnamese interpreter who saved him, and it goes, 'Will you forgive me?' 'There's nothing to forgive.' Manly tears. I thought it was utterly trite and unnecessary, and lowered a good movie to the usual dreck. Years later, David Putnam or Jofee the director, I forget which, told me that the scene was a re-shoot, added later, in response to previews . . . I'd rather slash my wrists. Anyway . . ."*

I understood completely the desire not to sentimentalize what had been a thorny relationship between Max and Jan from the beginning, and I was not any more interested in "manly tears" than Stoppard was. I was just anxious for the scene to have some forward momentum and to make a degree of emotional sense to an audience. Most Americans watching *Rock 'n' Roll*, for example, would not have known what the consequences would have been of having a secret police file found in post-Communist Prague. For whom would the file matter? Was Max actually in trouble? Was it a kindness that Jan gave him his file to deal with, or some form of humiliation? How could we parse the emotional undercurrents of the scene when we were not exactly sure what was at stake on a purely superficial plot level? Of course, if we had understood the emotional logic of the scene, the surface logic would have mattered less, but we did not. Not yet.

Stoppard continued his valiant effort to explain: *"So why does Max remain unbending, even truculent? Again—because he does, because he's Max, because there's too much commissar in him—and most of all because he doesn't know what's coming. He already knows, or suspects, what Jan is telling him, but he is genuinely surprised by 'I ask your forgiveness'"* (for having come to Cambridge under false pretenses). So, in Point 12, he acknowledges, *"I know—and have known for a long time— that the story of this part of the scene would be clearer without the three speeches which follow 'make myself indispensable'. Yes. I do know that . . . I tried to move those three speeches but I couldn't make them fit elsewhere."* "Nevertheless," he insists in Point 13, *"that is the story of the scene. Jan's confession falls on very unsentimental ground because Max is unsentimental (cf. cancer scene). In fact his first reaction when he realizes Jan could have kept quiet, is to begin to laugh, because the realpolitik of Marx-Leninism, 'you didn't have to tell me', is a cynical reaction. Finally—finally— Jan's tears are what breaks through to Max enough to get a 'human' response from him."*

On the final page of this long hand-written epistle, Stoppard finally arrived at Point 14. When I read it, I had to laugh, because in fact what he articulated there (full of cross-outs and evident frustration) was all that I actually needed: *"I do find it difficult to 'explain' Max, but not difficult to write him. Why is he still being cynical ("unkind") on 'What did you do with yours?' Max is not 'nice'. In fact he's damaged, in some way, out of any niceness—from childhood I guess—from the beginnings, and 'the God that failed' has somehow left him knotted up. I suppose. I hate trying to analyse these things."*

These few sentences were invaluable to me. *Damage* is something an actor can understand, and play. Stoppard was telling us that his Max, like Pinter's Max in *The Homecoming,* was too broken to behave well or logically. To my mind, it would have been useful to get a few more glimpses of Max's "brokenness" over the course of the play to prepare us for that penultimate scene, but for now it was enough for Stoppard to explain that this was a man who was damaged "from childhood." There is thus something about Max that is almost incapable of empathy or kindness. He is an ideologue out of *fear* more than out of conviction, which means that his arguments are only part of the equation. Even his dying wife has to plead with him, "I don't want your 'mind' which you can make out of beer cans. Don't bring it to my funeral. I want your grieving soul or nothing." I should have recognized the dynamic with Jan from Max's earlier scenes with Eleanor: clearly, Max invests so deeply in materialism because matters of the heart are both foreign and threatening to him, even when dealing with a wife he dearly loves. Similarly, he neither intuits Esme's feelings for Jan nor his own subsequent desire for Lenka, he simply knows he's grieving. I was moved that this explanation had come from a playwright with an immensely complicated past who was in the midst of uncovering the sorrow and trauma of his own family history and who was, perhaps, unclear what to do with the knowledge he was acquiring.

Once Jack Willis understood that Max's response was that of an emotionally stunted man who was too broken himself to sympathize with or truly understand Jan, the scene became richer and more interesting to play. Max's behavior did not have to be logical, or even completely connected to what Jan was saying, it simply had to be vulnerable. Faced with the return of this young man, Max was at a loss. The stage directions to play him "angry" were in fact not as useful as the notion of playing him "broken." (Years later, during rehearsals for *The Hard Problem*, Stoppard told us "I tend to use the word 'roused' as an all-purpose indicator of uplift," and perhaps this applies to Max as well.) Jan was Max's own specially chosen bright boy. When this surrogate son returns to the garden bearing evidence not only of Max's complicity with an enemy regime but of his own caring for Jan and his attempt to free Jan from prison, Max feels exposed. Vulnerability embarrasses him; it is not a state he is used to. He gets snarky ("Why don't you take this file and fuck off back to Prague") because he is not sure what the appropriate emotional response should be. Once we understood how "untidy" the scene could be, rehearsals became much more spontaneous and alive.

I felt badly for eliciting Stoppard's dutiful attempt at exegesis, when perhaps I should have simply asked for a clue to Max's emotional state. In his aforementioned toast at the occasion of my twentieth anniversary at A.C.T., Stoppard quipped, "A friend of mine, an elderly lady, told me once that going to the theatre had something in common with going to church, namely that there's no point in going at all unless you're prepared to meet it

FIGURE 14 *Jack Willis and Manoel Felciano in the file scene of* Rock 'n' Roll, *A.C.T. and the Huntington Theatre, 2008. Scenery by Douglas Schmidt, lighting by Robert Wierzel, costumes by Alex Jaeger. Photo by Kevin Berne.*

half way. I doubt that Carey would agree with that. With her, while you're deciding whether to meet the play halfway, you're likely to find your shoulders pinned to the back of your seat with your play in your lap." I hope that is not the case, but I am fairly relentless in trying to get to the bottom of things I do not understand or cannot quite bring to life. Emotional clues are hard to come by with Stoppard; he is as protective of his characters as he is of himself, and rarely gives away where they are vulnerable or in hiding. This is particularly true in his later plays. The arguments, as important as they are to the "themes" of the play, can occasionally be a distraction, because winning the intellectual point has stopped being a primary goal.

The scene we struggled so hard to unearth turned out to be about *grief,* pure and simple. Max's grief at losing Eleanor is coupled with his grief that a belief he had held onto so passionately all his life was being roundly discredited. Max's pain is made worse because the messenger is Jan, a man who has meant so much to him at a happier time in his life. Stoppard intuitively knew that by placing Jan in Max's garden (the locus of his marriage with Eleanor), the pain and pleasure of that past would come rushing back to both of them. The scene is full of regret, suffused with betrayal. Jan has lied to Max all along, which feels especially cruel when both acknowledge how hard Max had worked to get Jan out of prison. There is a feeling of failure on both sides. If Jan expected warmth or welcome from this Professor who had meant so much to him, he was clearly deluded. Sentiment was impossible. They should both have done better. Communism should have done better. Ideals should have lasted. Love should have triumphed. But everything had changed.

As with *Indian Ink,* the last few moments of *Rock 'n' Roll* were a work-in-progress right through to opening night. There was a "London version" of the ending (published by Faber), a "New York" version, and, apparently a "middle version" which was ours. The goal (as Stoppard reminded me later) was to get as quickly as possible from the final reunion scene in Cambridge to the stadium in Prague where the Rolling Stones were playing, without losing the wonderful story of Havel's first speech as President and the occasion of Ferdinand and Esme meeting. In the London version, the final scene takes place in Prague between Jan, Esme, and a Waiter, and begins with: JAN: We should eat something before the concert. ESME: I'll wait till we get home.

Esme then talks dirty to Jan on the assumption that the Czech Waiter will not understand, only to discover that he speaks perfect English. By the time the play had arrived in San Francisco, the Waiter's lines had somehow been transferred to Ferdinand, Jan's best friend. Then the question became, what was the best line with which Ferdinand could reveal his knowledge of English? We started with, "Okay, I'll see what I can do" and ended up with, "Okay, no problem"; Stoppard later said he thought that was too short to convey the joke, and that he preferred the Waiter's longer line which was "That's two beers and a cheese sandwich then." Regardless, one of my favorite discoveries, in going back to my rehearsal notes, was Stoppard's minute moment-to-moment explanation of how the final sex talk should be played. "The sexual connotation does not include Jan until 'First I'd like . . .'," Stoppard carefully explained. But "Esme is heading for sex from 'I know'." He proceeded to annotate each line, as follows:

Jan   That's too long to wait. (*"meaning food"*)

Esme   I know. (*"beginning to mean sex"*)

Jan   You can have anything you like. (*"still meaning food"*)

Esme   Anything I like? (*"definitely meaning sex"*)

Jan   Yes. (*"still food"*)

Esme   Promise? (*"sex"*)

Jan   (?). (*"what are you talking about?"*)

Esme   First I'd like the all-over kissing, and then the shagged senseless, and then just lie there—so tell Ferdinand to tell Havel to tell the Stones to get a move on. (*"Sex sex sex"*)

Ferdinand   Okay, no problem. (*"I understand you perfectly"*)

This delicious exchange took a great deal of finesse, first on the part of the writer who pared it away until it had just enough language to carry the requisite freight, and then on the part of the actors who had to operate on different trajectories until the final punch line, which released all three characters into laughter, romance and, one hopes, a better future, underscored by Esme's "I don't care, I don't care, I don't *care!*" "I want the absolute minimum," Stoppard has told actors during rehearsal. "I don't want to write over-explicitly."[3] This fear of explicitness, however, is coupled with deep feeling (and occasionally, deep pleasure) that has to be mined.

Douglas Schmidt's set design for *Rock 'n' Roll* featured an upended building seen from within, as if three walls of a house had been stood on their side; every scene in the play had to land inside that skewed perspective. Stoppard's text revealed the upending of human relations that happens when political systems become agents of deception and lies, and all values seem backwards or inside out. He had mined this idea beautifully in *Hapgood*, in which the Russian love interest and double agent Kerner compares the West and the Soviet Union: "The West is morally superior, in my opinion. It is unjust and corrupt like the East, of course, but here it means the system has failed; at home it means the system is working." In such a universe, trust is hard to come by, and confession can be death. In order to realize *Rock 'n' Roll* on stage, we had to allow the characters to be as messy, incoherent and full of contradictions as the situation in which they found themselves. We also had to find a way to sustain a beautiful thread of desire which is revealed in the first scene and is finally fleshed out in the final moments of the play. In the end, the more *Rock 'n' Roll* became an emotional reflection of Stoppard's own ambivalent but idealistic heart and soul, the more effective it was as theater.

A happy accident during our production of *Rock 'n' Roll* was meeting the band that helped inspire the play. As a nod to the role their music had played in the events of Czech history, the Plastic People of the Universe had reconstituted in 1997, twenty years after Charter 77, and had loosely stayed together since then. During the run of *Rock 'n' Roll* at A.C.T. the band played San Francisco. We could not quite believe that these famous "pagans" had shown up on our doorsteps just as we were trying to tell their story onstage. The night before their gig at the Independent, they came to see our production (in which we had used their music at strategic moments), and afterwards met with the audience, chatted with the cast, and sold merchandise which we all eagerly bought. Manoel Felciano, who played Jan, was a musician and rock 'n' roll devotee himself; he found the encounter with those anarchic musicians profoundly moving, a feeling that shaped his performance as Jan subsequently. The next night, when our curtain came down, we all descended upon the music venue in our "Plastic People of the Universe" t-shirts, exulting at the sight of a group of passionate aging Czechs playing their unique brand of cacophonous, rebellious rock 'n' roll. The rest of the San Francisco audience, totally unaware of what this band had done

FIGURE 15 *Sketches for the set design of* Rock 'n' Roll *by Douglas Schmidt, A.C.T. and the Huntington Theatre, 2008. Sketches courtesy of Douglas Schmidt.*

to change the world, bopped along, happy in their ignorance. It was a surreal and moving example of life meeting art.

Two major national events were happening during our production of *Rock 'n' Roll*: the Great Recession had begun, and Barack Obama was elected President. In spite of the looming financial crisis, the play seemed suffused with the spirit of hope that Obama's election promised. A co-production with the Huntington Theatre in Boston, *Rock 'n' Roll* played in San Francisco in September/October 2008, and then traveled to Boston in November, where we were in technical rehearsals on Election Night. The sound of the Plastic People of the Universe thundering into the Huntington auditorium will forever be associated in my mind with the wild emotional journey of that evening: we ended rehearsal at 9 p.m. just as the election returns were starting to come in, roaming the streets of Boston for hours afterwards until we ended up in Harvard Square right before midnight, when victory was declared for Obama. My daughter Lexie, whom Stoppard always associated with Thomasina in *Arcadia*, was a sophomore at Harvard that year, and I remember thinking (naively in retrospect) that the Obama era was going to be a watershed for her generation, a time of political engagement and a renewed belief in the positive power of government. "Yes we can" was the slogan of the day. This meant that for audiences watching *Rock 'n' Roll*, the message that art actually mattered and that despite the messiness of history, change could happen, felt apropos and alive. For a brief period, we ignored Jan's warning that if "all systems are blood brothers," one had to be careful of simply replacing one system with another. After the duplicity of the Bush years, in which surveillance was described as "patriotism" and harassment as "cleansing," we suddenly had a President of infinite verbal felicity who believed that the language could be reclaimed from the debasement of political discourse.

Back in San Francisco, I began struggling with how to re-invigorate a major theater in the wake of financial collapse and how to re-define "meaning" for an audience in need of sustenance. *Rock 'n' Roll* seemed to lay out the issues so clearly. Maybe commercialism was not the key. Maybe trying to fit the norm, to impress the *New York Times*, to "grow" our subscriber base and measure success by numbers of tickets sold was not the answer. Maybe it was time for some pagan idealism again. I thought of what Jirous, the Artistic Director of the Plastics, had articulated so beautifully in his 1975 "Report on the Third Czech Musical Revival": "In Bohemia, the situation is essentially different, and far better than the West, because we live in an atmosphere of complete agreement: the first (official) culture doesn't want us, and we don't want anything to do with the first culture. This eliminates the temptation that for everyone, even the strongest artist, is the seed of destruction: the desire for recognition, success, winning prizes and titles, and last but not least, the material security which follows." How ironic that this play about a rebel band that helped bring down Communism was written by a knighted English artist of immense prestige and wealth. But Stoppard's outsider perspective and idealism about the power of art to make order out of chaos had remained with him.

One of the interesting themes of Stoppard's later plays is the inability of emotionally-damaged people to articulate their pain. Finding ways to actively protect the secrets of inner life while revealing just enough to keep an audience hooked is a balance which must be carefully shaped by the director and actors throughout the rehearsal process. I had a second challenge with a Stoppardian male character who refuses to yield up his secrets a decade after *Rock 'n' Roll*, during rehearsals for *The Hard Problem* in 2015. This time, that character was not an irascible older man but a sexy young scientist who *seemed* like he was going to be our friend. And unlike with *Rock 'n' Roll*, on this occasion I had to ultimately let go of the desire to find emotional logic and try to stay focused on the passion of the argument instead.

The Hard Problem was deliberately minimal; Stoppard, claiming to be envious of contemporary playwrights who manage to write ninety-minute one-set plays, wanted *The Hard Problem* to be as spare as possible. But as always with Stoppard, he had much more to say than would comfortably fit into a ninety-minute format, and I felt that the emotional life of his characters in *The Hard Problem* was slightly under-nourished as a result. It was up to the actors to bring a history and inner life to scientists, quants, and Pilates teachers whose motives and behavior were occasionally oblique. The exception was the central character, Hilary, whose story echoed a true event in the life of Stoppard's former lover Sinead Cusack; at age seventeen, just as she was starting out as an actress at the Abbey Theatre, Cusack had had a brief affair with legendary Irish actor Vincent Dowling; the result was a "shame baby" that Cusack was forced to give up and whom she grieved about for many years. Thirty years later, having had a successful stage career herself, Cusack finally made connection with her son. He was Richard Boyd Barrett, a Socialist politician in Ireland, and the two quickly bonded (so much so that in some sense Richard became the love of her life, and Cusack no longer needed Stoppard in the same way, leading to their sad but highly amicable break up). The story of Cusack's teen pregnancy and its aftermath ultimately provided the heartbeat for, and framework of, *The Hard Problem*, in which Hilary (a young neuroscience researcher and mother of a baby born out of wedlock and given up when she was fifteen), is trying to prove that altruism is an innate feature of human consciousness. The study she undertakes over the course of the play, as described by her tutor and occasional bed partner Spike, "points to a strong indication that we start off nice and learn to be nasty, instead of the received wisdom that we start off nasty and learn to be nice." Hilary believes there is such a thing as *goodness*; every night, she prays for forgiveness for having abandoned her daughter. Needless to say, this behavior does not sit well with the scientists she encounters, particularly Spike, who finds her thinking embarrassing. "Let me make three points about your round-table presentation," he tells her later in the play. "Don't circulate it. If you circulate it, don't put your name on it. If you put your name on it, don't put the Krohl's name on it. (*an afterthought*) If you circulate it with your name and the Krohl's on it, don't call it, 'Is God the last man standing?'"

The faith/reason dialectic has found fertile ground with Stoppard on many previous occasions, and as always, he managed to find bits of himself on both sides of the argument in *The Hard Problem*. By temperament, Stoppard is more like Spike, the witty self-confident intellectual who dismantles Hilary's arguments with razor-sharp analysis. But emotionally and spiritually, Stoppard stands with Hilary. He cannot fathom a world in which the mysteries of the human mind, a mind capable of the sublime as well as of horror, can be reduced to the complex operations of a mechanistic brain. "The cases made for reductive materialism get better and better as science proceeds," Stoppard told Hermione Lee, "but I for one remain unconvinced."

On the first day of rehearsal for *The Hard Problem* at A.C.T., in one of those moments of coincidence that occasionally happen in the insular world of the theater, we discovered another personal connection to this play: the actress playing Hilary, Brenda Meaney, an Irish beauty from a distinguished theatrical family, turned out to be the grandchild of Vincent Dowling and thus the niece of Sinead Cusack's newly discovered son Richard. We listened in stunned silence around the table in the rehearsal room as Brenda described going home to Dublin one Christmas and meeting, at a family party, a man none of her relatives had known existed, and whom her own mother, Bairbre Dowling, never got to encounter before her death. Hilary's circumstance was thus very resonant to Brenda; Stoppard was, of course, fascinated to hear her story and seemed moved by the way that the past is always present, and history returns to make itself felt just when one least expects it. In a play filled with theories about the nature of coincidence ("Dad, what's coincidence?," Cathy asks Jerry in Scene 4, engendering a long disquisition from Jerry ending with, "Everything that makes the coincidence smaller and smaller till you decide it's worth betting your pound, is information"), it astonished us that the "shame baby" who inspired the play turned out, coincidentally, to be the uncle of the actress starring in our production. Stoppardian "luck" asserted itself once again.

Hilary is the most fleshed-out character in this densely argued play; it is her emotional journey we follow as she struggles to find her footing at the Krohl Institute for Brain Science, where she has been given a research position. Her nemesis, as I said, is her tutor Spike, an aptly named scientist with a keen wit and a deep antipathy toward any argument that denies the brain its function as a "thinking machine"; many of his arguments have been well-rehearsed by Max in *Rock 'n' Roll*, and Hilary's ripostes often echo more emotional outbursts of Eleanor's. Perhaps because Spike and Hilary's dialectic had such strong thematic connections to Max and Eleanor's, I initially assumed it must have some degree of emotional heat, but, at least according to the playwright, I was wrong. Hilary's sorrow is not connected to Spike, it is private and pre-dates her meeting him. It is when Spike calls motherlove "genetically selected behavior to maximize (the survival of genes)" that Hilary gets upset, and we begin to understand why this debate is fraught for her. There is no way that Spike, not yet privy to the story of Hilary's baby, can understand her response; still, as we rehearsed the play, we found his callousness bewildering, particularly since Hilary continued to seem eager to sleep with him.

This was one of the questions I brought with me when I traveled to Dorset in August 2016 to spend the weekend with Stoppard and his wife, Sabrina Guinness. We sat in his remarkable study, overlooking a garden redolent of *Arcadia*, and worked our way through the play in preparation for rehearsals in San Francisco in September. We began by discussing those anglicisms that might be worth changing for an American audience, such as a "two one" (a high second-class degree) and "Opal Fruits" (an English candy) for which we found expressions that would be less opaque. (Because the play trafficked in contemporary lived experience much more than had Pinter's *Mountain Language,* the references could be shifted without

damaging the linguistic muscle in a way that was impossible with the Pinter.)
Then there were "quick change" issues to be resolved regarding costumes
(for example, Hilary finishes Scene 2 in her nightgown and must immediately
launch Scene 3 in her interview clothes), and speculations about how much
help an audience might need in following the secret of Hilary's abandoned
child. ("Yes, I was asking too much of the audience," Stoppard told me,
"Definitely perverse of me, which is why I like it.")

But the thorniest conversations revolved around Spike. "I'll come back to
that, and of course to poor Spike whom everybody hates except me," he
wrote me after our meeting, but by the time we went into rehearsal, the
questions remained. Intellectually, Spike is the perfect foil for Hilary: he is
appalled to see her pray and to think that someone so intelligent would
stoop to what he considers mindless faith, while she is appalled by his
unthinking adherence to a utilitarian and literal interpretation of the brain:
"What is to be done with the sublime if you're proud to be a materialist?"
she demands. The thinness of Spike's argument is exposed when Hilary, in
Venice, asks Spike if he would do her a favor and pray for Catherine (her
baby). He resists, telling her it would be meaningless, to which she replies,
"If it's meaningless, what's your problem?" and Spike memorably replies,
"I'd be betraying everything I believed in." Which of course makes her smile.
Materialism, she argues, is just another form of faith. Everyone has to
believe in something. Why not God?

The issue we were having in rehearsal, somewhat similar to that which
troubled us with Max and Jan in *Rock 'n' Roll*, was how to make the arguments
more than just intellectual sparring and how to keep the momentum of the
play moving forward. Put another way, we had to discover what was at *stake*
for the two characters. When I asked Stoppard whether, by the time Hilary and
Spike find themselves in bed together at a conference in Venice, we had not
"moved on from the intellectual arguments of Scene 2," he countered, "I don't
agree that the relationship has moved on from the 'intellectual arguments' of
Scene 2. On the contrary, it's the argument which characterizes the relationship,
and I think it's quite funny that they're still where they left off." Once again, I
felt badly asking him to analyze something which obviously made perfect sense
to him, but the issue of Spike had bedeviled the first London company of the
play and ours as well. "Spike. We are at odds," he wrote.

I'm not interested in 'tracking his growing affection for her'. He's hardly
thought about her. She's hardly thought about him. Here's what I'm
doing: they go to bed and the next time we see them they go to bed again,
after which is his first line, 'So how've you been?' and her first line is
'Have you got a date?' I'm being anti-formulaic. It's not a rom-com. She's
not affronted, I think she's slightly amused. Spike is still Spike. He's a bad
boy but still intellectually engaging . . . I realize how bald this paragraph
must seem to you but it would take me another hour to unpack Spike–
Hilary now. He's like an obscure radio station she found five years ago

and now she's found it again. The love-making is an add-on. I'm finding all the wrong words in trying to convey myself to you . . . I'll try later.

These occasions are where the directorial process becomes complex. It sometimes happens that a director (or indeed, an actor, designer, or other collaborator) finds sections within a play that feel confusing, opaque, or somehow not workable. Regardless, a solution must be found if the theatrical "event" is to succeed. For some directors the solution is to cut (which is not usually permitted if the script is by a living playwright), for others it is to build something around or inside a given moment to help flesh it out or give it life. Casting can be a lifesaver. In this case, in order to tackle Spike in *The Hard Problem*, I knew I first needed to find someone for the role who was innately appealing and warm, not someone who would rely too heavily on argument or who would feel predatory. I cast a wonderful young actor named Dan Clegg, whom we had trained at A.C.T., and he quickly found Spike's charm and sense of humor.

Secondly, over the course of rehearsals, I tried to help Meaney understand that Spike was not emotionally important to Hilary, what was important was her lost baby. By investing too much in Spike, we were putting the stakes in the wrong place. The loss of her child was so unexpectedly profound to Hilary that she had not formed alliances since that time (in the room, Stoppard told Brenda Meaney that Hilary was "happily self-sufficient" and "uninterested in romantic entanglements"); thus, Spike needed to be viewed as a sparring partner without any hope that he might become "boyfriend material." What this meant in practice is that Catherine, the lost daughter, had to remain foremost in Hilary's mind even in, or perhaps especially in, the scenes with Spike. The way to give those scenes heat was not to create an emotional bond between Spike and Hilary but to make sure that Hilary was constantly vulnerable to her own secret. She feels shame about her child, and fear that the child may have turned out to be unhappy or unloved. Spike may be useful as a math expert and intellectual foil, and he is certainly good for a laugh and some quick sex now and then, but Hilary's emotional investment lies elsewhere. No wonder she mystifies him. His passionately held beliefs about brain science crash into her enormous need to hold on to a belief in goodness for her child's sake.

Even with these precepts in mind, it was hard to know how to help an audience parse the Spike–Hilary scenes. This balancing act was particularly difficult to manage in the cathartic party scene in which, surrounded by friends gathered to celebrate the publication of Hilary and Bo's study of altruism in children, Spike publicly skewers her published argument. Hilary's only response to his behavior is to say: "Don't imagine for a moment you're staying the night." In the greater scheme of the play, one could perhaps argue that Spike's obnoxious take-down of Hilary's research paper is its own form of altruism, since he is trying to save her reputation from being sunk by a flawed experiment. Nevertheless, it was hard to watch the heroine of the play being humiliated by her sometime bed-partner (who is, admittedly, drunk) without understanding how we were meant to feel about it.

But Stoppard is always more interested in surprise than in sentiment. Love, in *The Hard Problem*, does not reside in the Spike sub-plot, it ambushes us in the person of Bo, the Chinese-born math genius and research assistant who fudges Hilary's experiment in order to please her with clean results. "Why are you wasting my time with this fan-dance?" fulminates Hilary's boss Leo when he learns of her mistake. "Are you in love with her?" To which Hilary replies, "She's in love with me." "Well," sighs Leo, "finally, something I understand." A brilliant young assistant has ruined her own experiment because she has fallen in love with her boss; that's the reversal that Stoppard was looking for. By the end of *The Hard Problem*, goodness trumps utility when Hilary takes the blame for Bo's data falsification, and we experience all over again Stoppard's love of "irrationality" —as he demonstrated in *Arcadia*, the most airtight and rational predictive system will collapse as soon as desire is involved. One can never predict human nature. So, in *The Hard Problem*, as in all of Stoppard's work, we had to stop trying to connect the dots and start looking for the surprises. What he was trying to explain to us about Spike was that *of course* the audience would assume the play was going to track a love affair between two attractive young intellectuals found in bed early on in the play, so why go there? Instead, in an unexpected reversal, the love of a junior researcher for Hilary upends the narrative.

Did it work? Our production was certainly helped by the depth of Brenda Meaney's performance and the cocky charm of Dan Clegg's Spike. From Clegg's point of view, Spike was clueless rather than cruel. He does not take Hilary up on her offer to travel around Tuscany with her because he knows he is too gauche to be a good traveling companion: "You wouldn't want someone hanging on to your skirts who thinks when you've seen one town in Tuscany you've seen them all." But ultimately, Spike exists in the play to push Hilary to clarify her own beliefs about consciousness, and to give the audience a fair number of good laughs. He is not central to the play's emotional core, and trying to force him into that role was a fool's errand.

Working on *The Hard Problem*, Stoppard reveled in the arcane dealings of the financial industry and the impossible dialectic of the mind/brain conflict; he always takes great pleasure at watching smart people do difficult things well, onstage or off. My main memory of our time together on *The Hard Problem* was seeing him out of the corner of my eye at the side of the rehearsal room, shaggy hair covering his eyes and a rumpled linen jacket over the back of the chair, having set up his work station exactly how he liked it, the table covered in coffee cups and forbidden sweets (purchased at a favorite shop on his walk to the studio), along with a copy of the script and a small notebook and pencil in which gnomic markings occasionally appeared. His fingers hovered restlessly near the cigarette packet which was ready to be deployed as soon as there was a break; fortunately, our rehearsal

FIGURE 16 *Dan Clegg and Brenda Meaney in* The Hard Problem, *American Conservatory Theater, 2016. Scenery by Andrew Boyce, lighting by Russell Champa, costumes by Alex Jaeger. Photo by Kevin Berne.*

studio opened onto a balcony, so the playwright could happily smoke cigarette after cigarette while looking out over the roofs of Chinatown and debating the finer points of the play with the actors. I remember how immensely gracious he was one lunchtime when a donor was invited to come to rehearsal to have a sandwich with Stoppard and proceeded to announce that "he preferred the earlier plays"; Stoppard nodded pleasantly and began inquiring about workings of the man's hedge fund.

One tricky bit of plotting in *The Hard Problem* involved introducing the catastrophe of the 2008 financial crisis into the middle of the play without calling it out explicitly; this also involved revealing to the audience that five years has passed between Scene 3 (2003) and Scene 4 (2008). During our work session in Dorset, we wrestled with how to make this passage of time clear; shortly thereafter, Stoppard wrote me: "At the moment I have no ideas about announcing that it's 2008 or that the financial crisis is in full swing. I'll try to insert both bits of info into the front of Jerry's phone call in a way that doesn't make me shudder." Some weeks later, he followed up with another email, shortly before we began rehearsals:

I know I'm procrastinating. I'm the Cunctator among your writers, but I know from experience that it's better to deal with alterations 'in public', that is, when I'm with the actors—who often have suggestions of their own. In the case of the five year gap between scenes three and four, it seemed to me that an audience would understand, firstly, that if there is talk about Hilary having given birth to a (missing) female baby in the past, and if the next scene begins with a girl child on stage, it surely means that the child is likely to be Hilary's baby; and secondly, if the child is (to quote Lady Bracknell) 'that baby', then several years must have elapsed; and thirdly, if the child is declared to be an adopted child, then only a perverse writer would reveal otherwise. I can't think of anything more clunky than the spoken equivalent of projecting '5 years later' on the back wall. HOWEVER!—you are of course right and I ought to find a way to alert us to the lapse of years.

Once he arrived in San Francisco and settled into our rehearsal process, a simple solution suddenly presented itself. One morning, Stoppard took Scene 4 as written and flipped the order within it so that instead of the scene beginning with a young girl, Cathy, having breakfast (and the audience wondering who that child was and what the time sequence had been), the scene began with Jerry dictating a correction to the *Financial Times* about an analyst's report saying Krohl Capital had "called the top of the market." Since it was clear from Jerry's demeanor that something serious was happening, the story of the financial meltdown was more easily introduced. The analyst Amal enters and Jerry punishes him for having indiscreetly spoken to a journalist about the over-leveraged market. It was then that we saw a twelve-year-old girl wander into the dining room for breakfast. Simply by re-ordering the two halves of the scene, we were able to create a context and timeframe for the child that made her identity clear. By the time Cathy asks her mother on the phone, "Am I an orphan? ... Sally says if you're adopted it means you're an orphan," we felt the viewer would have had time to put the pieces together and discover with pleasure that this must be Hilary's lost daughter. Indeed, all was clear when we put the play in front of an audience.

Stoppard was extremely pleased to have found a solution that had integrity without feeling baldly expositional. Halfway through our run, we had another "aha" that further refined the infamous Scene 4. As written, Amal makes a crucial discovery as he exits Jerry's apartment after having been humiliated by his boss: "But I wasn't wrong," Amal has insisted about his assertion that the market was over-leveraged. "You were early, which is the same thing," Jerry retorts. Amal takes a beat and then realizes, with admiration, what Jerry's strategy is: "You're going to short the market?" To which Jerry simply replies, "Use the service stairs." Once again, Jerry is ahead of everyone else, as was Mike Ryan, who was playing the role in our production. After a matinee one day, Ryan sent me the following email:

While I am reaming Amal, I say, "meanwhile you sit in your corner and share your limp-dick, short-the-market wisdom with nobody except your supervisor." It occurred to me yesterday that line implies Amal has suggested that we should be shorting the market. The problem with that, of course, is that Jerry is not, in fact, one step ahead of him, and there's no discovery at the end of the scene for Amal.... (*whereas*) my understanding from conversations I have had with you and Tom is that Amal has simply called the *top-of-the-market*, probably suggesting that it was time to sell . . . A simple line solution would be to say, "Meanwhile, you sit in your corner and share your limp-dick top-of-the-market wisdom with nobody except your supervisor."

When I forwarded this thought to Stoppard, he responded immediately: "Dear Mike, I absolutely love your 'new line'. Not only does it make better sense, it makes better sound. As you rightly suspect, I wasn't setting myself a high standard of nuanced expertise here, but I thought—wrongly—that I should use a term Amal was going to repeat. I see now that it's stronger for Amal to take the wording a step forward. Stop the presses! Yours ever, Tom." The intricate financial logic of the scene finally made sense, reminding us once again that theater at its best is an iterative art form, especially when you are dealing with a Stoppard play.

The process of collaboration on *The Hard Problem* affirmed Stoppard's willingness to wrestle with thorny details until a satisfactory way forward can be found for all involved. He is happiest when the process is collaborative and when the artists in the room, whether actors, designers, director or even stage manager, are part of "molding the clay." Together we focused on another complicated moment in *The Hard Problem* which revolves around a cake Hilary produces in the party in Scene 9. The party takes place on Guy Fawkes Day, which we had changed to "Bonfire Night" for the benefit of American audiences. Stoppard wanted the audience to understand that the cake was actually baked in honor of Catherine's birthday ("She was six in November. Guy Fawkes. The sky was exploding," Hilary has told Julia). Stoppard urged Brenda Meaney to really look after "the sky was exploding" in Scene 3, so that, when we arrived at Scene 9 and heard "*the distant noise and illumination of modest fireworks,*" we would connect this to Catherine's birthday. But it is a subtle clue. In the original draft of the script, Hilary comes out of the kitchen distraught and says to Julia, "Guess what? I burnt her cake, too." The reference is easy to miss, which was a shame because knowing that the disastrous dinner party coincided with Catherine's birthday helped explain why Hilary was so fraught: it was not just because she was a terrible cook or because she was nervous about the publication of her experiment, it was again about her lost child.

After a week or so of watching the scene in rehearsal, Stoppard decided to add two short lines: when Hilary says, "I burnt her cake too," he asked the actress playing Julia to query gently, "Did you really bake her a cake?" and Hilary to reply, "I always do." We then found a quiet spot downstage where this private exchange could take place. Undoubtedly, the event still went unremarked by many audiences in performance, but the burnt birthday cake became part of the texture of Hilary's struggle, which felt useful and satisfying.

Stoppard graciously acknowledged the challenges of bringing *The Hard Problem* to life in his opening card, in which he described it as "a play which doesn't forgive. I think this 'brisk' text is on a tightrope, unlike, say, *Real Thing* or *Arcadia,* which will be more or less okay wherever. So I owe you!" Stoppard has often commented that, with rewrites and rehearsal changes, you are really just tinkering with five percent around the margins. But in the intricate fabric of a play in production, that five percent can tell the tale.

The other great pleasure of *The Hard Problem,* for me in particular, was developing the score. Because the play took place in 2008 and was about brain science and the most current neuroscientific debates, I was interested in using music that was muscular, contemporary, and electronic, rather than the Bach that was used for the original London production. My son Nick (aged twenty-one at the time) was an accomplished DJ and song writer who was about to arrive on the scene as "Wingtip" with a viral hit, *Rewind,* that got him a record contract with Republic Records. Stoppard began listening to Nick's music and was hooked—a longtime lover of rock 'n' roll, Stoppard was drawn to Wingtip's dance beats and propulsive, sexy feel. The slightly ironic lyrics amused him as well. Our sound designer Brenden Aanes therefore took dozens of Wingtip tracks and turned them into cues for the show, culminating in the party scene which featured *Rewind* playing at full blast from the speaker system in the Geary. As I look back upon my many collaborations with Stoppard, one of my fondest moments was walking into a technical rehearsal one evening and finding Stoppard and my son at the back of the house, headphones on, listening to tracks with profound concentration as they sought to find the perfect moment in the song to launch the party. On opening night, Stoppard left me a note that said, "I hope Nick looks back on *The Hard Problem* at A.C.T. as a big moment in his career. He's done so brilliantly for us." I think it moved him that the small blond boy he had first met crawling around the Geary had become a tall and surprising twenty-something who helped infuse a play about neuroscience with the dynamism of an infectious tune.

I want to close this chapter with some brief thoughts about perhaps my favorite Stoppard play and the one most congenial to my own background, *The Invention of Love* (2000). If *Rock 'n' Roll* and *The Hard Problem* presented Stoppard's collaborators with the challenge of excavating the emotion behind complex political and scientific arguments, *The Invention of Love* presents arguments about classical scholarship and textual emendation that only the most rarified of audiences might have familiarity with. *Rock 'n' Roll* ends with Esme yelling joyfully, "I don't care! I don't care! I don't care!," and that was my own delighted response when Stoppard slipped me an early draft of *The Invention of Love.* I knew the play would be difficult to realize, immersed as it was in the intricacies of philology and translating Latin. It was also an expensive proposition, featuring a large cast of mostly middle-aged men and many set locations. But I didn't care; I found the writing wildly imaginative and absolutely heartbreaking.

Like Stoppard, I have always been obsessed with the fragments that have come down to us from the ancient classical world. From the age of seven, I wanted to be an archaeologist, and spent much of my youth excavating sites in the American Southwest, with one eye always on Greece. My dream was to uncover the next great Bronze Age site, so I went to Stanford to study with archaeologist Michael Jameson. It was in my first-year Greek class, taught by Helene Foley, that I fell in love with theater. Her approach was inspired: even when learning the alphabet, drama was central to our understanding. We read "Brekekekex koax koax" of Aristophanes' *The Frogs* on the second day of class, and my delight in hearing the language of Greek drama in its original tongue never left me. Foley's class set me on the path of a theater career. But the metaphor if not the practice of archaeology has remained central to me as a director: my task is to excavate clues that give me insight into the behavior, belief, and ideas buried inside a play.

Stoppard let me read *The Invention of Love* during rehearsals of *Indian Ink* in 1998, and we took advantage of his presence in San Francisco to hold a press conference announcing our intention to do the American premiere of the new play the following season. With *The Invention of Love,* I felt I had come home. I understood what it was to parse a difficult passage of ancient poetry, how complex it was to transform the subtleties of an inflected language into English equivalents, how heartbreaking the poetry of repressed love is throughout the classical era, and how complex it was to find in the fragments that have been left to us a wholeness of experience. Furthermore, San Francisco was one of the most important gay communities in the world; my Stanford thesis advisor Jack Winkler was the first person I had known to die of AIDS in the 1980s, and the pain and struggles of being gay in America were immediate to our audience. Stoppard's exploration of Housman's "forbidden" love was a story I wanted to bring to A.C.T. We were able to secure the rights to the American premiere of *The Invention of Love* in part because many American producers, having seen it in London or read it on their own, found the play too abstruse and intellectual to take the risk. Three hours of unknown classicists wandering across the stage arguing about textual emendations and unrequited passion was not everyone's idea of a good night out. But that did not matter to me. It was the Millennium, I was turning forty, and I wanted to do the play almost as a gift to myself.

The Invention of Love is a dream play, structured as a series of ever-recurring images and events in the mind of the poet A.E. Housman shortly before his death at age 77. It is also, among other things, a debate between Housman and playwright Oscar Wilde about the relationship of art to life. Stoppard freed himself from historical and biographical accuracy and from linear narrative by creating an eccentric and highly unreliable narrator on the cusp of death. AEH defends his mental peregrinations thus: "not so out of court as to count as an untruth in the dream-warp of the ultimate room. . . . And yet not dreaming either, wide awake to all the risks—archaism, anachronism, the wayward inconsequence that only hindsight can acquit of *non sequitur* ... and the unities out of the window without so much as a window to be out of." In the mind of aging A.E. Housman, anything was possible. As the play begins, AEH is standing on the shores of the River Styx; that river then morphs, in a magical way, into the River Cam upon which his young self is punting with a fellow classicist, Pollard, and his great love, the scientist Moses Jackson.

Stoppard's ingenious solution to the question of how to get inside the heart of the deeply repressed Housman was to bifurcate the character. Of course, in many ways the historical Housman had already bifurcated himself: "A poet and a scholar" says the boatman Charon as if waiting for a second man to appear on the River Styx. "I'm afraid that must be me," says AEH ruefully. Stoppard was clearly fascinated by the duality of this seemingly desiccated and lonely classicist who also turned out to be a passionate poet whose writing became a monument to an impossible love. AEH beautifully embodied the Romanticism/Classicism dialectic that had shaped *Arcadia*, and the process of writing about him inspired in Stoppard a frenzy of reading and investigation that felt excessive even to him. I believe he told me that he had read eighty-five volumes on Housman and the Roman poets before even beginning the play. But he adored the research (many of the volumes were kept neatly in a traveling bookshelf-cum-satchel that had been purpose-built for Stoppard and which he carried with him to rehearsals) and the dialogue with eminent classicists from around the world. Here was a man who had never gone to university, finally in conversation with Oxford's finest minds on the subject of textual emendations in Propertius.

In order to activate Housman's conflicts, Stoppard hit upon the solution of dividing the character into his younger self, called Housman, and his old self, called AEH. As I noted in Chapter 1, the duality of warring identities is something that has preoccupied Stoppard since *Rosencrantz and Guildenstern are Dead*, and his own ongoing exploration about his past and his younger self only made this more potent. The divided self of his lead character in many ways echoed his own duelling personalities: the glamorous celebrity playwright never without a quip juxtaposed with the shy romantic hoping not to be exposed. The beauty of the divided-self solution in *Invention of Love* is that, unlike in life, the older man can influence his younger self as the younger man struggles to make sense of his conflicted heart. I wondered if in some way the play gave Stoppard an opportunity to imagine what he would have said to his own younger self at that moment had the occasion arisen. The play was completed a year after his mother's death, and his own reckoning with his past and with mortality had clearly begun.

The device of the "two Housmans" also offered innumerable opportunities for comedy: "Where can we sit down before philosophy finds us out?" asks AEH his younger self when they first meet. "I'm not as young as I was. Whereas you, of course, are." Further comic potential could be found in the situation of an elderly poet who arrives at the edge of death desperately needing to pee; there are chamber pots and urination jokes throughout. At the same time, the play is infused with Stoppard's own obsession with knowledge for its own sake, and with the moral imperative of *learning*.

Having carefully chosen those particular classical texts (from Catullus to Horace) which are connected to the invention of the "love poem" as we know it, Stoppard's exercises in translation seemed more seamlessly woven into the emotional life of these lovelorn characters than, say, the Sappho translations are woven into *Rock 'n' Roll*. If understanding the nature of Max's emotional damage was challenging in *Rock 'n' Roll,* with AEH, the wound was clear. This was a man who loved men in a culture that ultimately criminalized that desire. Although classicists had long understood that the feelings Greek men exhibited for each other in the poetry of Horace or the plays of Euripides were what we would later call "homosexual," AEH lived in a censorious Victorian era in which "sodomites" were arrested and prosecuted. The tensions between paganism and Christianity, and between modernism and Victorianism, give the play its muscle.

The "double" for AEH in *The Invention of Love* is Oscar Wilde, who lived his life as flamboyantly and unabashedly as AEH lived his in rectitude and repression. Their collision crystallizes the seminal question of how to measure a successful life, and whether Wilde's decision to "burn with a hard gem-like flame" is more admirable than the way Housman buried that flame while leaving a poetic monument behind. Stoppard has as much or more empathy for the poet who chose rectitude and repression as for the one who chose flamboyance and self-declaration. After *Invention* opened, he got caught up in a futile war of words with classicist Daniel Mendelsohn in the *New York Review of Books*, who accused Stoppard of making Wilde the more sympathetic character, a charge Stoppard vehemently disputed. But Stoppard had always given the best arguments to the opposing counsel— that was, in his mind, a mark of good playwriting. He did tell Jamie Cromwell, who played AEH at A.C.T., that he believed AEH's private devotion to the love in his heart, and the poetry that this love inspired, was something to be revered and admired.

Exploring AEH's emotional reticence occupied much of our rehearsal time: the temptation, of course, is to reveal his anguish early on and, equally, to make clear to the audience that he is gay. But in this case, I felt that the more buttoned up AEH was, the more heartbreaking the play became. It was not an issue of obtuseness, as with Max in *Rock 'n' Roll*, because in the case of *Invention*, we were given AEH's younger self as a key emotional counterbalance. It seemed important that young Housman be full of all the emotional ardor Wilde would have admired, without fully understanding his own feelings. His loneliness is heartbreaking: "I was waiting for them (his friends) on a bench by the river and it came upon me that I was alone, and there was no help for anything." *Invention* is infused with that deep sense of loss discussed in Chapter 1 in relation to Stoppard's Jewish legacy: "Scholarship is a small redress against the vast unreason of what is taken from us," Housman explains to his friend Pollard. We watch Housman fall in love with Mo, navigate his own feelings, try to stay close to him after Cambridge even if it meant destroying his own academic career, and finally, in the "bedsit scene," be "outed" and decide to move away. That scene, a precursor to the Durance proposal scene in *Indian Ink*, is a masterpiece of taut understatement at the heart of a highly loquacious play:

Housman   Will you mind if I go to live somewhere but close by?

Jackson   Why? Oh ...

Housman   We'll still be friends, won't we?

Jackson   Oh!

Housman   Of *course* Rosa knew—of *course* she'd know!

Jackson   Oh!

Housman   Did you really not know even for a minute?

We spent hours on this one tiny exchange, trying to infuse it with both the depth of feeling it demanded and the desperate inarticulateness the moment required; as AEH reminds Chamberlain, "Confession is an act of violence against the unoffending." Because it was a dream play, there were many opportunities to stage scenes from the past in conjunction with the older AEH looking on from a distance at the confusion of his youth. Multiple points of view could be consistently sustained and compared, offering a huge variety of visual options throughout. *The Invention of Love*'s theatrical structure mostly solves the problem of didacticism that has occasionally plagued Stoppard's plays. Each time a specific argument threatens to overwhelm the proceedings, AEH's "lucid dreaming" floats the scene away and we move on to something new. "I heard Ruskin lecture in my first term. Painters belayed on every side," Housman quips at the end of his first long scene with AEH, and suddenly the kaleidoscope shifts: "I think we're in danger of going round again," AEH replies, and indeed we are.

Designing these dreamlike transitions was a delight for the creative team; we made elaborate storyboards with drawings of every iteration of the set's moving parts and spent many hours counting crew members to make sure we had enough manpower to fly one piece of scenery, track a second, and prepare a third all at the same time. For the most part, Loy Arcenas' elegant and supple design worked seamlessly. A notable exception was the boat, which was meant to glide magically across the stage, romantically carrying the three young men along the River Cam past the stationary old poet. The night of our first preview, a cable underneath the stage snapped and the boat ground to a halt, forcing the three actors to "walk on the water" in order to finally exit the stage (which amused us since in AEH's last speech he comments that "walking on water is not among my party tricks"). We were forced to take a 45-minute break in the middle of Act 1 to repair things, which allowed delighted members of the audience to surround the tired playwright and engage him in vigorous conversation.

At the climax of *The Invention of Love* rehearsals, my house nearly burned down. This was the result of ashes left over from a fire we had had on New Year's Eve to welcome the Millennium, an irony that was not lost on me since *Invention* is a play filled with fire imagery and culminates in the bonfires of the Queen's Diamond Jubilee: "It was a grand sight. I counted fifty-two fires just to the south and west," as AEH comments. *The Invention of Love* was a millennial play being rehearsed at the dawn of our own new century; one of our fears at the time was that the "Y2K bug" would shut down computers worldwide and prevent planes from flying, designers from arriving, and computers from running to program our lights and sound. As it happened, the out-of-town company of *Invention* was at my house celebrating New Year's Eve as we prepared to enter the twenty-first century. Having put the ashes in a bag by the garbage in the basement, I went to the theater the next day to begin technical rehearsals. The dire warnings about Y2K had not materialized, our lighting designer Jim Ingalls had made it in from Amsterdam, and all was proceeding according to plan when my assistant appeared just after lunch to inform me that there were fire trucks surrounding my house and I had better go home. When I arrived at the house shortly thereafter with my husband and children in tow, firemen were breaking down the doors to let the smoke out. Although in the end there was minimal damage, our house proved uninhabitable for six months and my family moved to an alternative apartment while it was repaired. Final rehearsals of *Invention* were conducted with me wearing the same clothes for days on end as we shaped the complex choreography and managed endless scene changes. But once again, I didn't care. The play ushered in the new century with the kind of capacious vision I longed for, with an insistence that the struggle to create beauty was worth it and had always been contentious. "Your life is a terrible thing," AEH tells Wilde, "a chronological error. The choice was not always between renunciation and folly." But Wilde resists AEH's assessment: "Better a fallen rocket than never a burst of light . . . I made my life into my art and it was an unqualified success. . . . I awoke the imagination of the century." Like AEH, we found ourselves on the cusp of a new era, an era in which debates about the nature and purpose of art have become as heated and passionate as they were in Wilde's own time. Is there still room for the notion of knowledge and beauty for their own sake, for a belief in the transformative powers of the imagination, and for the love of investigating the fragments that have been left to us? Can we develop a relationship to our past that is generative and not toxic? Only time will tell.

The Invention of Love ends not with a dramatic conclusion but with a simple release of breath. We wrestled in previews with the most satisfying way to convey that kind of "dot dot dot" ending. AEH is standing on the shore of the River Styx, about to give way to death. He makes a tongue-in-cheek reference to urinating: "And now I really do have to go." And then he looks out at us and finally admits, "How lucky to find myself standing on this empty shore, with the indifferent waters lapping at my feet." It is a gentle moment, as if AEH's tormented soul were finally being untethered. How to best render that visually? We tried many staging ideas for those last moments and a variety of music cues, but nothing quite satisfied until, during the final rehearsal before the last preview, lighting designer Jim Ingalls had an idea. He had hung several lights equipped with moving templates called "twin-spins" for the water sequences in the play, to give a sense of the river flowing on the floor as the boat travelled across the stage. On an impulse, Ingalls suddenly put those lights into the final cue of the show, so that across Jamie Cromwell's face, as the stage started to go dark, a wash of gentle lights began to move and swirl. It felt as if a last breath of life was passing across AEH and disappearing into the ether. We sat in the silence of the theater, feeling the dissipation of time and the graceful end to a difficult and often tormented existence. Stoppard smiled at Ingalls, enchanted and grateful as he always was when another artist found the perfect solution. Ingalls' magical light cue released the play in a way that could only happen in the theater. A new century was dawning, at the same moment as we watched A.E. Housman gracefully exit his own.

Conclusion

As Harold Pinter has so frequently demonstrated, memory is elusive and inconsistent. While writing this book, I often recalled an image or a production moment with great vividness, only to look at a photograph of the event and realize that it had actually happened slightly differently ("It was in your kitchen"!). The rehearsal process is all-consuming, time-driven, and present-tense; in order to make the best possible decisions in the moment, one has to be alive to what is happening in the room. Which means that the ability to archive a rehearsal while it is happening is always compromised. I took copious notes during my explorations with Pinter and Stoppard, making sure to quote their statements as accurately as possible in the margins of my scripts. But capturing the spontaneity of a process is a complex effort, and I have had several phone calls with Stoppard over the course of this writing which have laughingly ended up with both of us acknowledging that we simply cannot remember precisely what engendered a certain script change, acting choice, or design idea.

Nevertheless, I hope this book will reveal not only the nature of my collaborations with Pinter and Stoppard, but why I believe the mysteries of their plays can best be understood inside the production process itself. Because so much has been written about their oeuvres from an academic perspective, there is often the perception that these were "titans on high," dispensing their remarkable plays without comment to an awaiting (and occasionally bewildered) public. But as I have tried to demonstrate, both Pinter and Stoppard not only relished the process of staging and investigating their work, they got their hands into the clay with alacrity and grace. The pleasure Pinter and Stoppard took in the practical creation of their work was palpable at every rehearsal I shared with them—nothing could be taken for granted, nothing shirked. The forensic pursuit of the perfect gesture, the perfect word, the perfect prop, occupied the day. Their appetite for *play* and their nose for the inherently *theatrical* were acute and contagious. This does not always mean that they knew how to solve a given moment or that I always agreed with a note; the richness of the process lay in a rigorous exchange of ideas, in the relentless desire to dig deeper and to keep exploring.

For me, one reason the collaboration worked so seamlessly was that both writers understood and respected the difference between the playwright and the director in rehearsal. This is not always the case. I have worked with playwrights who want to dictate every move the actors make, and I have been in rehearsal rooms in which the playwright refuses to engage in any meaningful dialogue. The balance is a tricky one: while it is true that the more the director understands the writer's intention, the easier it can be to access the material, it is equally true that because writing is an intuitive process, playwrights will often be at a loss to "explain" a moment or anatomize a character. In truth, that is not their job. The responses Pinter and Stoppard gave to our rehearsal queries often had to be teased out or translated into actions the actors could play. For me, that is part of the pleasure. The world a writer creates is unique and distinct, particularly when you are dealing with writers as brilliant as Pinter and Stoppard. No two productions of their work will ever be alike. But if the writer and the director are congenial and trust each other, a production can evolve which feels organic and alive, which is true to its source material without being slavish or overly respectful. As a director, it is rare to find writers with whom one has that intuitive connection. Without that mutual sympathy, the process can become contentious and frustrating, but with it, the journey is one of celebration and exhilaration.

This does not mean that my collaborative experiences with Pinter and Stoppard followed the same trajectories. Pinter was rarely interested in changing or cutting his text (at least, not at the behest of a director), and was meticulous that every punctuation mark, pause, and silence be honored. Stoppard has always been much more open to considering textual emendations that suited the particular circumstances of a given production. Conversely, Pinter had performed in plays all his life, and thus had an intuitive understanding of an actor's language and an actor's process that was easy to follow. Stoppard's lens is always that of the writer; he knows exactly how he wants a line to sound, but the process of arriving there for an actor is one that the director will often have to help orchestrate. Pinter and Stoppard set up difference puzzles for the director to solve, and permit different parameters. But in both cases, I have found enormous freedom within the rigor of their work. They leave room for an "event" to happen on stage; there are enough empty spaces, enough mysteries, and enough silences to allow artistic collaborators to find room for their own creative discoveries. With that comes the responsibility to work through all obstacles to bring the plays to life. While a critic can point out fault lines in the text, a director must find a way to make the building stand, no matter what.

Staging Pinter's and Stoppard's work is thus like a rigorous athletic event that requires every ounce of one's energy, focus, and intelligence; the process seems to make better artists of those who attempt it. Over many years of rehearsing their plays, my appreciation for both the craft and the audacity of their work grew. These are not radical plays with no underpinning in theatrical tradition, but neither are they conventional plays dressed up as something new: both Pinter and Stoppard were so steeped in the traditions of English drama that they were able to build upon a deep structure while utterly re-inventing it at the same time. It moved me that both writers felt so much respect for the actual process of making theater. They wrote subversive and unusual plays and then housed them (for the most part) in traditional proscenium spaces. Director Bill Gaskill remarked about the early days of his tenure at the Royal Court that "it's perhaps significant that the contemporary work of the English Stage Company should have thrived in an old-fashioned proscenium theatre," and that same tension between a traditional "frame" and a radical re-imagining was clearly a fruitful one for both Pinter and Stoppard

My work with Stoppard and Pinter was shared with a group of actors and designers (including A.C.T.'s "Core Company") who brought that work to life onstage over many decades. I have always believed that, as was the case with Sophocles, Brecht, and Moliere, playwrights should write for acting companies. This almost never proves to be possible in the contemporary theater, particularly in America, where actors rarely have the chance to become part of a long-standing troupe. But like an orchestra that grows adept at playing a certain kind of music, actors and directors access writing with far greater fluency once they have experienced its particular sound and structure, and it was certainly the case that A.C.T.'s Core Company, along with a key group of designers and composers, became virtuosos at handling the demands of Pinter and Stoppard through their constant exposure to that writing. Having a Core Company also meant that even the smallest roles would be filled by major actors (such as Marco Barricelli playing Oscar Wilde) or by excellent young actors-in-training. "The idea of an ensemble haunted all our dreams," said director Bill Gaskill about the founding of the Royal Court,[1] and so it has always been with me. Part of my journey with Pinter and Stoppard over the decades has been watching artists hand over their well-honed knowledge to each other, generation after generation. Theater is at its heart an oral tradition, and the most valuable things often happen in the wings between scenes, or in the green room after a performance. I remember the night David Strathairn and Peter Riegert, who played Stanley and Goldberg in my 1989 production of *The Birthday Party* in New York, came to San Francisco to see Firdous Bamji and Scott Wentworth essay the same roles in 2018; none of them needed a secret handshake, they clearly knew they were part of a magical fraternity that had experienced the mysteries and challenges of bringing those indelible characters to life.

The outsider voice is compelled to sing its own tune. Pinter and Stoppard began at the outskirts of British culture and ended up taking center stage by sheer force of will, imagination, hard work, and linguistic genius. The passion of both playwrights to re-animate spoken English gives their work its muscle and surprise. As Wittgenstein said in 1940, "Sometimes you have to take an expression out of the language, to send it for cleaning, and then you can put it back into circulation,"[2] an apt description of the process Pinter and Stoppard engaged in through their playwriting careers. One could argue that these two Central European Jewish writers did more to salvage theatrical language in English drama than any other playwright of the twentieth century with the exception of Beckett. The right words can save us from barbarity and cliché. Pinter and Stoppard have consistently reminded the theatergoing public that language is to be revered and celebrated, it is an active tool of engagement, not because it is confessional or transparent but because it dances to its own music, hides a vulnerable heart, skewers pretension and exposes banality, keeping silence at bay and inviting a laughter of both recognition and fear.

"Where were you born then?" Aston asks Davies in *The Caretaker*. This is a question that would seem completely innocuous in the hands of almost any other playwright. But not in Pinterland. "What do you mean?" Davies replies (*"darkly"*). Suddenly, we are brought up short. A world of possibility opens up in front of us. Nothing is taken for granted. What *does* it mean to ask about someone's origins? How do any of us actually know, or indeed prove, who we are and where we come from? What game is being played, as Davies challenges Aston? These questions can be analyzed forever, but their theatrical power is best discovered in the rehearsal room, in real time, as actors experiment, iterate, and expose what is lurking underneath. After all, only an actor could assert, as does the Player in *Rosencrantz and Guildenstern are Dead*, "I extract significance from melodrama, a significance which it does not in fact contain; but occasionally, from out of this matter, there escapes a thin beam of light that, seen at the right angle, can crack the shell of mortality." If the most profound questions a play can ask are "who am I?" and "how did I get here?," it is no surprise that two playwrights with such complex and shifting identities felt so completely at home in a comic existential universe in which nothing is a given and everything is possible. "When we have found all the mysteries and lost all the meaning, we will be alone, on an empty shore," Septimus tells Thomasina in *Arcadia*. "Then we will dance," she replies.

It is my belief that Pinter's and Stoppard's work will keep dancing far into the future. As I was completing this book, musing from the isolation of my pandemic lockdown about what significance these plays might have in our post-Covid theatrical lives, I chanced to hear a comment by the noted Indian professor and director Abhishek Majumdar. He confided to Frank Hentschker in a recorded interview that "I don't think I would have survived the deaths in India during the pandemic if I hadn't simultaneously been reading Tom Stoppard's *The Coast of Utopia*."[3] Majumdar went on to explain that, surrounded by anxiety, disease, and governmental abdication throughout India, he had found deep comfort in the aesthetic and humanist arguments of literary critic Belinsky, one of Stoppard's finest recreations. "I'm losing my health and making enemies all over the shop," exclaims the struggling Belinsky in Part One of *The Coast of Utopia*, "because I believe literature alone can, even now, redeem our honor, even now, in words alone, that have ducked and dodged their way past the censor, literature can be . . . become . . . can," at which point he runs out of breath and self-confidence for a moment before resuming, "Art has the right to be useless, an end in itself, for its own sake. . . . It only has to be true . . . Not true to the *facts*, not true to appearances, but true to the innermost doll, where genius and nature are the same stuff. That's what makes an artist moral." It seemed so fitting to me that those passionate and sputtering words, put by Tom Stoppard into the mouth of an idealistic Russian critic in the 1830s, could save a contemporary Indian artist from despair during a global pandemic in the twenty-first century. What more could a playwright ask for?

NOTES

Introduction

1 Harold Hobson, "The Screw Turns Again," *Sunday Times*, May 25, 1958.

2 Kenneth Tynan, "Withdrawing with Style from the Chaos," *New Yorker,* December 19, 1977.

3 Mel Gussow, *Conversations with Stoppard,* New York: Grove Press, 1995, p. 35.

4 Mel Gussow, *Conversations with Stoppard,* New York: Grove Press, 1995, p. 21.

5 Mel Gussow, *Conversations with Stoppard,* New York: Grove Press, 1995, p. 21.

6 Tom Stoppard, interviewed by Shusha Guppy, "The Art of Theater No. 7," *Paris Review* 109 (Winter 1988).

7 Quoted in Hermione Lee, *Stoppard: A Life*, London: Faber and Faber Ltd., 2020, p. 759.

8 Mel Gussow, *Conversations with Pinter,* New York: Grove Press, 1994, p. 24.

9 From Pinter's private archives, June 1986, as quoted in Ian Smith, *Pinter in the Theatre*, London: Nick Hern Books, 2005, p. 9.

10 Mel Gussow, *Conversations with Pinter,* New York: Grove Press, 1994, p. 79.

11 Mel Gussow, *Conversations with Pinter,* New York: Grove Press, 1994 p. 108.

12 Ian Smith, *Pinter in the Theatre,* London: Nick Hern Books, 2005, p. 118.

13 Hermione Lee, *Stoppard: A Life*, London: Faber and Faber Ltd., 2020, p. 273.

14 Kenneth Tynan, *"Tom Stoppard": Profiles,* New York: Harper Perennial, 1989, p. 296.

15 Robert Brustein, *Dumbocracy in America,* Chicago: Ivan R. Dee, 1994, p. 256.

16 Susan Hollis Merritt, "A Conversation with Carey Perloff, Bill Moor, Peter Riegert, Jean Stapleton and David Strathairn," *The Pinter Review: Annual Essays,* 1989, p. 76.

17 Hermione Lee, *Stoppard: A Life,* London: Faber and Faber Ltd., p. 193.

Chapter 1

1 Christine Pittel, *New York Times,* January 8, 1989.

2 Steven Berkoff interviewed by Simon Round in the *Jewish Chronicle*, January 22, 2009.

3 Arnold Hinchcliffe, "Preface" in *Harold Pinter,* London: St. Martin's Press, 1967, p. 3.

4 John Boorman, *Conclusions,* London: Faber and Faber Ltd., 2020, pp. 78–79.

5 Michael Billington, *The Life and Works of Harold Pinter*, London: Faber and Faber, 1996, p. 4.

6 Michael Billington, *The Life and Works of Harold Pinter,* London: Faber and Faber, 1996, p. 2.

7 Gussow, *Conversations with Pinter,* New York: Grove Press, 1994, p. 104.

8 John Russell Taylor, *Anger and After: A Guide to the New British Drama,* London: Methuen, January 1969, p. 285.

9 Harold Pinter quoted by Henry Hewes, "Probing Pinter's Play," *Saturday Review,* April 8, 1967, p. 56.

10 Miriam Gross, "Pinter on Pinter", Observer, October 5, 1980, p. 25.

11 Jonathan Wilson, "Virginia and the Woolf," *The Tablet,* May 13, 2020.

12 Amos Elon, *The Pity of it All: A Portrait of the German-Jewish Epoch, 1743–1933,* New York: Picador, 2002, p. 398.

13 Michael Billington, *The Life and Works of Harold Pinter,* London: Faber and Faber, 1996, p. 41.

14 Michael Billington, *The Life and Works of Harold Pinter,* London: Faber and Faber, 1996, p. 9.

15 Harold Pinter in an Interview with Mireia Aragay and Ramon Simo, Universitat de Barcelona, in *Various Voices,* London: Faber and Faber Ltd., 1998, p. 64.

16 Michael Billington, *The Life and Works of Harold Pinter,* London: Faber and Faber, 1996, p. 17.

17 Daniel Sonabend, *We Fight Fascists: The 43 Groups and their Forgotten Battle for Post-War Britain,* London: Verso Books, 2019.

18 Harold Pinter, interviewed by Laurence Bensky, "The Art of Theatre No. 3," *Paris Review* 39 (Fall 1966).

19 Francesca Coppa, "Comedy and Politics in Pinter's Early Plays," in *The Cambridge Companion to Harold Pinter*, Cambridge University Press, 2009, p. 50.

20 Leslie Kane, "The Weasel under the Cocktail Cabinet: Rite and Ritual in Pinter's Plays," *The Pinter Review* 2, 1988.

21 Harold Pinter in an interview with Nick Hern in *One for the Road*, London: Methuen, 1984, p. 9.

22 Harold Pinter, "A Speech of Thanks," in *Various Voices,* New York: Grove Press, 1998, p. 57.

23 Leslie Kane, "The Weasel under the Cocktail Cabinet: Rite and Ritual in Pinter's Plays," *The Pinter Review* 2, 1988, p. 22.

24 Debra Shostak, "Marginal Writers: Or, Jews who Aren't," in *The Edinburgh Companion to Modern Jewish Fiction,* edited by David Brauner and Alex Stahler, Edinburgh University Press, 2015, p. 169.

25 Ian Smith, *Pinter in the Theatre,* London: Nick Hern Books, 2005, p. 175.

26 Michael Billington, *The Life and Works of Harold Pinter,* London: Faber and Faber, 1996.

27 John and Anthea Lahr (eds.), *A Casebook on Harold Pinter's The Homecoming,* New York: Grove Press, 1971, p. 161.

28 Ian Smith, *Pinter in the Theatre,* London: Nick Hern Books, 2005, p. 12.

29 Harold Pinter in *The Jewish Chronicle*, February 1960.

30 George Ross, "On the Horizon: 'Death of a Salesman' in the Original", *Commentary Magazine*, February 1951.

31 Tom Stoppard, "On Turning out to be Jewish," *Talk Magazine,* September 1999, p. 242.

32 Hermione Lee, *Stoppard: A Life,* London: Faber and Faber Ltd., p. 315.

33 Maya Jaggi, interview with Tom Stoppard in the *Guardian*, September 5, 2008.

34 As quoted in Kenneth Tynan, *Show People*, New York: Virgin Books, p. 71.

35 Shusha Guppy, "The Art of Theater" No. 7, *Paris Review* 109 (Winter 1988), pp. 298–299.

36 Hermione Lee, *Stoppard: A Life,* London: Faber and Faber Ltd., p. 634.

37 Tom Stoppard, "On Turning Out to Be Jewish," *Talk Magazine*, September 1999, p. 242.

38 Amos Oz, *Dear Zealots: Letters from a Divided Land*, New York: Houghton Mifflin Harcourt, 2018, p. 47.

39 Hermione Lee, *Stoppard: A Life,* London: Faber and Faber Ltd., p. 632.

40 Marjorie Perloff, *The Vienna Paradox*, New York: New Directions Books, 2003, p. xv.

41 Mel Gussow, *Conversations with Stoppard,* New York: Grove Press, 1995, p. 83.

42 Hermione Lee, *Stoppard: A Life,* London: Faber and Faber Ltd., p. 344.

43 Marjorie Perloff, *The Vienna Paradox*, New York: New Directions Books, 2003, p. 236.

44 Hermione Lee, *Stoppard: A Life,* London: Faber and Faber Ltd., p. 370.

45 Marjorie Perloff, *The Vienna Paradox*, New York, New Directions Books, 2003, pp. 42–43.

46 Shusha Guppy, "The Art of Theater" No. 7, *Paris Review* 109 (Winter 1988), pp. 298–299.

47 Hermione Lee, *Stoppard: A Life,* London: Faber and Faber Ltd., p. 845.

48 Marjorie Perloff, *The Vienna Paradox*, New York: New Directions Books, 2003, p. 235.

49 Quoted in Michael Billington, *The Life and Works of Harold Pinter,* London: Faber and Faber, 1996, p. 180.

Chapter 2

1 David Thompson, *Pinter: The Player's Playwright*, New York: Schocken, 1985, p. 19.

2 Kenneth Tynan, "Dead Language (The Lack of New Writing)," November 21, 1954, in *Theatre Writing*, selected by Dominic Shellard, London: Nick Hern Books, 2018.

3 Quoted in Dominic Shellard, *British Theatre Since the War*, New Haven: Yale University Press, 1999, pp. 21–22.

4 Ian Smith, *Pinter in the Theatre*, London: Nick Hern Books, 2005, p. 125.

5 Richard Hoggart, *The Uses of Literacy*, London: Penguin Classics, 1957, p. 114.

6 Terry Teachout, "The Future With, or Without, Tom Stoppard," *Commentary Magazine*, May 2021.

7 Peter Hall, *Making an Exhibition of Myself: The Autobiography of Peter Hall*, London: Sinclair, Stevenson, 1993, p. 190.

8 Mel Gussow, *Conversations with Stoppard*, New York: Grove Press, 1995, p. 3.

9 John Russell Taylor, *Anger and After*, London: Methuen, 1962, p. 11.

10 Mel Gussow, *Conversations with Pinter*, New York: Grove Press, 1994, p. 114.

11 Mel Gussow, *Conversations with Stoppard*, New York: Grove Press, 1995, p. 22.

12 Mel Gussow, *Conversations with Stoppard*, New York: Grove Press, 1995, p. 124.

13 Mel Gussow, *Conversations with Stoppard*, New York: Grove Press, 1995, p. 110.

14 Elizabeth Brodersen, "An Interview with Tom Stoppard," *American Conservatory Theater Playbill*, 1998, p. 27.

15 Harold Pinter, "Speech upon receiving the David Cohen British Literature Prize," in *Various Voices*, New York: Grove Press, 1998, p. 57.

16 Ian Smith, *Pinter in the Theatre*, London: Nick Hern Books, 2005, p. 121.

17 Mel Gussow, *Conversations with Pinter*, New York: Grove Press, 1994, p. 142.

18 Miriam Gross, "Pinter on Pinter," in the *Observer*, October 5, 1980, p. 25.

Chapter 3

1 Richard Hoggart, *The Uses of Literacy*, London: Penguin Classics, 1957, p. 85.

2 Austin Quigley, *The Pinter Problem*, Princeton University Press, 1975, p. 275.

3 Mel Gussow, *Conversations with Pinter*, New York: Grove Press, 1994, p. 44.

4 Ian Smith, *Pinter in the Theatre*, London: Nick Hern Books, 2005, p. 187.

5 Michael Billington, *The Life and Works of Harold Pinter*, London: Faber and Faber, 1996, p. 148.

6   Michael Billington, *The Life and Works of Harold Pinter*, London: Faber and Faber, 1996, p. 64.

7   Austin Quigley, "Pinter, Politics and Postmodernism," in *The Cambridge Companion to Harold Pinter*, ed. Peter Rabey, Cambridge University Press, 2001, reprinted 2009, p. 17.

8   Harold Pinter, "*On The Birthday Party 1*: Letter to Peter Wood," in Harold Pinter, *Various Voices*, New York: Grove Press, 1998 p. 8.

9   Harold Pinter, "On Being Awarded the German Shakespeare Prize in Hamburg," 1970, in Harold Pinter, *Various Voices*, New York: Grove Press, 1998, p. 41.

10 Used in the sense of "total visual world," as articulated by Arnold Aronson in his edition of essays *The Routledge Companion to Scenography*, London: Routledge, 2018.

11 Rolf Fjelde, "Forworde" to *Ibsen: Four Major Plays*, Signet, 2006, as quoted in Austin Quigley, "Theatrical Language," in *The Routledge Companion to Scenography*, London: Routledge, 2018, p. 94.

12 Helen Sheehy, *Eva Le Gallienne: A Biography*, New York: Alfred A. Knopf, 1996, p. 240.

13 Mel Gussow, *Conversations with Pinter*, New York: Grove Press, 1994, p. 33.

14 Michael Hallifax, *Let Me Set the Scene: Twenty Years at the Heart of British Theatre 1956 to 1976*, New Hampshire: Smith and Kraus, 2004, p. 176.

15 Giles Havergal, in conversation with the author, May 2020.

16 Quoted in Clive Barker, "Games in Education and Theatre," *New Theatre Quarterly* 5 (August 1989), pp. 227–235.

17 Tom Stoppard, *Squaring the Circle*, London: Faber, 1984, p. 8.

18 Stoppard, "Introduction" to *Rock 'n' Roll*, New York: Grove Press, 2006.

19 Hermione Lee, *Stoppard: A Life*, London: Faber and Faber Ltd., p. 750.

20 "Introduction" to *The Seagull*, a version by Tom Stoppard, London: Faber and Faber Ltd., 1997, p. ix.

21 Paul Delaney (ed.), *Stoppard in Conversation*, University of Michigan Press, 1994.

22 Gussow, *Conversations with Stoppard*, New York: Grove Press, 1995, p. 57.

23 Gussow, *Conversations with Stoppard*, New York: Grove Press, 1995, p. 62.

Chapter 4

1   Harold Pinter, interviewed by Laurence Bensky, "The Art of Theatre No. 3, *Paris Review* 39 (Fall 1966) p. 263.

2   Harold Pinter, "*On The Birthday Party* 1: Letter to Peter Wood," in Harold Pinter, *Various Voices*, New York: Grove Press, 1998 p. 8.

3   Michael Billington, *The Life and Works of Harold Pinter,* London: Faber and Faber, 1996, p. 95.

4   Harold Pinter, "On the Birthday Party ll," letter to the Editor of *The Play's the Thing,* October 1958, reprinted in *Various Voices,* New York: Grove Press, 1998, p. 15.

5   Susan Hollis Merritt, "A Conversation with Carey Perloff, Bill Moor, Peter Riegert, Jean Stapleton and David Strathairn," *The Pinter Review: Annual Essays,* 1989, p. 79.

6   Susan Hollis Merritt, "A Conversation with Carey Perloff, Bill Moor, Peter Riegert, Jean Stapleton and David Strathairn," *The Pinter Review: Annual Essays,* 1989, pp. 73–74.

7   Richard Hoggart, *The Uses of Literacy,* London: Penguin Classics, 1957, p. 62.

8   David Thompson, *Pinter: The Player's Playwright,* New York: Schocken, 1985, p. 34.

9   Richard Hoggart, *The Uses of Literacy,* London: Penguin Classics, 1957, p. 88.

10 Irving Wardle, Review of "The Birthday Party," *Encore,* July-August, 1958.

11 Quoted in Lawrence Shainberg's "Essay on Beckett" in the *Paris Review,* 104 (1987).

12 Kenneth Tynan, *Observer,* June 5, 1960.

13 Ian Smith, *Pinter in the Theatre,* London: Nick Hern Books, 2005, p. 204.

14 David Thompson, *Pinter: The Player's Playwright,* New York: Schocken Books, 1985, p. 15, quoting Ronald Harwood, *Sir Donald Wolfit: His Life and Work in the Unfashionable Theatre,* 1971, p. xiv.

15 Simon Gray, *An Unnatural Pursuit,* London: Faber and Faber, p. 70.

16 David Thompson, *Pinter: The Player's Playwright,* New York: Schocken Books, 1985, p. 15.

17 Susan Hollis Merritt, "A Conversation with Carey Perloff, Bill Moor, Peter Riegert, Jean Stapleton and David Strathairn," *The Pinter Review: Annual Essays,* 1989, p. 79.

18 Ian Smith, *Pinter in the Theatre,* London: Nick Hern Books, 2005, p. 189.

Chapter 5

1   Hermione Lee, *Stoppard: A Life,* London: Faber and Faber Ltd., p. 750.

Chapter 6

1   Mel Gussow, *Conversations with Pinter,* New York: Grove Press, 1994, p. 128.

2   Michael Billington, *The Life and Works of Harold Pinter,* London: Faber and Faber, 1996, p. 66.

3 As discussed in Michael Billington, *The Life and Work of Harold Pinter,* London: Faber and Faber Ltd., 1996, p. 166.

4 Michael Billington, *The Life and Works of Harold Pinter,* London: Faber and Faber, 1996, p. 163.

5 Mel Gussow, *Conversations with Pinter,* New York: Grove Press, 1994, p. 78.

6 Mel Gussow, *Conversations with Pinter,* New York: Grove Press, 1994, p. 115.

7 John and Anthea Lahr (eds.), *A Casebook on Harold Pinter's The Homecoming,* New York: Grove Press, 1971, p. 165.

Chapter 7

1 Hermione Lee, *Stoppard: A Life*, London: Faber and Faber Ltd., p. 451.

2 Hermione Lee, *Stoppard: A Life*, London: Faber and Faber Ltd., p. 737.

3 Hermione Lee, *Stoppard: A Life,* London: Faber and Faber Ltd., p. 820.

Conclusion

1 William Gaskill, *A Sense of Direction*, New York: Limelight Editions, 1988, p. 55.

2 Ludwig Wittgenstein, *Culture and Value*, Revised Edition, ed. G. H. von Wright (Oxford: Blackwell, 1998), p. 44e.

3 Abhishek Majumdar, interviewed by Frank Hentschker for the Segal Talks at the CUNY Graduate Center, New York, May 2021.

INDEX